Reimagining Philosophy of Religion

Expanding Philosophy of Religion

Series Editors:
J. Aaron Simmons, Furman University, USA
Kevin Schilbrack, Appalachian State University, USA

A series dedicated to a global, diverse, cross-cultural, and comparative philosophy of religion, Expanding Philosophy of Religion encourages underrepresented voices and perspectives and looks beyond its traditional concerns rooted in classical theism, propositional belief, and privileged identities.

Titles in the series include:
Philosophical Hermeneutics and the Priority of Questions in Religions,
by Nathan Eric Dickman
Philosophies of Religion, by Timothy Knepper
Diversifying Philosophy of Religion, edited by Nathan R. B. Loewen and
Agnieszka Rostalska
Collective Intentionality and the Study of Religion by Andrea Rota
Engaging Philosophies of Religion by Gereon Kopf, Purushottama Bilimoria
and Nathan R. B. Loewen
Rethinking Religious Conversion by Jack Williams
Philosophies of Liturgy, edited by J. Aaron Simmons, Bruce Ellis Benson
and Neal DeRoo
Art, Desire, and God, edited by Gereon Kopf, Purushottama Bilimoria
and Nathan R. B. Loewen
Art Making as Spiritual Practice by Lexi Eikelbloom and David Newheiser
Rethinking Philosophy of Religion with Wittgenstein by Thomas D. Carroll

Reimagining Philosophy of Religion

Understanding, Commitment, and Making-Believe

Amber L. Griffioen

BLOOMSBURY ACADEMIC

LONDON • NEW YORK • OXFORD • NEW DELHI • SYDNEY

BLOOMSBURY ACADEMIC
Bloomsbury Publishing Plc
50 Bedford Square, London, WC1B 3DP, UK
1359 Broadway, New York, NY 10018, USA
29 Earlsfort Terrace, Dublin 2, Ireland

BLOOMSBURY, BLOOMSBURY ACADEMIC and the Diana logo are trademarks of
Bloomsbury Publishing Plc

First published in Great Britain 2025

A catalogue record for this book is available from the British Library.

A catalog record for this book is available from the Library of Congress.

ISBN: HB: 978-1-3503-2847-1
        PB: 978-1-3503-2850-1
        ePDF: 978-1-3503-2848-8
        eBook: 978-1-3503-2849-5

Typeset by RefineCatch Limited, Bungay, Suffolk
Printed and bound in Great Britain

For product safety related questions contact productsafety @bloomsbury.com.

To find out more about our authors and books visit www.bloomsbury.com
and sign up for our newsletters.

In memory of Helen De Cruz (1978–2025).

"Does striving become impossible once one has accepted success as impossible?"

"No. But it thereby becomes irrational*" [. . .]*

"Undoubtedly, so long as success *is the goal of the striving—the finish line the primary aim of the runner. But what if the striving were an* aim in itself? *If there was no finish line to be achieved, or (what is the same for the contestants), only one infinitely far away? What if the journey wasn't undertaken for the sake of the destination but rather the destination set for the sake of the journey—so that one could experience the orientation of the course, and precisely* not *its terminus?" [. . .]*

Religion is not the (theoretical) belief that a kingdom of God will come; rather, it is the striving *to bring it about, even if one believes it will never come [. . .]."*
Friedrich Carl Forberg, Apology of his Alleged Atheism

To many, the form of this "exposition" might appear strange; it will seem to them too rigorous to be edifying and too edifying to be rigorously academic. As far as the latter is concerned, I have no opinion. As for the former, however, [. . .] if it were indeed too rigorous to be edifying, then I would consider it a failure.
Søren Kierkegaard, The Sickness Unto Death

Contents

Preface   x

Acknowledgments   xvii

Introduction: Playing at Being a Discipline?   1

Part One: Reorientation

1   Beyond Help? Fairies, Idols, and the View from Nowhere   11

2   Beyond Knowledge: Toward a Social Epistemology of Understanding   25

3   Beyond Nowhere: Doing Religious Epistemology from Somewhere   43

Interlude—From Reorientation to Reform: Implications for the Discipline   63

Part Two: Reform

4   Beyond the Cognitive: Faith, Commitment, and the Religious Life   71

5   Beyond the Doxastic: Recovering the Role of Imagination in Religion   107

6   Beyond the Indicative: the "Ultimate Horizons" of Pretend Play   127

7   Beyond Faith: Make-believe and the Religious Life   147

Interlude—From Reform to Revolution: Playing the "Spoilsport"   167

Part Three: Revolution

8   Beyond Theodicy: Faith-shaking Trauma and the "Purely Intellectual" Approach   175

9   Beyond Closure? "Re-mystifying" Analytic Philosophy of Religion   207

Works Cited   223

Index   239

Preface

This book, quite honestly, was a struggle to write. Or, perhaps better put, it is the result of various struggles. The germs of it were formed all the way back in 2009–10. I was an adventurous, single, US-American grad student trying to complete a PhD thesis for the University of Iowa on the nature and dynamics of self-deception, and I was myself still very naïve (perhaps even a bit self-deceived?) about the inner workings of the philosophical discipline I was about to enter. I was living hand-to-mouth on a poorly paid (but generously offered and perfectly timed) graduate scholarship in Marburg, Germany—where I hung around with semi-ruly Protestant German theology professors, dipping my toes in the waters of *Kulturprotestantismus* and *Schleiermacherei* and experimenting with half-baked ideas about "atheist religious experience."

Although I had planned to leave Germany after my initial stay in the Marburg theology department, as of the date this manuscript goes to press, I am still here. Indeed, by the time this book appears, I will have somehow transformed into a mid-career, married, expat philosopher of religion, teaching remotely at a Chinese university from my home of fifteen years in Konstanz and planning a career change that will likely take me out of full-time academia. I have had the immense luck and privilege of becoming a permanent resident of Germany, presenting my work all over the world, conducting collaborative research stays in Iran and South Africa, getting hitched in the same German cathedral that witnessed the resolution of the Western Schism (seriously!), and giving birth to a beautiful child who is the light of my life. I have also survived continuous job contingency, punctuated by various periods of unemployment in an often ridiculous and toxic academic job market—as well as a pandemic, infertility, pregnancy loss, birth trauma, chronic pain, and the balancing act that is navigating motherhood with an unstable career in one's forties.

During my decade as a contingently-employed scholar on various contracts at the University of Konstanz, I would somehow manage to "fall into" the field that has become the subject of this book, namely analytic philosophy of religion (henceforth in this book referred to as APR). At the same time, I was somehow able to carve out space to cultivate an eclectic set of philosophical and theological interests. (I think we're supposed to call them "areas of competence"?) I became an expert on various facets of medieval Christian and Islamic mystical and contemplative thought (including women thinkers in these traditions), and I worked on projects promoting the pluralization of the so-called philosophical and theological "canons." I explored questions of "truthiness" and "bullshit" in the public sphere and dipped my toes (and the rest of me) into feminist thought and social epistemology. I taught on the philosophy of games, play, and sport and published articles on baseball and sports jurisprudence. (Hint: I'm an umpire voluntarist!) And my own fertility journey led me to dive uterus-first into the metaphysics and philosophical theology of pregnancy and pregnancy loss. These academic "side-hustles" have, ironically, made me less marketable on the academic job market (funny how that works), but they have all exercised a profound influence on the content of this book, and I think appropriately so.

Having now decided to leave full-time academia to pursue a career as an existential coach for individuals dealing with reproductive struggle, I look at these chapters, and I see the evolution of my own thought and outlook over the past fifteen years. The book began as a planned *Habilitation* monograph on non-doxastic faith, a topic which itself was largely influenced by the death of my Protestant-Reformed grandmother and my dawning realization of the insidious effects that a certain kind of normative doxasticism can have in the religious sphere. Some of these earlier ideas have made their way into what is now Chapter 4. At the same time, as my own encounter with other faiths, languages, and cultures shaped my experience over the years that followed, I came to see the philosophical faith-literature as ultimately unsatisfying in a way that I think comes out in that chapter and those that follow it. Similarly, what began as a gnawing annoyance with certain discourses in the discipline became a full-blown critique as I began, on the one hand, to be invited to participate more actively in APR circles, and, on the other, to encounter more work in feminist and liberation thought, social epistemology, and medieval mysticism. (It is, perhaps, no coincidence that my approaches to perfect-being theology in Chapter 1 and theodicy in Chapters 8 and 9 bear striking parallels to those of Grace Jantzen and Dorothee Sölle, both of whom, like me, were immersed in medieval mysticism—and especially in texts produced by, with, or for women.) My work in philosophy of sport changed the way I thought about the "rules of the game" in philosophy of religion—and also deeply influenced the development of the ideas surrounding the imagination and religious make-believe that I develop in Chapters 5–7. Finally, the transformation of my half-baked ideas from my Marburg days into what ultimately became a central argument of this book and the explicit focus of Chapters 2 and 3 stems, in part, from all-too-brief discussions with Muhammad Legenhausen over NA beers in Konstanz and while hiking the Khidr Nabi Mountain in Qom—as well as from the many, many conversations over cigarettes and decidedly non-NA beers with my friend and former colleague in Konstanz, Jochen Briesen. Despite our pronounced differences in philosophical orientation and inspiration, Jochen's work in analytic epistemology and aesthetics has always dovetailed in surprising and exciting ways with my own work in APR. (Perhaps Dina Emundts was on to something when she hired us both as post-docs to her *Lehrstuhl* all those many years ago.)

In any case, if this book feels a little uneven or unsettled in places, that's because it is. It stitches together, not always perfectly, the ideas and approaches that have troubled, excited, fascinated, or otherwise occupied me in philosophy of religion since breaking through into the discipline over a decade ago. Similarly, if it sounds critical and sometimes angry, that's also no accident. I am dissatisfied with APR in a lot of ways, especially because I think, given the quality and ingenuity of its scholars, it could be and do so.much.more. That being said, I have also found many friends and sympathetic souls, both outside the discipline and within it, who practice what I preach here better than I ever could and whose work has encouraged and inspired me along the way. I have also made the acquaintance of a number of folks in the discipline who, although they rarely see things the way I do, are still an absolute joy to spend time with, and who have provided me with valuable "epistemic frictions" over the years, keeping me from getting too comfortable in my own perspective.

For what it's worth, I do not think APR is wholly broken, nor that it need come to an "end," whatever that might mean in scholarly circles. (I tend to think less apocalyptic approaches are preferable when manageable.) Still, I do think the discipline needs some fresh perspectives if it wants to remain relevant and some serious shifts (or, minimally, expansions) in focus if it wants to grow. The structure of this book therefore references two *geographic* metaphors that, together, capture the central theme of this book:

First, to channel Hans-Georg Gadamer, another philosopher similarly interested in the connections between understanding and play, the notion of the opening horizon gestures both at the idea of a "limit" and the idea of a "beyond" that is almost, but perhaps not quite (yet), visible. There are various ways to interpret this metaphor. It might be understood unidirectionally as an expansion *into* new or previously uncharted "territory"—one that "goes beyond" its previous limits by redefining its boundaries or reshaping its contours in an outward direction. Alternatively, it may be understood more multilaterally as the opening or loosening of previously closed borders *between* spaces to permit a mutual traversing and transgressing of those boundaries in ways previously prohibited. These interpretations are not mutually exclusive, of course, but the emphasis of the former on expansion might raise worries about the potential co-opting or colonization of the spaces the discipline expands into, while the latter's emphasis on porousness and mutual influence risks the potential loss of disciplinary demarcations—and with them, perhaps, a more concrete sense of identity.

I think APR is capable of "opening up" its horizons in both of these ways without dominating other discourses or losing its own identity. In fact, I suspect it already has the tools within its own history and resources to see past what, I will argue, are rather arbitrary and self-imposed disciplinary limits. For this reason, each chapter title gestures at one way in which I think the discipline can go *beyond* its more traditional, mainstream limits by both expanding its emphases and spheres of interest outward and creating internal space for marginalized and excluded voices to enter, contribute to, and enrich the discourse, even where such "incursions" might involve the disruption of the *status quo*. These ways of opening up the discipline represent an opportunity to create a more welcoming and inclusive space for fruitful philosophical exploration—one that has the potential to make the field itself more relevant from the standpoint of both the academy itself and the public at large.

A second, more dynamic—and "mystical"—metaphor is that of *turning*. In many cases, shifting our focus or attention requires a fundamental "re-orientation" of our more comfortable ways of thinking or modes of discourse and a corresponding "re-formation" of some of our approaches. My attempt in this book will be to enable more "revolution-ary" transformations in APR down the road by turning us (at least temporarily) away from the overemphasis on particular (realist, knowledge-centric, intellectualist) ways of thinking about what philosophy of religion is and does and toward alternative (more ontologically open, understanding-centered, praxis-oriented) approaches. Indeed, if we allow ourselves to be "turned" in these ways, I think we can, first, better *diagnose* how our discipline fails with respect to those who might actually need us or find our deliverances relevant and, second, better set about *transforming* our discourse in ways that can both address those needs and enrich the discipline itself. I have thus inserted two interludes that reflect the importance of thinking of the development of analytic philosophy of religion going forward not only as a matter of expanding or opening our field of vision, but as *turning our attention* toward bodies of thought and practice we often (sometimes willfully) ignore.

Another advantage of these metaphors is their relevance within the religious sphere. As I will discuss, religious practice takes us to the *limits* of what we can imagine—and, in many cases, postulates something "otherworldly," just *beyond* our immediate grasp. Religions present us with imaginative narrative frameworks that both constrain and kindle our imaginations, and which help (re-)orient us in the world around us, even sometimes *converting* us to new ways of thinking, feeling, and willing. (Think here of the Latin *conversio* or the Greek μετάνοια.) When religions function beneficially, they can be empowering and liberative—and show us how to love. They turn us inward toward self-discovery, outward toward our fellow human beings, and toward each other in solidarity. They provide us with identity and direction, grace us with nuanced aesthetic preferences, and open up a horizon of meaning that can "color" everything we see and do. In short, they can make us morally better, more sensitive, more *interesting* people. When they function harmfully, they promote self-deception and close us off to others; they make us partisan and jingoistic, hateful and afraid; they can force us into social roles that hurt us or others; they can make us worse off as people and the world worse off overall, sometimes in ways that are unlikely to be made good again.

I therefore do not want to shy away from the harm that religions can (and often do) inflict with respect to human and world flourishing. But I also remain in the camp of those who think (or hope anyway) that there can be something genuinely valuable about the religious life—and even if I am wrong about this, it is at least valued by individuals and communities to such an extent that I do not think we can and should dispense with philosophy of religion. That being said, I am worried that the way philosophy of religion in the analytic mode is currently conducted does not adequately bring out why religion *matters*, nor how it is or can be genuinely epistemically valuable. (In fact, it rarely addresses *religion* or the *religious life* at all.) I therefore think APR as it is often practiced is actively contributing to its own irrelevance and dispensability, and it is this concern that underlies the themes of this book.

A few caveats are in order before I proceed.

First, what I say concerning APR is by no means intended to apply across the board to all corners of the discipline, nor to every one of its members. There is a lot of work being done in APR right now that virtuously models what I am advocating for in this book, and there is reason to be encouraged by the directions this research is taking. My main concern is that of certain *tendencies* that one finds—especially in the more mainstream and public faces of the discipline—as well as in the way philosophy of religion still tends to be taught in many Anglo-American-European classrooms.

Likewise, when I talk about various intellectual or moral vices that certain ways of philosophizing can lead to, I do not mean to be claiming that all APR scholars operating within that tradition are epistemically vicious (though I suspect some are), nor that those APR scholars whose work exhibits such tendencies are themselves epistemically or morally blameworthy (though some might be). Sometimes ignorance and "good intentions" exculpate, sometimes they do not, and I am not taking it upon myself to define this line in the case of APR, nor to excuse myself from criticism. Instead of focusing on backward- or sideways-looking attributions of *blame*, I am more inclined to adopt a more forward-looking model of *responsibility* like that of Iris Marion Young's "social connection model," which focuses less on retrospective "finger-pointing and blame-shifting" and more on how all of us in the discipline "who participate by [our] actions in the structural processes that produce injustice" bear a level of collective responsibility for correcting such injustices (Young 2006: 124 5). Indeed, insofar as the large majority of APR scholars I know are genuinely kind, humble, and well-intentioned individuals, I would expect them to minimally be willing to think about where and how we in the discipline collectively fall short and to acknowledge our shared responsibility to ameliorate these shortcomings where we can. This book attempts to take a step in this direction.

Second, although my own preference is for a more radical change in the approach and subject matter of APR, I wish to emphasize here that many of the attentional shifts I propose in this book are consistent with APR continuing to pursue the kinds of projects it has traditionally explored. However, my hope is that they would be pursued with a different kind of awareness, accompanied by a commitment to fostering a more polyphonic research and discussion climate within those projects, while simultaneously resisting tendencies toward monotonic assertion and adversarial "duel-ism."

Third, as I discovered in my research for this book, more than a few of the ideas discussed here are already implicitly or explicitly present in earlier work by philosophers who paved the way for my generation of scholars, even if my own approach frames them somewhat differently. This has struck me as at once heartening and demoralizing. On the one hand, reading these thinkers has helped me see that I am not alone in my concerns, and their work has greatly assisted me in better sketching the contours of my own ideas. I have thus tried to hearken back to this literature wherever possible in what follows so that readers can go back and rediscover these rich texts for themselves. On the other hand, it is frustrating to know that concerns articulated already decades ago have still not received the serious attention and respect they deserve in the discipline. I can only hope that the current philosophical and academic climate is more conducive to disciplinary change than it has proved itself to be in the past.

That being said, what I write here is unlikely to please everybody. In fact, it may not wholly please anybody. It may be too "far-out" or "woke"-sounding for some of the more deeply entrenched scholars in the dominant APR in-groups, while not going far enough for those who would like to see more radical changes in the discipline. For many scholars of religion in the social sciences, it will likely still appear too monolithic, too essentialist, too monotheism-centric, and above all too *theological* to be the kind of genuine philosophy of *religion* I myself call for—while many analytic philosophers will view it as painting the concepts of religion and (especially) religious belief with strokes too broad for their comfort. It will talk too much about God for some scholars and too little for others. It might be too "metaphysical" for my postmodern theologian buddies and too "antirealist" for my analytic theologian friends.

I will be the first to admit that, in leaning heavily on the APR tradition in which I cut my philosophical teeth—and in attempting to address the discipline largely on its own turf and terms—the scope of what I can accomplish here is regrettably limited. I am also wary of overstepping the bounds of my own expertise and background knowledge in ways that do more harm than good. But it is my hope that, even if it pleases no one fully, there will be something that piques, irks, or incites reflection in most readers, even those relatively unfamiliar with the discipline under discussion—especially given the way APR's discourse both reflects and influences a not-insignificant amount of what we see in contemporary Anglo-American Christian religiosity in the public sphere. In this sense, even if I don't end up accomplishing the fruitful Socratic midwifery I aim to practice in my philosophy, perhaps I can at least play the vexing Socratic gadfly I have sometimes been accused of being. At the end of the day, I will be happy if, as famed Iowa football coach Hayden Fry might have put it, I am simply able to "scratch the discipline where it itches."

Acknowledgments

The completion of this book would not have been possible without the support of an entire constellation of colleagues, friends, and family over the years.

Professionally, I would like to thank the Center for Philosophy of Religion at the University of Notre Dame, North-West University Potchefstroom, IKIU Qazvin, and the (now defunct) *Kulturwissenschaftliches Kolleg* in Konstanz for hosting me as a visiting scholar, giving me space to pursue individual and collaborative research, and letting me try out many of this book's ideas on various faculty members and students. I am especially grateful to Mike Rea, Justin Sands, Mohammad Sadegh Zahedi, and Dorothea Weltecke in this regard. I would also like to thank Duke Kunshan University for keeping me afloat institutionally post-pandemic and being family-friendly enough to have let me teach remotely from Germany. I was proud to be part of the experiment in higher education you are undertaking.

I have complicated feelings toward the University of Konstanz, but I am glad for the nearly ten years of office space, for the various students I had the pleasure of teaching and supervising during that time, and for several of my similarly contingently-employed colleagues in the *Mittelbau*. A Margarete von Wrangell fellowship from the Baden-Württemberg Stiftung funded five years of my research there, and various smaller internal and external scholarships and grants allowed me to travel, network, and organize conferences related to that research. I also owe a lot to the Uni-Konstanz Office for Equal Opportunity and Diversity who provided continued support, even after I left the university.

Sarah Buss and Dina Emundts were both important mentors for me in my formative grad school and postdoc years, and they each showed me different ways of being a kick-ass woman in philosophy. Thank you for being great role models. Conversations with Evan Fales, Muhammad Legenhausen, Roderich Barth, and Jörg Lauster also played not-insignificant roles in the ideas for this book. You kept me intellectually and theologically honest in a variety of ways.

Personally, I am forever grateful to Christina Van Dyke, Lacey Hudspeth, the members of "the refuge" (you know who you are), and all the women in my online AWOWR writing group—not only for encouraging me professionally but also for supporting me emotionally through some of the most psychologically taxing periods of my adult life. I also want to express my appreciation to Jochen Briesen whose company, friendship, and humor always buoyed my spirits when they flagged (and they flagged a *lot*). Special thanks go to Eva Popp for being an incredibly competent student assistant, a fearless mountain-road driver, and a dear friend over the years. Your tenacity and get-it-done attitude have always inspired me. To Melanie Spangehl, whose unwavering enthusiasm and support since her freshman year has shown me that I, too, can be a mentor: It's been a pleasure to watch you blossom into such a thoughtful, smart, and increasingly confident philosopher. And to Jess, Sanne, Kim, Pete, Kris, Dan, Laura, Shawn, Christoph, the regulars at the *Foxhead*, and all the rest of the old IC crew: Your friendships helped make me who I am as a philosopher and a person, and I am thankful for all of you.

Finally, to my family: Mom and Dad, you have always supported my personal and intellectual endeavors—including my decisions to move and remain abroad—which has not always been easy, especially through times of great uncertainty (not to mention global shutdowns and travel bans). It is to you I owe much of my spiritual formation (and the ever-cranky reflective attitude that accompanies it), as well as my love of all things baseball. You are, simply put, *really good parents* and even better grandparents. Make sure to have the big red plastic bat and wiffle ball ready for the next time we come home.

To my spouse and partner in life shenanigans, Daniel Schumacher, you have been a rock of consistency on which I have been able to lean throughout this journey. The fact that you put up with me on a daily basis never ceases to blow my mind. We have endured a lot together, and you have seen me through difficulties, both personal and professional, that I don't think I could have navigated alone. (You also taught me objectively better ways of folding clothes, though I'll still leave the ironing to you.) I am excited to embark on this next phase of our relationship, wherever we end up.

Last in the order of size and age, but first in the order of my heart, my dear Charlotte Rae: I am always hesitant to call things "blessings" or to believe that petitionary prayers really are answered, yet I cannot help but regard you, Charlie, as a true gift from the Godhead and a continual lesson in humility, patience, and wonder from Lady Wisdom. You simultaneously exhaust and invigorate me, and you remind me daily what it means to really *be present*. I somehow managed to grow your little body as part of my body, and you—just by virtue of being *you*—are growing me every single day as a mother. May our little *Selbdritt*—our distant, dusty mirror of that uniquely singular social trinity—remain united in love and enjoy many more off-key *gemütliche Singkreise* in the years to come. This book is dedicated to you.

Playing at Being a Discipline?

Here the Disciple found a wonder that warranted laughter. It seemed there was a silver ball [of wisdom] rolling among the scholars, which [. . .] bestowed glory and honor upon those who held it. [. . .] When this ball bounced around among them, those present tried not indeed to grasp it for themselves, but rather to do all they could to knock it out of each other's hands and snatch it and show that the other did not have it. [. . .] And sadly there were among them bewildering arguments and uproars and contradictions about this ball, and in the minds of many who were listening this produced great boredom and distaste. For they derived no benefit from these things, but complained that they were at some sporting event or stupid show.

Henry Suso (d.1366), *Horologium Sapientiae*

In many academic circles, analytic philosophy of religion (or "APR") does not enjoy the best of reputations. A growing number of scholars external to the discipline view it as archaic, apologetic, biased, and/or obsolete. On the one hand, such critics maintain that, insofar as analytic philosophers of religion concern themselves with objects and entities that (according to the objectors) do not exist, APR takes *too* seriously something "enlightened" scholars recognize as a waste of time. For example, although a "fan of philosophy as a whole," biologist Jerry Coyne has called philosophy of religion straightforward "garbage"—a field akin to "the philosophy of fairies" (Coyne 2014). On the other hand, APR is sometimes also charged with displaying a certain *lack* of seriousness. Viewed by many on the outside as an enterprise overwhelmingly consisting of theistic (usually Christian) apologists, the claim is that APR is largely engaged in mere "puzzling" or a kind of "metaphysical gerrymandering" ("pure mental masturbation," as Coyne puts it) in the service of epistemically reinforcing already-held theistic worldviews. Both charges, however, imply that APR is not to be taken seriously as an academic enterprise but should rather be viewed as a sort of "ideology" that, in one way or another, merely "plays at" being a serious discipline. APR is thus often regarded with a degree of distanced suspicion or even outright derision, as when one philosopher provocatively tweeted that publishing in philosophy of religion "should disqualify one from sitting at the adult table."

Now it should be noted that these criticisms are not entirely fair. First, the "masturbatory" side of APR mirrors much of what goes on in analytic philosophy at large, such that criticisms of its playful or even onanistic aspects might be extended to much of what falls under analytic philosophy in general. (Of course, having a partner in crime doesn't make one innocent, and, as I will discuss, part of APR's relevance problem has to do with its insularity, which is not entirely unrelated to the contentedness of many analytic philosophers with the abstraction of the proverbial "ivory tower.") Second, some of the concerns about APR stem from authors who have little acquaintance with what actually goes on in the discipline. For example, not every APR scholar is a theist, or even religious. Some atheist or secularist scholars thus agree with Coyne that the term "God" is extensionally equivalent to that of "fairy," but they nevertheless consider APR a serious and worthwhile philosophical enterprise. Third, many topics and discussions in APR overlap with those in non-APR philosophy, and the influence between these two spheres has not been solely unidirectional. Work in religious epistemology and metaphysics has influenced research (and entire research programs) outside APR in ways that have had a significant impact on analytic philosophy as a whole, and there have been several fruitful exchanges between theistic philosophers and non-theistic philosophers on topics in various philosophical subfields.

At the same time, criticisms like these do not arise *ex nihilo*, and it is important that analytic philosophers of religion be prepared to reflect critically on the discipline's shortcomings in method, subject matter, and audience, taking measures to correct and extend its approach in ways that are both philosophically respectable and socially inclusive. In the remainder of this introduction, I want to lay out a few of these shortcomings in detail before turning in Part One to a more detailed discussion of two fundamental objections to the discipline itself that APR ought to take more seriously—one from outside philosophy of religion and one from within philosophical theology. In Chapter 1, I argue that the discourse between APR and its critics has been overwhelmingly centered around a particular version of theological realism and an unhelpful approach to objectivity—foci that have not only led APR to adopt a largely defensive (and somewhat unambitious) stance but which also promote a way of approaching its subject matter that may ultimately be epistemically and morally detrimental. I suggest that the discipline might do better to move beyond its traditional debates concerning this form of realism and to **reorient** itself differently with respect to objectivity.

In Chapters 2 and 3, then, I go onto explore how I think such a move might be accomplished—namely, by shifting from a knowledge-centric to an understanding-focused epistemology. The shift from knowledge to understanding, however, dethrones the central emphasis on the rationality of religious belief that currently stands at the center of religious epistemology in APR, making room for attitudes other than belief and additional values besides truth, and allowing that religion need not be factive in order to be of significant epistemic value. Relatedly, I suggest that the dominant role that the cognitive aspects of religion play in APR is itself drastically overblown and distorts our very understanding of what matters to the religious life.

In Part Two, I therefore think about how we might **reform** APR in light of the reorientation suggested in Part One. Chapter 4 considers what religious faith might look like if we decenter the cognitive and allow religious practice to regain the primacy it actually enjoys in the religious life. In so doing, I will conclude that religious faith is more doxastically permissive than even most non-doxasticists about religious faith in APR are willing to admit. Chapter 5 argues that the religious *imagination* is what allows faith to be doxastically permissive in this way and that religious imaginings are often sufficient to play the cognitive role in the life of religious faith. Chapters 6 and 7 go even further by exploring the role of "serious imaginative play" in religion and suggesting that the religious life at its "highest and holiest" comes out in a form of what I call *earnest make-believe* compatible with a life of authentic religious faith as discussed in Chapter 4 and capable of leading to an especially rich kind of hermeneutical understanding of the kind discussed in Chapter 3.

In Part Three (Chapters 8 and 9), I use examples from my own experience of miscarriage to "play the spoilsport" with respect to the way APR conducts much of its discourse surrounding theodicy and the problem of evil, suggesting that we need to **revolutionize** the way we approach such issues. I conclude my discussion by hearkening back to medieval mystical literature to locate a framework for constructing better and more compassionate forms of theodical discourse in APR.

I should note here that Chapter 2 on the epistemology of understanding and Chapter 6 on pretense, play, and make-believe temporarily step away from the case of religion to explore these phenomena on their own in more detail. I think this is important to motivate the views in question, but it is also a way of showing the relevance of certain contemporary discussions from outside APR for thinking about what can happen inside the discipline—and it gestures at ways that APR might itself be able to make a contribution to these discussions, at least insofar as it is willing to engage in a genuine philosophy of *religion* and not just the pursuit of issues relating to whether and how religious (usually monotheistic) belief can be justified, warranted, or otherwise rational(ized).

However, before embarking on this journey of reorientation, reform, and revolution, it is worth briefly examining some of the ways in which the current state of APR requires us to "look beyond" its traditional boundaries to locate new and innovative ways of doing philosophy of religion in the analytic mode. I will not be able to address each of these problems in the chapters that follow, but it is important to be aware of them and to keep in mind that this book represents only a small part of what is needed to make APR into a genuinely inclusive philosophy of *religion*.

The constricted horizons of APR

Although APR has seen significant thematic diversification in the past 20 years (Hasker 2005; Timpe 2015), the discipline remains remarkably narrow in various ways. First and foremost, it remains an area of philosophy largely rooted in questions surrounding the metaphysics of classical[1] monotheism and the epistemology of belief-systems grounded in so-called "perfect-being theology"— an idealized, theistic vision endorsed by only a limited number of religious traditions (and to varying degrees within these traditions). Some, like William Wood, even define the *specific task* of APR as using "the tools of philosophy to investigate arguments for and against the existence of God, as well as [. . .] the properties or attributes that the major monotheistic traditions would ascribe to God" (Wood 2021: 7). As a result, as Kevin Schilbrack notes, "it is rare to find any treatment [. . .] of the ethical, political, and ritual practices in which the majority of religious people seek to learn and perfect their piety" (Schilbrack 2014: xii). This may not come as much of a surprise to those in the discipline, given APR's contemporary fashioning of itself as inheriting the legacy of (what turns out to be a rather narrow understanding of) medieval scholasticism. Yet it has moved quite far away from philosophy of religion's actual disciplinary roots in the work of the seventeenth-century Cambridge Platonists, who saw their theoretical pursuits as fundamentally tied up with moral, social, and political concerns (Taliaferro 2005: 13).

Indeed, given its designation, one unfamiliar with the discipline would likely expect a philosophy of religion to have as its primary focus a cluster of phenomena that is inherently socio-cultural, namely *religion*. It might thus come as somewhat of a surprise to find that APR has spent so much energy on the content and rationality of a very small set of religious beliefs (even if those beliefs express certain fundamental propositions of particular religious traditions) while paying so little philosophical attention to what religion actually is and does, let alone to the phenomena that many religious adherents take to be central to their way of life. APR has thus become predominantly theoretical and intellectualist in its orientation, generally content to leave discussion of the practical and cultural aspects of religion—not to mention the definition of "religion" itself—to religious studies and the social sciences (Schilbrack 2014; Strenski 2012). Yet insofar as APR has largely failed to productively engage with the research in these latter fields, it has also remained largely indifferent with respect to the important cultural critiques and postcolonial discourses that have arisen within the contexts of their research. Whether due to a mere lack of interest or an unfortunate suspicion of cultural and area studies, this represents a significant blind spot in the focus of the discipline.

Now certainly the scope of APR is not strictly beholden to all the myriad empirical manifestations and analyses of lived religion on the ground. After all, much philosophical reflection concerns itself with thought experiments and counterfactuals intended to refine and enhance our overall understanding of the concepts we use and the practices in which we engage, even if the average person employing such concepts and engaging in such practices might not characterize them in this way. At the same time, if, for example, the philosophy of sport portrayed the mental attitudes of athletes in ways that made the activities of sport nearly unrecognizable to actual athletes, or if the philosophy of science described the activity of scientific inquiry in ways that belie the way the majority of scientists actually proceed, we might think this one reason to be suspicious of such analyses. Similarly, if APR consistently puts forward views of religion or religious adherents that are, as Terence Cuneo has put it, "detached from the religious life in such a way that it threatens to offer a distorted picture of what is important to this way of life" (Cuneo 2016: 6), this might count as a strike against the way the discipline tends to proceed.

Another major gap in the APR literature in Anglo-American-European contexts is, predictably, the lack of non-Christian perspectives. The discourse remains largely dominated by discussions concerning concepts and ideas central to Western Latin Christendom at the cost of excluding important voices from other traditions and subtraditions. Given APR's prominence in largely Christian Anglo-American-European academic contexts, this may come as no surprise. However, where those operating in these contexts also see themselves as setting the standards for what is considered "genuine" or "quality" scholarship in the discipline, worries about self-selection bias loom large. And although the number of non-Christian APR scholars has increased in recent years, they not rarely encounter difficulties in engaging with their Christo-centric counterparts. On the one hand, non-Christian philosophers are often forced to frame their discussions in terms of familiar Christian concepts (e.g., "sin," "faith," "atonement," "incarnation") in order to be granted a seat at the APR table. Simultaneously, however, especially where a scholar is invited to present or write as a token member of a non-Christian tradition, there is pressure to show the ways in which one's approach is distinctively representative of their particular tradition (De Cruz 2020). This puts non-Christian—and especially non-(mono)theistic—scholars in a special sort of scholarly double-bind that can make it difficult to gain a foothold unless one does work that is commensurate with larger projects of interest to Christian philosophers. Moreover, the difficult question is raised of how to *teach* philosophy of religion in a more global way or in contexts where the dominant religious traditions are *not* interested in proofs for the existence of the God of classical theism.[2]

Some scholars skirt this concern by restricting themselves to employing the tools of analytic philosophy as a methodological "helpmeet" in the service of specifically *theological* endeavors within a particular religious tradition. Proponents of the self-styled *analytic theology* movement (hereafter AT), for example, explicitly and openly limit themselves to the confines of specific religious and doctrinal commitments (Arcadi 2017; Rea 2009). Now in and of itself, this is not problematic (at least insofar as one thinks it legitimate for theology in general to be restricted in this way). However, the moniker itself, understood as a distinctly contemporary movement within philosophical theology, has until relatively recently been almost synonymous with Christian AT.[3] And even if it is not inappropriate from a disciplinary standpoint for AT to restrict itself to a particular tradition in this way, a dialogue between Christian AT and non-Christian theologies, analytic or otherwise, is still largely lacking. We therefore cannot (yet) really speak of a robust *comparative theology* from an analytic perspective. Likewise, with some exceptions, both APR and AT have largely kept their distance from feminist, queer, postcolonial, liberation, and other less "orthodox" or "mainstream" theologies, though this too is beginning to change.

Ultimately, both APR and AT remain relatively insulated within certain theoretical, disciplinary, doctrinal, and stylistic confines. For some, this represents an advantage: The object of study is well-defined (the God of classical, usually Christian, perfect-being theism), the methodology straightforward (employing the argumentative tools of analytic philosophy), and the rhetorical style precise and coherent (at least from the standpoint of analytic philosophers themselves). It is also clear who the predominant participants in the discussion will be—or at least who they are likely not to be. (The additional lack of gender, ethnic, social, and economic diversity, although a general problem for analytic philosophy as a whole, is one from which APR rather acutely suffers.) What is not clear, however, is whether having such "well-defined" contours is really what is best for the discipline. In fact, one might think that such an insular, arguably protectionist, approach severely limits what APR can do and in which debates it can legitimately participate. There is also a very real question of how long it can continue to be relevant for the academic sphere, let alone for anything outside it.

It is my contention in this book that APR can be and do more. However, in order for it to retain a strong theoretical leg to stand on, it must, first, take more seriously two contemporary (though deeply historically rooted) challenges that threaten to undermine its credibility as a discipline and, second, locate ways to more productively grapple with its critics in these domains than on its current approach, which places it largely at an impasse with both. It is to a discussion of these critiques I now turn.

Notes

1 I should note here that I am *not* using "classical monotheism" here as a contrast to "monotheistic personalism." I am grossly dissatisfied with the use of "classical" to simply mean something like "(neo-)Aristotelian," and so I use the term here merely to indicate that much of the perfect-being theism discussed in APR has roots in Greek and Latin philosophical traditions.

2 For two very promising approaches, see Burley (2020); Harrison (2020).

3 Ramon Harvey's recently concluded project on Muslim Analytic Theology and Samuel Lebens' work in Analytic Judaism represent important contributions to the growing non-Christian literature and research programs in AT. I take up Lebens' work later in this book.

Part One

Reorientation

1

Beyond Help?

Fairies, Idols, and the View from Nowhere

The trail of the human serpent is thus over everything. Truth independent; truth that we find merely; truth, no longer malleable to human need; truth incorrigible, in a word; such truth [. . .] means only the dead heart of the living tree, and its being there means only that truth also has its paleontology and its "prescription," and may grow stiff with years of veteran service and petrified in men's regard by sheer antiquity.

William James, Pragmatism

Two fundamental objections to APR

There are two central objections to APR that have often been (at least implicitly) viewed as posing a serious threat to the discipline's standing as an academic enterprise. One of these objections comes largely from outside philosophy of religion, whereas the other arises within the context of philosophical theology itself. I think both are worth taking seriously.

The first of the two objections we may call the *ontological critique*. At its most acerbic, it is encountered in the polemics of the (now somewhat musty[1]) "new atheist" movement, popularized by such public figures as Richard Dawkins, Daniel Dennett, Sam Harris, and Christopher Hitchens. But it is also an objection that one sometimes encounters from secular students and colleagues in the academy.[2] Why, the ontological critic asks, should we continue to discuss and debate God's existence and attributes—or even to inquire into the rationality of religious belief in the first place—when we live in an "enlightened" society that has long since recognized the failure of the classical arguments for the existence of God and the possibility that someone may live a good life without accepting the God-hypothesis? Put more succinctly: If a (or the) central task of APR is to examine objects and relations that our best science tells us are false or superfluous, why should we take it seriously as a discipline?

The second objection, which we may call the *ontotheological critique*, addresses APR from within the confines of philosophical theology. This objection is most commonly encountered in phenomenological and postmodern thought, which takes its inspiration largely from the critiques of metaphysics put forward by Kant and Heidegger (though aspects of this line of thought can be traced at least as far back as Pseudo-Dionysius and come to various forms of expression in the apophatic and mystical theology of late antiquity and the middle ages[3]). This approach does not view philosophy of religion itself as a backward or otherwise unscholarly enterprise but rather objects to the *way* in which APR proceeds, insofar as the latter insists on a metaphysical and rationalistic approach to philosophy of religion that construes the Divine most fundamentally as a *causa sui*—as the rational, discursively describable, causal explanation for the existence of the universe and all its contents. The broadest version of this critique regards all "metaphysical" approaches in philosophy with suspicion. In a narrower sense, however, it criticizes APR's particular attempts to transform the God of theism into a mere "being among beings," thereby purportedly sacrificing the transcendence and radical alterity of the Divine for a rationalized, objectified *Sein-an-sich*.[4] In this more restricted sense, the postmodern theological objector claims that the "god of philosophy" distorts the nature of the Divine in such a way as to make it no longer valuable to that domain where it finds its most profound meaning, namely in the life of faith. As Paul Tillich put it: "If God is brought into the subject-object structure of being, he [*sic*] ceases to be the ground of being and becomes one being among others [. . .] he [*sic*] ceases to be the God who is really God" (Tillich 1973: 172). With Heidegger, then, the anti-ontotheological objector might be inclined to worry that before this kind of God one can neither sing nor dance nor fall to one's knees in awe and worship (Heidegger 1969: 72).[5]

Hence, whereas the ontological critique centers on the fact *that* APR tries to speak seriously of God, the ontotheological critique focuses on *how* it does so. APR thus finds itself in an unfortunate bind: The former objection implies that the subject matter and investigations of APR are evidentially untenable, given what we have learned from our best scientific theories, as well as from reflections on the problem of evil and other plausible challenges to theism—and thus are simply *irrational*. The latter objection implies that APR proceeds *too rationally*, insofar as it proceeds from a "hyper-rationalized" approach to the Divine that produces a theologically misleading image of what God is or could be. So what is to be done? Can APR escape this bind and come into fruitful conversation with both poles of criticism? Or is it doomed to remain largely restricted within its own borders, its internal vibrance and innovation marred by a failure of relevance and sad lack of concern for those outside its disciplinary city-limits?

The contours of the debate

To begin addressing these questions, it is important to note that all three parties to this discourse—APR, new atheism, and postmodern theology—are to some extent "playing on the same pitch." It is a playing field whose discursive boundaries are largely defined by recourse to a particular form of *metaphysical realism*—not, of course, about the social reality of religion itself[6] but rather about the existence of the God of perfect-being monotheism and the relevant properties, powers, activities, relations, etc. that are purported to attach to that God.[7]

Unfortunately, the contemporary philosophical literature is littered with discussions of realism and antirealism, and what is meant by these terms in one philosophical context often differs from the way it is used in another. In what follows, I am using the term 'realism' to refer roughly to the following set of claims within the context of some particular theistic tradition:[8]

1. The objects of theistic discourse appropriately designate at least one actually-existing superempirical[9] or otherwise transcendent entity/reality, and the existence of such an entity/reality is not dependent on any human attitudes, experiences, or actions concerning them. (That is, their existence is not the sole product of social construction or individual or group projection.)
2. Where theistic discourse is assertive or otherwise entails propositions about objects of the kind set out in [1] or about states of affairs involving such objects, those assertions are truth-apt, irreducible, and purportedly fact-stating—and at least some of them are true.

Here, I do not strictly equate theistic realism with theological cognitivism as many semantic approaches do. My characterization of realism allows that non-cognitivist theological expressivists will generally count as realists, whereas cognitivist error-theorists will not. I think that this more "ontological" or "existential" approach better tracks the contours of the debates in philosophy of religion (and what motivates many of them), even if other characterizations of (anti-)realism in the literature draw these lines somewhat differently.[10] It also removes the necessity of making all relevant "God-talk" in theistic discourse a matter of the evaluation of propositions.

On this rather common-sense understanding of realism, both the ontological and ontotheological critics of APR adopt a broadly *antirealist* stance with respect to the purportedly superempirical objects, properties, or relations of the theistic discourse in question, though the scope of their antirealism differs. The ontological objector opposes theistic realism *tout court*, whereas the ontotheological objector takes exception to the *metaphysical robustness* of the theistic realism proposed by APR. Put a bit differently, the former camp denies that *God* exists (i.e., they reject the claim that there is any such reality), whereas the latter camp is inclined to deny that God *exists* (i.e., to reject the category of existence as applying to the God under discussion in the same way it applies to other "things").

APR, for its part, has been predominantly concerned with protecting itself from the perceived threat of secular atheism at the cost of largely ignoring (or simply dismissing) the more heavily theological postmodern critique. In this respect, APR scholars over the past fifty years or so have cultivated a broadly *defensive* stance aimed at demonstrating the reasonableness of (belief in) a version of what we might call *metaphysically robust theistic realism* (henceforth MaRTeR) which is generally implied to be compatible, if not coextensive, with Christian monotheism. This defense of MaRTeR has involved a return to and, where deemed necessary, a revision of the traditional scholastic proofs for the existence and nature of the God of perfect-being theology, as well as the development of further (admittedly innovative and thought-provoking) arguments using the tools of contemporary analytic philosophy. At the same time, these contemporary defenses of MaRTeR tend to be less akin to Anselm's prayerful and impassioned *fides quaerens intellectum*, focusing instead on the rather unambitious tasks of avoiding epistemic blame and defending the rational permissibility of theistic belief in the face of contemporary scientific and atheist challenges to this form of theistic realism (Harris 2005: 117).

This has led the theism-atheism debate in the Anglo-American (and, to some extent, European) intellectual context to become increasingly framed as an essentially *evidential* issue[11] concerning the plausibility of MaRTeR—which, in turn, has contributed to APR's largely treating religion as an essentially *cognitive* enterprise centered around the attitude of justified, warranted, or otherwise epistemically permissible theistic *belief* and the possibility (if MaRTeR turns out to be true) of genuine religious *knowledge*. Yet an approach to religion on which belief (in the rather dry and sterile sense generally employed by analytic philosophy) stands overwhelmingly at the center of the discourse fails to take into account the sheer diversity of religious forms of life, even those heavily informed by MaRTeR, which yet again threatens to distort analyses of religion in ways that make the object of that discourse largely unrecognizable. By "diversity" here, I mean not only the plurality of religious traditions but also the variety of religious attitudes found amongst the adherents of any particular tradition. Not only does APR tend to overlook the multitude of affective orientations, volitional commitments, embodied practices, and social experiences that constitute the bulk of lived religion, it also fails to recognize the wide doxastic spectrum on which actual religious practitioners find themselves, whether this refer to the varying levels of doxastic commitment found among different religious individuals in a particular social context or to the fluctuating degrees of confidence entertained by any particular religious subject over a given span of time. Moreover, as Kelli Potter (2013; forthcoming) has rightly pointed out, it also fails to take seriously the *radical heterodoxy* found within most religious traditions. At the end of the day, religious believers simply do not believe identically, nor do their individual credences or levels of confidence remain static over time. In fact, as I will suggest later on in this book, one might come to think that the religious believers whose beliefs are so vehemently defended by APR are themselves a socially constructed fiction.[12]

The overemphasis on MaRTeR and the rationality of theistic belief also signals a failure to appreciate the very real *practical* and *moral* concerns at stake in the concerns of APR's critics (Harris 2005; Jantzen 1999). Importantly, both the ontological and ontotheological critiques are generally driven by more than just epistemic worries. While some atheists may wish to reject theism solely on the basis of its presumed falsity, the force of the ontological critique (especially in the case of many contemporary humanist movements) also rests on the very real and plausible concern that religion, and especially theism, might do more harm than good. Similarly, the ontotheological objector is not just concerned that APR's version of MaRTeR has at its center an incorrect or distorted image of God but also that a philosophical theology informed by this kind of theistic realism is potentially *idolatrous* or *sacrilegious*—or that it precludes the kind of response that would be appropriate to the Divine. In both cases, then, the objector is not merely (or perhaps even primarily) worried that the theist of the APR persuasion is simply getting it wrong or defending unwarranted propositions but also that adherence to a religion centered around such propositions may be (and has historically shown itself to be) morally, socially, or theologically *pernicious*.

Likewise, from a purely pragmatic standpoint, by continuing to frame the discourse solely in terms of MaRTeR, APR and its critics seem unlikely to be able to engage in constructive dialogue with each other that can take the concerns of all sides seriously. The debates between the defenders of MaRTeR and their ontological critics have not generally been particularly friendly or cooperative[13] and have often served to further polarize the relevant parties, with APR realists and secular new atheists respectively (though not always respectfully) digging themselves into ever-deeper ideological trenches, while largely ignoring the theological "no-man's-land" of postcolonial, feminist, queer, or liberation approaches.[14] This does not mean that questions concerning MaRTeR or the epistemic justifiability of theistic belief need be abandoned. But when a particular discourse concerning something of such social and political importance as religion comes to an impasse in which no amount of argumentation or debate appears able to move the discussion forward (or even sideways)—when the framing of the discourse makes it nearly impossible for the various participants to interact virtuously with one another—one might be justified in asking what is really being achieved by continuing to engage in such discussions, scholarly or otherwise, and whether or not there are alternative modes of discourse that could do better.

I contend that by putting all or most of its eggs in a defensive intellectualist basket framed by MaRTeR, APR has pigeonholed itself into a very small and rather unambitious discursive space—one largely defined by the attempt to defend the religious subject's "right to believe" along the lines of MaRTeR and to demonstrate the mere *possibility* that such belief, if true, could amount to objective, factual knowledge. This has often led the discipline to pursue what Basil Mitchell referred to as "minute philosophy," or a preference for focusing only on those very limited metaphysical and epistemological topics that can be treated "with exemplary clarity and rigour" (Mitchell 2005: 22). It tends to "put a premium on tight manageable themes," where "the prevailing orthodoxy [is] reinforced by gestures, tones of voice and figures of speech" (22) that often serve to police the boundaries of the discipline. In this sense, APR has trained itself to avoid the messiness of the religious life (or of particular religious *lives*) in favor of a rather philosophically conservative project aimed at preserving the possibility of detached and disinterested theistic knowledge.

Viewing God from nowhere?

Indeed, APR's sustained normative emphasis on the idealized stance of detachment and disinterestedness itself gestures at a more deeply rooted problem, one which will occupy us in some form or another throughout the rest of this book: By trying to defend the idea that theistic belief *could*, in some limited instances, conceivably amount to knowledge, APR has moved increasingly further away from the *actual* experiences, feelings, and imaginings of the divine espoused by the adherents of particular religions, endorsing instead the attempt to articulate a concept of God that would be acceptable to any "rational," "impartial," "unprejudiced" epistemic subject were they to step *outside* the particular, subjective, potentially biased perspectives of religion "on the ground." That is, the dominant model of epistemic objectivity in APR has tended to either implicitly or explicitly endorse the adoption (or at least approximation) of a kind of "view from nowhere," in order to defend a stripped-down version of MaRTeR that can successfully counter the ontological critique.

Unfortunately, neither the view from nowhere nor the MaRTeR-style perfect-being theism that results are as objective or value-neutral as their proponents might be inclined to think. In fact, the view from nowhere the defender of MaRTeR is asked to take up when investigating questions of the existence and nature of the Divine is, somewhat ironically, one that takes the very epistemic values exemplified in classical perfect-being theism as its starting point. It valorizes a largely *abstract* and *disembodied* stance—that is, a "purely intellectual," ahistorical and aperspectival approach to issues that remains as impartial and detached from its objects as possible. Where possible, it is *universal* as opposed to particular, and values like *simplicity* and *unity* are preferred over complexity and multiplicity.

It is thus no coincidence that the view from nowhere is also often termed the *God's-eye view*. Yet although purporting to endorse a supposedly "universal, neutral, objective rendering of the way things are" (Jantzen 1996: 100) and thereby implying that this vantage point is not itself informed by a particular perspective, the ideal(ized) epistemic stance on this approach is ultimately one that might itself end up reinforcing a particular, idiosyncratic view of God (namely that of traditional perfect-being theism) more than it neutralizes one from such bias. Put a bit differently, the mutually reinforcing ideas of a certain version of MaRTeR and a particular philosophical conception of what it means to be "rational" at once determine both which conceptions of God are worth defending and who it is that can be in a position to rationally defend them (Griffioen 2021a). Those who endorse epistemic standards standing in tension with the standards promoted by the view from nowhere are seen as having no business trying to develop a philosophically defensible conception of God, while those whose preconceptions, experiences, or interpretations of the divine fall outside this understanding of what it means to be *aliquid quo maius nihil cogitari potest* are excluded from participation in rational philosophical inquiry from the outset. In this sense, the question posed a quarter-century ago by Grace Jantzen is not merely rhetorical: "Whose values are reflected in the putative 'view from nowhere'?" she asks. "The lame response that 'this is just what the philosophy of religion consists of' obviously begs the question of why, and in whose interests, that particular 'consistency' is held to and [. . .] zealously defended" (Jantzen 1999: 206). The same might be said for the model of God that emerges from this stance.

APR's failure to adequately address this question not only displays a lack of critical reflection regarding its own approach, it may ultimately end up doing an epistemic *disservice*—both to those who endorse such an approach and to those epistemic subjects affected or excluded by the kinds of conclusions it draws. To begin, there is a concern that the kinds of philosophy and philosophical views traditionally favored by the dominant voices in APR are often uncritically assumed to be those that actually best instantiate the values of the view from nowhere, while alternative perspectives are simply taken to be "unphilosophical" or to lack philosophical "rigor." The way APR proceeds may thus sometimes promote a disciplinary form of what José Medina calls *epistemic arrogance* with respect to potential alternatives—one that can ultimately lead to a kind of *closed-mindedness* or even to the *incapability* of seeing alternative viewpoints that can further serve to "erode[ ] reliability, epistemic trust, and one's general capacity to learn" (Medina 2013b: 34).

Additionally, the inability or unwillingness of APR to interrogate its own presuppositions also severely limits its ability to take seriously the *experiences* of certain epistemic subjects, insofar as they do not fit the favored mold, and this can perpetrate further harm to all parties concerned.[15] For example, as I will explore further in my discussion of intellectualist theodicies in Chapter 8, a subject's particular experience (e.g., of horrendous suffering, religious trauma, or divine absence—or as a member of a socially oppressed or marginalized group) may make them unwilling or unable to take up the affectively distanced stance of "disinterested neutrality" required by the APR approach, thereby excluding their testimony from the arena of rational discourse and relegating them to the realm of mere irrationality (or even to that of a dehumanizing *a*-rationality). And insofar as they are not invited to the discursive table so long as they are not (at least pretending) to adopt this "ideal" stance, their experiential testimony is unlikely to be taken very seriously by those operating within the dominant perspective, thereby further policing what can count as genuine counterevidence to the perfect-being theology in question and potentially leading to distorted perceptions of who is qualified to speak on such matters.

Finally, given that the purportedly "neutral" standpoint of the view from nowhere endorses the *de-particularization* and *de-contextualization* of the "rational" religious subject in the interest of "objective" religious knowledge, this may not only exclude alternative voices as discussed above, it can ultimately promote the dismissal and neglect of epistemically relevant *differences* in the objects of study. For example, it can lead to forcing ideas and practices of those religious traditions outside the disciplinary *status quo* into particular conceptual molds as conceived by the dominant tradition under discussion. It can also serve to erase relevant differences with respect to race, gender, sexuality, ability, class, and so on, which, in some cases, also likely underlie important religious differences. Thus, by raising a particular version of MaRTeR to the level of the "most general" theism—belief in which would be rationally defensible or at least epistemically permissible—APR threatens to *homogenize* religious subjects and traditions by erasing the religious and cultural differences that give their faith shape and meaning, as well as by ignoring the wide varieties of attitudes, orientations, and identities that may be significant for understanding the significance of the religious life.

Taken together, these two first-order insensitivities (lack of awareness of other perspectives and lack of sensitivity to relevant religious difference) can serve to cultivate a kind of more general *meta-insensitivity* on the part of APR— as Medina describes it, an overall "inability to recognize and acknowledge [its] limitations and blind spots" (Medina 2013b: 150). It can thereby end up manifesting an "ignorance about [its] own positionality and relationality with respect to those ignored others [and] ignorance about certain aspects of [itself] that [it] is unable to recognize" (162). This carefully (though rarely reflectively or intentionally) cultivated and systemically embedded *shared self-ignorance* in APR can serve to further reinforce the presupposition that any approach to the Divine which cannot be "folded into" the God of MaRTeR theism must be irrational and thus not worthy of philosophical exploration.

Conclusion

In the end, if APR's view-from-nowhere approach to defending MaRTeR against the ontological critique epistemically exculpates generic, idealized theists at the cost of promoting in its practitioners an inability to appropriately and reliably form non-distorted beliefs about their own epistemic status, that of their fellow human beings, and the traditions that make up the objects of their study, we must ask ourselves whether this is really an epistemically preferable way of proceeding. Indeed, this is not only an epistemic problem, but potentially a social, moral, and political concern of some significance, especially where those persons and groups who are the objects of such distorted belief are thereby excluded from contributing to the discourse. It also points to the possibility that the epistemic values championed by APR, as well as the conception of God that arises from the desire to defend MaRTeR against its ontological objectors, might not be the only possible values—or the only appropriate view of God—in the game. So what should we conclude from this? Has APR outlived its moment? Must it stop everything it's been doing and start doing something else?

My answer is both yes and no. On the one hand, I think APR can and must move beyond the confines of (largely defensive) discussions concerning the plausibility of MaRTeR. It must become a discipline that is less isolated, more ambitious, and genuinely socially relevant—and it should do so in a way that both engages productively with its conscientious objectors and enriches the discipline itself. This, I think, can best be accomplished by exploring alternative epistemic values and approaches and by making certain focal shifts within the discipline. On the other hand, making these shifts need not mean the end of all that APR holds dear (though it may call for an epistemic reframing of these enterprises or a shift in attitude with respect to alternative positions). Likewise, calling the view-from-nowhere approach into question is *not* the same as rejecting the importance of reason and rationality. It is merely to note that, since these values do not themselves arise from a perspectiveless "nowhere," they can thus perhaps be extended, supplemented, complemented, or corrected—especially if it turns out that they tend to exclude perspectives and interests that are of epistemic and moral relevance to projects we care about. As Jantzen writes: "Critical reason need not be replaced by a sardine can opener, but it could very beneficially be supplemented by [...] a wider understanding of reason that includes sensitivity and attentiveness, well-trained intuition and discernment, creative imagination, and lateral as well as linear thinking" (Jantzen 1999: 99).

At the same time, when we start to explore alternative values and methods to those proposed by the view-from-nowhere approach, we may also end up with something other than the God traditionally championed by APR MaRTeR-dom. In, fact, even if one *agrees* with the defenders of perfect-being theology that the divine attributes should amount to something like idealized or maximized versions of certain epistemic or moral values we find in non-divine reasoning agents, it is unclear that the candidates for maximization traditionally employed uncritically by APR are the only—or even the best—standards in the game. If, for example, we are willing to entertain the possibility that particularity and partiality may be more important than universality and neutrality for certain forms of moral or political reasoning,[16] that complexity or intricacy may sometimes be preferable to simplicity,[17] that diversity and disagreement might be more relevant for epistemic objectivity than singularity and consensus,[18] and so on—then, even were we to continue to insist on a form of perfect-being theology, the corresponding view of divine perfection based around such values might still end up looking radically different from that currently espoused by many proponents of APR.

In the following chapters, then, I will attempt to show the beginnings of what such an analytic philosophy of religion might look like. Ultimately, I think that while we can and should appreciate the work the debate over MaRTeR has done for APR, the time is perhaps coming to "sacrifice" the MaRTeR debate in the interest of the growth and diversification of the discipline. Importantly, I am *not* recommending we all become theological antirealists. Far from it. The approaches I recommend below, as I will discuss, are compatible with realist and antirealist approaches. Further, the project of defending MaRTeR will still have a contextualized place in APR. But, to crib from an esteemed thinker much more eloquent than I,[19] the "dogmas of the quiet past" in APR are simply no longer adequate to our "stormy present," nor to our overall epistemic task as philosophers of religion. It will therefore be necessary to at least gesture at how we as a discipline can "disenthrall ourselves" from MaRTeR—and how, in moving *beyond* our current self-imposed constrictions, we can begin to "think and act anew" in ways that both "save" the phenomena and justify APR's legitimacy as a discipline.

Notes

1   Whether the movement was ever "new" is up for debate. Its self-styled image as inheriting the "rationalist" legacy of the Enlightenment demonstrates its own admitted lack of novelty. Indeed, both its deeply engrained misogyny and its perpetuation of common misunderstandings of Enlightenment thought reveal unfortunate ways in which it is wholly unoriginal. Although I think it would be overall better if APR could divorce itself from its combative focus on defending itself from this movement (with whom it unfortunately has come to share certain values, concerns, and talking points), given the cultural force that the "new" atheism has become, such an extraction is unlikely and perhaps (at this point, anyway) ill-advised.

2   I write here as a US-American scholar working within two different academic
    cultures (Germany and China) in which students and faculty tend to come from
    largely secular backgrounds.

3   There are subtle and relevant distinctions to be made regarding the different strands
    of this more apophatic line of thought, which I unfortunately cannot go into here. It
    will have to suffice to note that although the various expressions of what I am calling
    the "ontotheological critique" all tend to maintain in one form or another that the
    category of the Divine "outstrips" in some relevant way our cognitive or descriptive
    capacities, they are not all uniformly suspicious of metaphysics, nor equally skeptical
    of our ability to genuinely know or speak of God. For one treatment that attempts to
    connect these strands, see Westphal (2007).

4   See, among others, Caputo (2013); Kearney (2011); Marion (1991); Westphal (2001).
    For a helpful (and constructive) overview of the "personal theism" of many APR
    scholars vs. the "alterity theism" of the ontotheological critics, see Stenmark
    (2015).

5   However, on this point, see also Marilyn McCord Adams' response that the "idea that
    we cannot sing and dance before the first cause fails to take seriously Who the first
    cause really is" (McCord Adams 2014:12).

6   I take it that most of the members in this debate would agree that religions have
    some sort of social ontological status or "reality." Of course, there is a relevant debate
    in religious studies concerning whether the concept of 'religion' as a social-scientific
    category has, as Arnal & McCutcheon have suggested, "outlasted its shelf life," such
    that "we would be better served setting aside not simply the word, but the very idea
    that it makes good academic sense to clump together, for description, analysis, or
    especially explanation, those diverse acts, institutions, objects, and claims that we
    normally call 'religious'" (Arnal and McCutcheon 2013: xiii). Yet this is *not* the
    concern that tends to drive the discourse between APR and its critics. Indeed, if APR
    wants to productively contribute to this latter debate (and I think it should at least
    have *something* to say on the matter), it may first need to move past some of the
    strictures imposed on its discourse through its adherence to the kind of
    metaphysically robust theistic realism I discuss here.

7   Anthony Pinn notes that "humanists and atheists often fail to make a distinction
    between theism and religion, although humanist and atheist rhetoric would suggest
    the former is the real target of disbelief" (Pinn 2015: 99). However, it is not only
    secularists who conflate the two. Much of the discourse in APR itself, as well as
    between APR and its objectors, fails to draw this distinction in any adequate fashion.

8   Here, I loosely follow the accounts of Eshleman (2016) and Le Poidevin (2019),
    except that I do not insist that realist discourse be propositional or truth-apt (though
    it may, as Eshleman suggests, be understood as entailing certain truth-apt
    propositions).

9	I borrow this term from Schilbrack (2014), who defines the 'superempirical' as "those [. . .] aspects of reality whose existence allegedly does not depend on empirical sources" (135).

10	While there are a number of much more nuanced views on (anti-)realism in the philosophical literature, I nevertheless think that the way I have formulated things here, while perhaps oversimplified, still gets at the core of what drives these various parties. For instance, even if one wants to call the ontological objector a realist because they think the utterance 'God exists' asserts a fact whose truth value depends on a non-epistemic state of affairs independent of human cognition that we can have true beliefs about (Insole 2006: 2–3), their beef with theists of a similarly "alethically realist" persuasion has to do with the *actual* truth or falsity of this utterance, not with whether such propositions are *capable* of being true or false. And this disagreement has traditionally been cashed out is in terms of producing and critiquing arguments concerning the ontological question. Likewise, although the question of whether there *is* an answer to the ontological question is distinct from the questions of whether we can *know* or *reasonably believe* that answer, both APR and its atheist critics have, by and large, responded to all three questions in the affirmative and have then set about quarrelling over what the answer actually is (or can reasonably be believed to be).

	The realist-antirealist debate is somewhat more interesting with respect to the ontotheological objection, since many of those who worry about ontotheology have pushed forms of semantic non-cognitivism or alethic (and sometimes epistemic) antirealism. But even here, I think the larger debate between APR and the ontotheological critics tends to boil down to questions concerning how we (should) conceive of the divine, with APR largely insisting on a God-qua-existent-being who can be the object of propositional belief and the ontotheological objector resisting this conception in some form or another.

11	While it is true that some APR scholars have taken a decidedly anti-evidentialist stance (especially in what has come to be known as Reformed epistemology), such approaches are still usually reactions to the ontological critic's *demand* for evidence, with the anti-evidentialist answering that epistemic permissibility is not always beholden to evidential considerations. See, for example, Plantinga (1983) and Wolterstorff (1976) for two seminal texts in this vein. See also Chapter 3 of Plantinga (2000).

12	One might object here that the "religious believer" as employed in APR by proponents of MaRTeR merely represents some sort of epistemically idealized religious subject. Yet if the "warranted belief" or "reasonable faith" defended by certain APR scholars is held by very few *actual* theists (even those of a realist persuasion)—and if heterodoxy within a religious tradition is as widespread as we have reason to think it might be—then it is unclear that the defender of MaRTeR has really answered the epistemic challenge they ought to be worried about if MaRTeR really matters. True, they have made room for the *possibility* of reasonable religious belief, but the charge that most-if-not-all *actual* believers are irrational remains a genuine concern.

13 The discourse tends to be somewhat more civil when occurring within the confines of APR itself, but even here it is unclear that the debate is really all that helpful in moving the discussion forward.

14 This is particularly unfortunate because it seems like both APR and its ontological critics could benefit (and find grist for their respective mills) from exploring these theological approaches more thoroughly.

15 Of course, here the distinction between epistemic and moral harm runs together— hence the term "epistemic injustice" employed in the literature.

16 See, e.g., Dancy (2004); Harding (1993); Williams (1981); Young (2011).

17 One may think here not only of works of music or art but also of the classical "principle of plenitude" and its contemporary inheritance (see, e.g., Jaeger 2016; Kane 1976), as well as of the rejection of Ockham's razor as requiring quantitative parsimony (see, e.g., Lewis 1973).

18 See, e.g., Anderson (2006); Longino (1993); Medina (2013b); Wong (2020).

19 See: Abraham Lincoln's 1862 Annual Address to Congress.

2

Beyond Knowledge

Toward a Social Epistemology of Understanding

The Master said, "You can study with some, and yet not necessarily walk the same path (dao 道); you can walk the same path as some, and yet not necessarily take your stand with them; you can take your stand with them, and yet not necessarily weigh things up in the same way. [. . .] The exemplary person pursues harmony rather than sameness (tong 同); the small person does the opposite."

Kǒngzǐ, Analects

Introduction

In the previous chapter, I claimed that analytic philosophy of religion (APR) would do well to move beyond the confines of its limited epistemological focus on defending the rationality of belief in what I called *metaphysically robust theistic realism*, or MaRTeR. In this chapter, I want to motivate the idea that there are other epistemological options available—and that these alternatives still allow for the claim implicitly championed by many APR scholars that religion can be (and at least sometimes is) an epistemically valuable enterprise. In fact, if I am right, the alternative epistemological approach I suggest here may help us better come to see what it is about the religious life that is of real epistemic value.

However, to motivate the epistemological shift I am recommending, this chapter will explore two domains from outside the sphere of philosophy of religion that we generally take to be relatively uncontroversial examples of epistemically valuable enterprises—namely, that of the natural sciences and mathematics. Drawing especially on the work of Catherine Elgin, I will argue that, even in these domains, the question of robust metaphysical realism and the epistemological emphasis on propositional knowledge in contemporary philosophy can be misleading with respect to how actors proceed and make progress within these domains—and that we might therefore need to reconsider the philosophical obsession with knowledge and true belief. Ultimately, I will claim that a social epistemology focused more on *understanding* and the pursuit of epistemic *harmony* than knowledge and the desire for cognitive homogeneity can both better explain how it is that these enterprises are epistemically valuable and provide a better normative framework for the pursuit of objectivity in these domains. In the chapter that follows, then, I will apply this approach to the religious domain, arguing that such an epistemological shift can help us better address the diversity of propositional (and other kinds of) commitments among religious adherents and can give APR the tools to productively transform itself in ways that demonstrate religion's potential to produce systems of epistemic value.

Science, mathematics, and the dispensability of realism

Let us begin by looking at the natural sciences. Although we tend to think of the sciences as encompassing those fields most immediately concerned with objective, impartial knowledge and the accurate description of the natural universe, Catherine Elgin (2006, 2007, 2017, 2022), Hank De Regt (2015), De Regt and Gijsbers (2016), and others have argued that a fundamental component of traditional theories of knowledge—namely, *truth*—is perhaps much less central to the scientific enterprise than we might expect. As Elgin notes: "Even the best scientific accounts are not true. Not only are they plagued with anomalies and outstanding problems, but where they are successful, they rely on lawlike statements, models, and idealizations that are known to diverge from the truth" (Elgin 2017: 14). To make matters even more complicated, scientists also sometimes employ incompatible models with regard to the same subject matter, as when water is alternately represented as a fluid or as a collection of molecules, or when light is modelled as a wave or as a particle, depending on which scientific purpose the representation is supposed to serve in a particular context (De Regt 2015: 3791–2; Elgin 2017: 267). Yet although models like the ideal gas law are explicitly acknowledged not to be true, and the wave and particle models with respect to light are admitted to be incompatible with one another, these falsehoods and incongruencies nevertheless still figure centrally in the scientific contexts in which they are employed. Elgin calls such representations "felicitous falsehoods," or those untruths whose inaccuracy does not undermine their epistemic function within the scientific enterprise and may even serve to enhance it (Elgin 2017: 3). Contemporary science, she maintains, is "riddled" with useful fictions of these kinds, yet importantly it is unclear that the use of such devices in scientific practice is likely to disappear—nor that their elimination would even be desirable—even if they may sometimes be replaced by new or revised representations as science pursues an ever more comprehensive understanding of the phenomena it observes (31).

The second epistemic domain I wish to consider is that of mathematics. Here, questions concerning the existence and ontological status of numbers and other mathematical objects are largely irrelevant to—or at least posterior to—the success of actual mathematical practice.[1] As Charles Hockett wrote with respect to a particular form of mathematical realism: "Nothing is gained for mathematics by assuming that such entities exist" and that, in many cases, mathematicians simply "*do not care*" (Hockett 1967: 20). More recently, Justin Clarke-Doane has observed concerning the unanimity in mathematical practice that "the mathematical, and generally scientific, community has decided to *use*, for example, the Least Upper Bound Axiom, even if the case for its truth, realistically construed, is contested" (Clarke-Doane 2020: 61).

Howard Wettstein has likewise claimed that it would be a "folly" to think that work in mathematics awaits a "philosophical underpinning" of the kind that would settle questions concerning "the existence and status of mathematical entities like numbers and sets" (Wettstein 1997: 257). We simply do not feel the need to settle the question concerning mathematical realism in order to justify mathematics as an epistemically valuable enterprise.[2] Why not? Wettstein chalks this up to the "primacy of the institution and its practices," as well as to our "confidence in mathematical practice" (257). Regardless of what we think about the existence or ontological status of numbers or other mathematical objects, we value what mathematics *does* for us, and we trust it to continue to do so reliably without first feeling the need to settle the ontological question. In this sense, realists, agnostics, and skeptics about mathematical objects can successfully engage in, say, proving or exploring the limits of a particular theorem, so long as they share an understanding of how those objects can be employed and manipulated to further their collective epistemic projects.

In both the scientific and mathematical domains, then, the question of the existence of some of the most fundamental objects of the discourse and of the "objective" truth of certain theories central to practice in these domains (in the sense of an isomorphic correspondence with some perspective-independent reality) is largely orthogonal to that practice itself. Yet if this is right, then a veritistic epistemology that places propositional knowledge (in the sense of justified or warranted true belief) at the center of its account is going to have a very difficult time explaining how it is that these domains are epistemically valuable. As Elgin puts it with regard to the sciences: "Knowledge requires truth. And there seems to be no feasible way to get the scientific accounts we admire to come out true" (Elgin 2017: 37). Something analogous might also be said with respect to mathematics, at least insofar as we can have little confidence about the truth of mathematical realism with respect to numbers and other mathematical objects but remain firm in our conviction that the mathematical enterprise employing such objects yields epistemically valuable results. So if knowledge is *not* the "the cognitive condition that good science standardly engenders" (37), and if the question of realism is of no pressing relevance to doing good mathematics, what is it that allows us to reasonably maintain that these practices are of epistemic value?

From knowledge to understanding

Elgin argues that it is the epistemic achievement of *understanding*, rather than that of merely justified or warranted true belief, that lies at the heart of the scientific enterprise—and which can better explain both the activities of scientists and the epistemic value of the sciences, as well as most other scholarly domains. According to Elgin, understanding "consists in accepting a system of commitments in reflective equilibrium," where the latter is construed as each of the elements of a network of commitments being "reasonable in light of the others, and the network as a whole [being] as reasonable as any available alternative in light of our relevant previous commitments" (Elgin 2017: 4).[3]

The focus of Elgin's account is less about the mere understanding of individual propositions and more about what she, following Kvanvig (2003), calls *objectual understanding*. Objectual understanding, or the kind of systematic, holistic "grasping" of a topic or subject matter characteristic of disciplinary understanding, involves (minimally) the ability to "wield [the object of understanding] to further one's epistemic ends" (Elgin 2017: 33; see also 44ff.) and is a broader and more comprehensive notion than that of propositional knowledge (at least as it tends to be discussed in traditional analytic epistemologies). Not only do we understand facts, she notes, we also understand "rules and reasons, actions and passions, objectives and obstacles, techniques and tools, forms, functions, and fictions, as well as [. . .] pictures, words, equations, and patterns," to name just a few (Elgin

1996: 123). Moreover, as Elgin notes, understanding need not be verbal or expressible solely via propositional assertions but can also be found in "apt terminology, insightful questions, effective nonverbal symbols, [or] intelligent behavior," where these latter expressions may be of equal or greater epistemic value than their propositional counterparts: "A mechanic's understanding of carburetors or a composer's understanding of counterpoint is no less epistemically significant for being inarticulate. Even a physicist's understanding of her subject typically outstrips her words" (123).

Understanding and propositional knowledge also differ with respect to their demandingness. On the one hand, understanding is more demanding than propositional knowledge insofar as the former is holistic, involving not just getting some particular thing or series of things "right" but also being able "to wield one's commitments to further one's epistemic ends [. . .], being able to draw inferences, raise questions, frame potentially fruitful inquiries, and so forth" (Elgin 2017: 3). On the other hand, understanding is less demanding than propositional knowledge insofar as knowledge is a veritistic notion, whereas accepting a system of commitments in reflective equilibrium need not be factive in order for its deliverances to count as contributing positively to the epistemic ends in question (Elgin 2007).[4] Indeed, viewing understanding as *non-factive* allows us to better make sense of the scientific proclivities toward idealization and the use of felicitous falsehoods, as well as of the irrelevance to mathematics of settling the question of realism prior to its practice, in ways that more veritistic knowledge-centered accounts cannot adequately capture. It also allows us to see why, for example, mathematicians might value proofs of propositions whose truth is not in doubt or to pursue multiple proofs of the same theorem. As Elgin puts it: "If truth were the sole concern, any subsequent proof would be redundant. Because a new proof exemplifies different mathematical relations, it is not. Such a proof enriches understanding of the relations among mathematical propositions" (Elgin 2011: 406).[5] Finally, unlike factive accounts of knowledge, understanding is not an all-or-nothing epistemic phenomenon. It can be a *gradual* or *comparative* notion, one that admits of degrees (Elgin 2017: 58).[6]

Henk de Regt has likewise argued that instead of focusing on the epistemic deliverances of science as merely taking the form of propositional knowledge requiring truth, we would do better to focus on scientific understanding as a kind of processual skill aimed at *intelligibility*: "Scientific understanding does not require that theories are (approximately) true but instead that they are intelligible, that is, they should have qualities that allow scientists to *use* them for constructing models of the phenomena" (De Regt 2015: 3795). Construed thusly, an epistemology that brings understanding to the fore allows for the development of an approach to science and mathematics that, to some extent, moves them "beyond realism," insofar as it can be consistent with both realist and antirealist approaches to scientific models and mathematical objects yet requires neither to make sense of how these enterprises are epistemically valuable.

Shifting to an understanding-centered, non-factive epistemology also shows us why it is not necessary for the success of the scientific or mathematical enterprises that their practitioners actually *believe* in the truth of the propositions associated with the representations in question but only that they *accept* such propositions as put forward by the relevant models. Acceptance in this sense is less a cognitive disposition to represent a proposition p as obtaining or to "feel" p to be true when asked whether p and more a volitional disposition to *act* in ways commensurate with p-relevant worlds. As Jonathan Cohen puts it: "[To] accept that p is to have or adopt a policy of deeming, positing, or postulating that p—i.e., of including that proposition or rule among one's premises for deciding what to do or think in a particular context, whether or not one feels it to be true that p" (Cohen 1992: 4). This may include asserting p in relevant scenarios, employing it in one's reasoning, or acting, where appropriate, as though p were true. Accepting that p is not incompatible with believing that p, and most people who believe a proposition also accept it, but belief is not necessary for acceptance, nor might it even be sufficient in some contexts.[7] But insofar as acceptance is put toward the epistemic aim of understanding, it may not be unfitting for a scientist or a mathematician to maintain a skeptical or agnostic doxastic attitude toward the truth of p, while at the same time being willing to assert, use, and act on the proposition in the relevant ways (Elgin 2017: 19). In this sense, two scientific practitioners in the same field operating with the same model need only agree in their *acceptance* and *use* of the relevant propositions and objects to do "good" science, even if they may ultimately disagree on their truth or ontological status.

Understanding's non-factivity notwithstanding, however, neither Elgin nor De Regt is claiming that the way things "really are" has no bearing on the epistemic value of the scientific or mathematical enterprises whatsoever. De Regt, for example, notes that "at the level of the empirical phenomena of interest the models should provide descriptions or predictions that are true in the [restricted] sense that they agree with the observations in relevant aspects and to a sufficient degree" (De Regt 2015: 3795). At the same time, he notes that truth interpreted in this restricted sense (which is always determined by context) will not necessarily track understanding, such that a higher degree of agreement need not entail a higher degree of understanding. Elgin, for her part, claims that part of what makes understanding epistemically valuable is that the elements of the system being understood are appropriately "tethered" to reality—or that they are somehow "answerable" to something external to themselves. This means, first, that a system must tie what is understood to the relevant community's prior epistemic commitments. That is, the community's understanding needs to be, "in a suitable but flexible sense, sustained by what its members were already committed to" (Elgin 2017: 183). Yet to ensure that not just any coherent system will make the proverbial cut, she argues that the system in question must also in some relevant sense be connected to the "phenomena they concern" (1). In this sense, she thinks astronomy as a scientific enterprise will be suitably tethered, whereas astrology will not. Still, there is a relevant sense in which one can be said to pursue and understand astrology, insofar as one's commitments are "tethered to the doctrine or account" itself, not necessarily to the phenomena the system purports to be about (45). In this way, an account itself can also be the object of understanding, even if its subject matter is not suitably tethered to the facts in the way Elgin has in mind.

Importantly, however, Elgin maintains that although a system's being suitably tethered is part of what makes understanding of the system epistemically valuable, truth is not the only suitable tether that can "moor" a system in this way. Channeling Nelson Goodman, she claims that *exemplification* can also serve to tie systems to the relevant theory-external phenomena to which they pertain. When something functions as an exemplar, it takes on the role of a *symbol*—one which "makes reference to some of the properties, patterns, or relations it instantiates" (Elgin 2017: 184). It may be literal or metaphorical, analogical or allegorical. For example, a Dm7-G7-Cmaj7 chord progression may be played in a certain register on a piano to demonstrate the so-called "two-five-one turnaround" when playing a 12-bar blues, even though this progression can be performed in any key and any register by any instrument or set of instruments capable of producing such chords. A crude model made of sticks and Styrofoam balls—although grossly inaccurate in many ways—may help young chemistry students come to better understand how molecules are structured. A medieval hagiography may use biographical scenes in a saint's life to point to more general moral or theological virtues and ways of living that the book's readers are encouraged to emulate. Or, as we find in Christian Gothic and Renaissance art, a pomegranate held by the Madonna or the infant Christ may symbolize and prefigure Jesus' eventual passion and death, even as it refers to Persephone's cyclical descent into the underworld in ancient Greek mythology.

Still, to employ a metaphor of our own, exemplars and the systems that employ them are importantly *not*—even ideally—"mirrors" that merely serve to "reflect" salient properties or to "replicate reality." As Elgin writes:

> To replicate reality would simply be to reproduce the blooming, buzzing confusion that confronts us. What is the value in that? Our goal should be to make sense of things—to structure, synthesize, organize, and orient ourselves toward things in ways that serve our ends. [. . .] Neither art nor science is, can be, or ought to be, a mirror of nature. Epistemically effective representations in both disciplines embody and convey an understanding of their subjects. Since understanding is not mirroring, failures of mirroring need not be failures of understanding.
>
> Elgin 2017: 250, my emphasis

Neither are exemplars mere "vehicles" of salience. In fact, they can often themselves be the *sources* of salience. An exemplar can highlight or help us access epistemically-relevant features of an object or situation that we may tend to otherwise disregard; or it can help us recognize certain properties when we encounter them elsewhere. It may even "marginalize conspicuous features in order to exemplify elusive ones" (Elgin 2017: 187). That scientific models and idealizations can do this seems clear. But we now also have a better way of seeing how, for example, mathematics can be appropriately tethered without answering the realist question. Numbers, variables, and other mathematical objects can be used and manipulated in equations, theorems, and proofs in ways that can make epistemically relevant patterns, structures, and relations intellectually salient without first (or ever) establishing that the mathematical objects themselves exist as construed by mathematicians or that they correspond directly to independently existing extra-theoretical entities in the world. The use of felicitous falsehoods or ontologically indeterminate objects is therefore to be viewed neither as an "unfortunate expedient" in the pursuit of factual knowledge that can be consigned to the periphery of a theory nor as something that would ideally be eliminated in these domains. It is rather a "powerful tool" essential to the enterprise itself, an instrument in the pragmatic pursuits of these disciplines, which a greater degree of understanding can help achieve (61).

Importantly, however, what counts as the relevant criterion or salient feature for exemplification depends heavily on *context*, including what function the understanding being pursued is ultimately intended to serve.[8] For this reason, the determination of which criteria are relevant or which features are salient to appropriately tether a model or theory—and the corresponding understanding to which it contributes—to reality is not necessarily (or even usually) a wholly epistemic matter, and even where epistemic it is not merely evaluable in terms of how truth-conducive it is. Whether a model is suitably tethered or what constitutes "fitting" or "adequate" model-driven understanding in a particular context depends not only (or, in some cases, perhaps not at all) on its truth-conduciveness but also (or rather) on how well such understanding can be utilized to successfully realize other epistemic and practical ends we value or to pursue further projects we care about. Put a bit differently: although understanding can itself be viewed as a cognitive achievement on its own,[9] its epistemic value in many contexts derives largely from other concrete things we care about doing—things like *explaining* why global temperatures are increasing or *predicting* the impact of climate change on the world food supply, *building* working automobiles or *cultivating* safer and less hostile online environments. And these goals, in turn, may derive their value from more overarching practical or political concerns like wanting to save the human race from destruction, or trying to help people get efficiently from point A to B, or promoting justice and human dignity.[10]

This pragmatic contextualism with respect to understanding, models, and their tethers is important as it points us to the fact that, ultimately, *understanding is as understanding does*, and what may determine both its epistemic value and its fittingness with respect to "objective" reality has much to do with what we want or need understanding to *do* in a particular context. In this respect, its function goes beyond the merely cognitive. For example, if the goal is to reduce the amount of plastic bought and consumed by the members of a community, the understanding afforded by a very basic model of climate change may be more effective than the more truth-conducive models employed by climate scientists, since the cognitive energy required for understanding the latter may actually make people less inclined to pay attention to climate change in the first place. The more basic model may still be epistemically valuable in this context, insofar as it provides ordinary citizens with the requisite grasp of the situation needed to awaken the right kind of feelings to motivate action. It is, as Elgin puts it, "true enough" to be action-guiding, even if such a model would not count as adequately tethered for a climate scientist who is trying to explain the environmental impact of plastic consumption or to predict how consuming less plastic would make a difference with respect to climate change. And even with respect to the latter, it is unlikely that mere truth-conduciveness will be sufficient to fully capture the epistemic value of the model in question.[11]

Resonance, dissonance, and the dynamism of understanding

Consequently, there is good reason to think that contextual and pragmatic considerations are not irrelevant to appropriate model and theory choice in the natural sciences and mathematics, and that this is not generally a bad thing. However, there is another sense in which the values that drive model preference or theory choice are not always exclusively cognitive—namely, insofar as it the latter are sensitive to certain *aesthetic* and/or *affective* attitudes of epistemic subjects that may not be straightforwardly reducible to truth-evaluable doxastic states. Many scientists and mathematicians, for example, report a sensitivity to and respect for such aesthetic values as beauty and elegance, which are often accompanied or driven by feelings of wonder and awe. For example, one study found that the more "beautiful" an equation was ranked by mathematicians, the more activity the researchers measured in the area of the brain correlated with visual, musical, and moral beauty (Zeki et al. 2014). This finding was unsurprising to mathematicians themselves, one of whom reported, "When I see a beautiful mathematical construction, or an unexpected and wonderfully intricate argument with precise logical interlocking pieces in a proof, I do feel the same way as when I see some art that amazes me" (Colin Adams, quoted in Moskowitz 2014).

In some cases, the beauty of a particular theory, or the response it inspires in the theorist who comprehends it, may lead to the preference of that theory over one equally or more likely to be true. For example, mathematician and physicist Hermann Weyl is quoted as claiming that his work "always tried to unite the true with the beautiful" but that, in cases where he had to choose, "I usually chose the beautiful" (quoted in Chandrasekhar 2010: 57). Theoretical physicist Richard Feynman likewise noted the motivational aspect of the feelings of scientific wonder: "The same thrill, the same awe and mystery, comes again and again when we look at any question deeply enough. With more knowledge comes a deeper, more wonderful mystery, luring one on to penetrate deeper still" (quoted in Chandrasekhar 1989: 16). In this sense, the experience of beauty and elegance and the related affective states of awe and wonder, are not necessarily mere "epiphenomenal" byproducts of scientific or mathematical practice but may themselves be a driving force behind the practice itself.[12]

We might, then, with Muhammad Legenhausen (2013), employ the metaphor of *resonance* to characterize a particular kind of responsive experience elicited by certain ideas or theories, by which acceptance becomes aroused and welcomed. Legenhausen himself focuses predominantly on cognitive attunement, in which a certain concept or proposal resonates with one intellectually, but in many cases the kinds of resonances elicited when considering a model are also (maybe even predominantly) emotional or aesthetic, such that the cognitive and the affective domains may not be neatly separable as we might like to think. Moreover, whatever the mode of resonance in question, it is often difficult to express such experiences propositionally in a way that is straightforwardly truth-evaluable.[13]

The experiential counterpart to resonance is *dissonance*. As Francis Bacon wrote in his 1625 essay on beauty, "There is no excellent beauty that hath not some strangeness in the proportion" (quoted in Chandrasekhar 2010: 61). Chandrasekhar himself claims that the general theory of relativity "reveals *strangeness* in the proportion at any level in which one may explore its consequences" (61). These elements of "weirdness" or "surprisingness," too, may be non-cognitive or not-exclusively-cognitive features of the scientific and mathematical enterprises. Many experiences of wonder and awe are elicited by the uncanny, weird, or sublime—by those phenomena and ideas that rub up against or do not fit neatly within our expectations or intuitions. This is part of what makes awe such an interesting emotion. From a phenomenological standpoint, it is often characterized not only by attraction to its intentional object but often also a kind of fear, repulsion, or cognitive resistance. This affectively "contradictory" kind of experience, characterized in its most extreme form by theologian Rudolf Otto (1958) as a response elicited by the apprehension of *mysterium tremendum et fascinans*, is (perhaps *pace* Otto's own view) not restricted to the religious realm but can also function as a response to "epiphanic experience" or the apprehension of "the breadth and scope of a grand theory," as well as to more tangible human artifacts and splendid works of art and architecture (Keltner and Haidt 2003: 310).[14]

Significantly, in addition to the beauty and/or strangeness that particular theories, models, or artifacts may display internally and which may play a causal role in an individual subject's willingness to accept them, the notions of resonance and dissonance are also important for the *social dynamics* of understanding— both with respect to how epistemic subjects come to understand their own models or theories in light of approaches different from their own and regarding how they come to better intersubjectively understand each other in such contexts. Indeed, rather than merely focusing on understanding as a synchronic state of an individual subject at a time, it is also important to think about the ways in which understanding is an ongoing *process*—one most often pursued in a social context with other epistemic agents, who may or may not agree with each other or find themselves similarly "attuned." Legenhausen, for example, introduces the concept of resonance within a discussion of epistemic peer disagreement. With respect to coming to understand another perspective (and, we might add, with coming to better understand one's own perspective in light of another's views), he claims that resonance between paradigms is necessary for *depth* of understanding (Legenhausen 2013: 38). Yet such resonance need neither stem from nor culminate in belief. One can allow certain views to resonate without thereby coming to believe them, thereby learning, as Legenhausen puts it, "to navigate the space of reasons" of other perspectives (39) in ways that may both promote understanding of the other and be transformative of one's own commitments, whether or not this ultimately leads to a subject's revising, switching, or adjusting their confidence in their preferred model. It may even in some cases make rational their doubling-down on it.

Nonetheless, "learning to resonate" in this way—to be open to alternative ways of approaching a subject matter—is not possible without the introduction of *dissonances*, especially in cases where allowing oneself to resonate in a certain way brings one into tension with one's own preferred perspective. In fact, it is not merely the (often temporary) achievement of reflective equilibrium that is most epistemically transformative within the dynamics of understanding but rather its *disruption*. The affectively or cognitively disruptive, resistant, or subversive elements of a particular model, or those dissonances that arise between competing models, can serve as what José Medina, using a more tactile metaphor, calls *beneficial epistemic frictions*. Far from being a threat to understanding, Medina claims, such forms of epistemic resistance are themselves often important, perhaps even necessary, for making epistemic progress: Just as we need friction to walk, to move forward, the introduction of epistemic frictions in the pursuit of understanding "enables us to acknowledge and engage alternative viewpoints and to reach epistemic equilibrium among alternative perspectives on a problem or phenomenon" (Medina 2013b: 176). First, epistemic frictions can draw attention to those aspects of an account that one has not yet comprehended or to where one's blind spots might lie, and this can lead one to seek out new or more comprehensive perspectives and ways of thinking about the subject matter. Second, they can disrupt comfortable reflective equilibrium by throwing subjects "off-balance" in a way that requires them to revisit their approach and "re-balance" themselves epistemically. In this sense, both resonance and resistance are, in some sense, inseparable in the pursuit of understanding. Or, to return to the aural metaphor, harmony is not equivalent to sameness; in fact, as Confucius points out in the epigraph to this chapter, it presupposes the difference that actually underlies our social interactions, even in the epistemic realm.[15]

The normative interplay of resonance and dissonance, equilibrium and imbalance, not only reminds us that understanding is a matter of degree; it also points to the fundamental *discursivity* and *incompleteness* of processes of understanding. The pursuit of understanding is rarely final and definitive. It generally requires being open to new or alternative perspectives and involves diachronic processes of interrogating and negotiating the various imaginative spaces we occupy in our epistemic pursuits. One can be better or worse at moving fluidly in and between these spaces and more or less skilled at utilizing them to achieve the mutual aims one shares with others in those spaces, but throughout this process understanding is best viewed as partial, and the ways to improve it are multifaceted. As Elgin and Goodman point out: "[F]itting symbols or ways of symbolizing in and making them work is a task as varied as are symbol systems, referential relationships, and situations and objectives" (Goodman and Elgin 1988: 161). Moreover, the fittingness of traditional symbols might itself change as new situations and challenges arise.

Focusing on the discursivity of understanding also helps us see how, even when truth sometimes takes a backseat in the ways we have seen above, the notion of *objectivity* need not, as demonstrated by Helen Longino's social approach to scientific objectivity, according to which objectivity is "characteristic of a community's practice of science rather than of an individual's" (Longino 1990: 74). In this respect, the pursuit of objectivity in the natural sciences may not be all that dissimilar to forms of inquiry in the arts and humanities, even if the modes of understanding in the various disciplines may be different.[16] Viewed as a social notion, objectivity is not only compatible with but also *requires* criticism from alternative points of view, since subjecting models, theories, and evidence to critical scrutiny is the very thing that prevents individual biases and subjective preferences from playing an inordinately large role in what comes to be accepted as scientific knowledge (76). As Longino writes: "Only if the products of inquiry are understood to be formed by the kind of critical discussion that is possible among a plurality of individuals about a commonly accessible phenomenon can we see how they count as knowledge rather than opinion" (74). Put in our preferred terms, the beneficial epistemic frictions provided by introducing multiple voices into the discussion allow us to distinguish "fitting" or "acceptable" models from wholly untethered or idiosyncratic approaches. Viewed in this fashion, objectivity—like understanding—can be a matter of degree. As Longino puts it: "A method of inquiry is objective to the degree that it permits *transformative criticism*" (76).

In a similar vein, Medina notes that taking into account multiple perspectives in our epistemic negotiations can help us "improve the articulation and justification" of our models and theories, thereby further contributing to the overall objectivity of our epistemic appraisals (Medina 2013b: 302). Importantly, however, Medina also takes care to point out that objectivity viewed as a social and polyphonic phenomenon need not aim at consensus or at "the configuration of a common vantage point from which we can all survey the world together" (304). Rather, epistemic subjects seek coordination and cooperation between perspectives, such that "standpoints become, not merged or fused together, but connected and attentive to each other, allowing the subjects who hold them to discharge their shared epistemic responsibilities" (305).

This also means that objectivity does not secure (or even really try to approximate) the God's-eye "view from nowhere" discussed in the previous chapter, nor does it aspire to the illusion of what Elgin calls "utter objectivity." Drawing on the work of Bas van Fraassen, Elgin notes that if scientific representations are to do what science actually requires of them, they cannot be wholly objective in the "God's-eye" way. Perspectival representations are largely a matter of preference or choice, are indexed to particular viewpoints, and may occlude or be noncommittal to other objects or properties that would be visible from other perspectives (Elgin 2017: 153–4). Such perspectivity is inherently limited (and limiting). Yet, as we have said above, these limitations do not make scientific or mathematical representations a wholly arbitrary matter. For some purposes a more coarse-grained perspective may be needed, for others a more fine-grained approach. And to fail to discern between which is best suited to which purpose can be to commit a grave error. This is one more reason why dissonance is just as important for understanding as resonance: epistemic frictions can function to disrupt the kind of epistemic arrogance or contentedness with the *status quo* that inhibits the ability to see that other options may better suited in a particular setting than one's preferred model or paradigm. Acknowledging and reflecting on these perspectival limitations, then, can help individual subjects cultivate an epistemically virtuous "meta-lucidity" which can serve to counter the intellectual vices associated with the "view from nowhere" discussed in the last chapter. By cultivating a "capacity to see the limitations of dominant ways of seeing" (Medina 2013b: 47), one may come to recognize that, even in the domains of purportedly "objective" subjects such as science and mathematics, one is simply in "*no position* to adopt a God's eye view" or to "say that *in absolute terms* one account is better than another" (Elgin 2017: 67).

However, on an epistemological approach that privileges understanding, we no longer rationally need something like the God's-eye view to see how one approach can be an improvement upon another—especially when reflective equilibrium with respect to our collective purposes is paired with something like the social account of objectivity discussed above. Since, as Elgin notes, "the method of reflective equilibrium is dialectical and its results are provisional," we can both put our various commitments and their revisions up against one another and "judge our criteria for being best on balance by seeing if they yield verdicts that we can on reflection endorse" (67). Thus, the shift from an epistemology focused on true belief and utter objectivity to one centered around holistic understanding in reflective equilibrium allows perspective and positionality to be recovered in a way that can actually contribute to our notion of epistemic viability, as opposed to threatening it.

Conclusion

To summarize, I think there is good reason to think that the focus on the truth of metaphysical realism and an epistemology centered exclusively around propositional knowledge might not do justice to many of our epistemic practices, even in domains whose epistemic value is not in doubt, like those of the natural sciences and mathematics. With Elgin and others, I have argued that, in order to do justice to the way these enterprises actually proceed and how they are epistemically valuable, philosophers would do better to shift their epistemological approach from a sole focus on the values of absolute objectivity and justified true belief to include those of perspectival understanding in reflective equilibrium— and to explore epistemically-relevant factors that go beyond the merely cognitive, which may be manifested in the affective or aesthetic resonances and frictions that may respectively arouse acceptance and disrupt comfortable balance in the dynamic processes involved in such understanding.

As the reader may suspect, I think something similar can be said for the way we approach religion in APR. Indeed, I maintain that if APR wants to become a genuine philosophy of *religion*, it must look beyond its obsession with defending the possibility that belief in MaRTeR could constitute utterly objective knowledge and think more carefully about the valuable roles that understanding might play in instances of actual individual and collective religious participation. I take this approach to be preferable in both a descriptive and regulative sense. That is, not only can an understanding-centered religious epistemology better account for much of what religion already does and thereby make room for religion as a potentially valuable epistemic enterprise; it can also provide helpful guidelines for APR (and, I think, for religious adherents themselves) to engage in more productive communication and dialogue, both with each other and with marginalized or critical voices.

Notes

1　This is not to say that mathematicians and mathematical philosophers have not busied themselves with answering the realist question. However, as in APR, the question is becoming how important it really is to defend mathematical (anti-) realism when it might be more productive to focus more on the philosophy of mathematical *practice* (Avigad 2018).

2　See also Sylvia Jonas' claim that "mathematics is widely accepted as a rational enterprise even though we have no clue how to make sense of its objects" (Jonas 2016: 70).

3　For a lengthier elaboration on what is involved in acquiring and maintaining reflective equilibrium, see Baumberger and Brun (2016, 2021).

4　The claim that objectual understanding is non-factive is not uncontroversial. For example, Michael Strevens (2016), Stephen Grimm (2006), and Jonathan Kvanvig (2003) have argued that understanding must be factive, though Kvanvig allows that understanding may involve "peripheral" falsehoods, so long as the "central" propositions of the relevant account are true, and Strevens maintains that, although felicitous falsehoods may actually enhance the explanatory power of certain models, the "difference-making" propositions must be true.

5　There may also be aesthetic considerations of beauty or elegance in play here, similar to those I discuss below.

6　For example, someone learning the game of baseball for the first time may have very little understanding of the sport or its rules. Yet someone who is familiar with sports like cricket or the German *Brennball* may have a better intuitive grasp of the game than someone wholly unacquainted with bat-and-ball games, even if the former still has an overwhelming number of false beliefs about how the game is played. And while to say such a person "understands baseball" *full-stop* is certainly a stretch, there is a very real sense in which we want our epistemologies to be able to say how it is that their grasp of the game has an epistemic advantage over the non-sports-fan. Similarly, although I have been a baseball fan for years, I do not understand the game as well as the manager or a player of any given professional team. I may not always be able to explain why the players are shifting toward one side or to predict what pitch is coming next, and I may have some false beliefs about, say, the infield fly rule.

But to say that I do not "really" understand the game, or that I only understand it in an "honorific" sense, as Jonathan Kvanvig (2003) appears to suggest, seems to discount my (not minimal) epistemic competence with respect to baseball in a way that may even degrade my status as an epistemic agent.

7   For example, the ability to successfully accept a proposition one believes may, as Miranda Fricker notes, "lag behind belief" in instances where strongly embedded biases and other "cognitive commitments held in our imaginations" continue to influence how we perceive our social surroundings, despite the our having long rejected any correlative beliefs and adopted strong beliefs to the contrary (Fricker 2007: 37).

8   Compare Elgin's claim that the way magnitude is defined "is largely a pragmatic matter; it depends on what we want to do with the information we glean" (Elgin 2017: 162). Nevertheless, this does not make the choice arbitrary, since "a viable magnitude must be suitably invariant under the conditions of interest." But neither is absolute invariance required, so long as the magnitude is "invariant enough" to serve our purposes in particular contexts (163).

9   See Pritchard (2010). Given his focus on propositional understanding and understanding-*why*, Pritchard is inclined to think of understanding as factive, which I, with Elgin, want to deny. Nonetheless, it seems to me that even non-factive understanding (e.g., understanding astrology or mythology) can be characterized as a cognitive achievement, in the sense that it is attributable to the agent's own abilities and involves the epistemic agent's "know[ing] his way around the field" (Elgin 2007: 35).

10 Of course, in some cases the relevant understanding may not be a mere tool toward some further end but is rather in some way *constitutive* of the end being sought. For example, if the only goal in a particular context is to satisfy one's curiosity about how certain concepts hang together or to arrive at a comprehensive analysis of some empirical phenomenon, there may be nothing more to achieving these goals than achieving the relevant form(s) of understanding. Likewise, as is common with respect to *autotelic* activities—i.e., activities pursued primarily for their own sake— those elements which may normally serve an instrumental purpose can be transformed into ends-in-themselves. This is the case with regard to many puzzles or games—and, perhaps, with respect to much thought-experimental work in analytic philosophy—in which the activity is, to some extent, also the goal. In these kinds of cases, the understanding that, in other contexts, is reserved for primarily instrumental purposes may be at least partially constitutive of what it means to successfully participate in such an activity in the first place. This, however, requires that understanding be construed dynamically, as I discuss in more detail presently. I discuss autotelicity (and its role in pretend play) further in Chapter 6.

11 For more on the promise of epistemic value pluralism for the epistemic justification of objectual understanding, see Baumberger and Brun (2016).

12 For more on the connection between aesthetic reasons and theory choice in the history of physics and the natural sciences, see Müller (2019). Whether science and

mathematics ultimately *ought* to be partially guided by these kinds of aesthetic considerations is an open question. For example, should it turn out, as Sabine Hossenfelder (2018) and Massimo Pigliucci (2019) have suggested, that aesthetic preferences with respect to, e.g., simplicity or beauty tend to be less reliable than theorists have tended to treat them, this may count against such considerations being employed in theory choice. Or it may count in favor of giving heavier weight to alternative aesthetic values like complexity or even ugliness. Nevertheless, I think what I say about resonance and dissonance below points to the idea that not only do scientists and mathematicians rely on considerations other than the purely cognitive in their epistemic pursuits, some non-cognitive or not-solely-cognitive factors may actually be *necessary* to make progress with respect to understanding. The question then becomes which non-cognitive factors are the relevant ones for epistemically beneficial resonance/dissonance and how these kinds of responses are to be cultivated and properly employed in the scientific or mathematical enterprises.

13 We may be nevertheless able to evaluate such feelings of resonance along the lines of *fittingness* or *appropriateness* with respect to their intentional objects or targets in ways that are independent of straightforwardly moral or strategic evaluations (see, e.g., D'Arms and Jacobson 2000; Deonna and Teroni 2012).

14 For a much more detailed account of the role and workings of wonder and awe in science, religion, and other areas of life, see the late Helen De Cruz' "wonderful" book, *Wonderstruck* (2024).

15 On this point, see Wong (2020). Wong himself prefers the metaphor of *gustatory* harmony, as when one makes a soup from different and counterbalancing ingredients, but the idea is roughly the same.

16 Longino writes in a footnote: "This is not to deny the importance of distinguishing between different modes of understanding—for instance, between scientific, philosophical, and literary theories—but simply to deny that objectivity can serve as any kind of demarcation criterion" (Longino 1990: 75, n.27).

3

Beyond Nowhere

Doing Religious Epistemology from Somewhere

By wisdom a house is built, and by understanding it is established.

Proverbs 24:3

The germs of an epistemology of religious understanding: finding meaning, making value

In this chapter, I want to extend the social epistemology of understanding as sketched out with respect to science and mathematics in the last chapter to the religious domain. As we shift our attention to religion, then, it will be helpful to think more carefully about the *kind* of understanding that might be most relevant to the latter. Whereas scientific understanding is often (though by no means exclusively) tied to the epistemic goals of explanation or prediction, and mathematical understanding might be said to trade more closely in the comprehension of salient patterns or structures (or perhaps in coming to better grasp "the nature of necessity"[1]), I suggest that religious understanding involves an epistemic aim that is essentially *hermeneutical* in nature. That is, whatever else religion might be, it is minimally a collective interpretive enterprise aimed at a kind of *existential meaning-making*.[2]

I thus submit that one central way in which religion (or, better put, a religious tradition) may be epistemically valuable is insofar as it provides the contours of a narrative cosmic framework through which human beings can come to productively understand their own experience, as well as their relations to each other, to non-human beings, and to the universe, in ways that (ideally) contribute to the flourishing of all concerned.[3] This approach to the epistemic value of religion dethrones belief as the sole—or even the central—attitude for investigation in religious epistemology, insofar as particular narrative cosmic frameworks or models of the divine within such frameworks can be legitimately accepted in ways that can beneficially contribute to existential meaning-making without being straightforwardly believed. (More on what this might look like in subsequent chapters.) Religious understanding in the hermeneutical sense focuses less on questions of truth-conduciveness, placing instead a certain kind of *existential* understanding at the epistemic heart of the religious enterprise. It also importantly places human beings, not the divine, at the center of that enterprise. But this is just as it should be. For whereas religion may concern itself with that which is "beyond" the natural or empirical world, religions themselves are empirical social phenomena which both arise within and pertain to the messy constellations of human concerns and subjectivities. And even where religions do point imaginatively[4] beyond empirically measurable realities, they are centrally concerned not only with the nature of that imagined transcendence but also with its relationship to or manifestation in the human experience and how that connection or expression can be meaningful to those who participate in particular forms of religious practice. Indeed, in contrast to what one might glean from much APR literature, religions are as much or more about *us* as they are about that which they often take as their intentional object (e.g., the divine, transcendent, or other purportedly superempirical dimension(s) of reality). Religion viewed under its hermeneutical aspect inevitably always "points back to us" (Pinn 2015: 97), and a religious epistemology centered on understanding must take this into account by ensuring that the human relatum remains relevant to the religious equation.

At the same time, the hermeneutical approach also places the religious individual in the context of a *cosmic narrative framework*. Religious concepts are not merely "imaginative one-offs" but rather derive much of their significance from the narrative contexts in which they are embedded. Of course, religious stories themselves may be local or global in scope, canonical or anecdotal. They may be passed down orally or textually, by images or performance, or in some other way. Yet what binds them all within a historical religious tradition has to do with the ways in which they figure in an overarching cosmic narrative framework within whose limits religious adherents can locate and make meaning.[5] By "cosmic" here, I mean not only "cosmological" or having some story to tell about the origin, history, constitution, and nature of the universe and humankind. Cosmic frameworks also provide the means for relating the cosmological to the personal, the sociopolitical, and the ethical by way of the divine, the ancestors, superempirical dimensions of experience, and so on. Moreover, although providing "narrative scaffolds" to orient and structure religious imaginings, such frameworks do not always provide a *totalizing* story that erases particularity, ensures systematicity, or aims at theoretical coherence. Cosmic narratives may be spelled out and systematized in these ways, especially when taken as objects for scholarly investigation (e.g., through the efforts of systematic theologians, social anthropologists, religious historians, and the like), but they need not.

APR itself may represent one such scholarly context in which cosmic narratives and frameworks may be examined for consistency or constructively systematized to produce or critique candidates for rational religious acceptance. But the discipline can also do more than this. For example, it can more closely explore the kinds of stories and objects to which a particular cosmic narrative framework gives rise and evaluate the ways in which such imaginings contribute (or fail to contribute) to epistemically or morally productive religious understanding. It may compare various religious frameworks to one another and attempt to locate resonances and dissonances, or it may seek to introduce new concepts or inject beneficial epistemic frictions into a particular framework. Alternatively, it may explore the ways in which religious narrative itself can be a way of philosophizing or can otherwise lead to important philosophical insight, as Eleonore Stump (2010) and Mikel Burley (2020) have suggested.[6]

Importantly, the reference to flourishing in the hermeneutical approach to religious understanding, together with the fact that the meaning-making in question is fundamentally existential, points to the fact that that religion's epistemic aims are not independent of its practical, ethical, and social ends. Whether or not the objects of religious discourse exist (or exist as they are represented by any particular tradition), the epistemic aspects of the religious life on this approach cannot be divorced from pragmatic concerns and moral commitments, from individual and collective values and experiences, from human beings' situated lives as embodied, social, and political organisms. Of course, even if this is especially true for the religious enterprise, it is also the case for many if not most of our epistemic undertakings. One of the great insights of feminist epistemology is that we cannot neatly separate our epistemic practices from our practical and moral concerns or from the social and political realities in which we are situated. Another is that analytic philosophy's attempt to try to detach epistemology from these kinds of considerations has tended to do more damage than it has alleviated in the name of "clarity and rigor."[7] If this is right, then any religious epistemology or attempt to evaluate the epistemic dimensions of a religious tradition would do well to consider the ways the epistemic and non-epistemic are intertwined, especially insofar as existential meaning-making and world-flourishing are concerned.

In this respect, an understanding-centered approach allows APR to recover the "primacy of praxis" that John Cottingham (2005) places "at the heart of the religious enterprise" and which unfortunately tends to be overlooked by APR in its focus on belief, rationality, and propositional knowledge. Cottingham argues that "it is in the very nature of religious understanding that it characteristically stems from practical involvement rather than from intellectual analysis" (6). I will return to this notion in subsequent chapters, but for now it is sufficient to notice the parallels between this case and the mathematical one discussed in Chapter 2. Theorizing about the ontological status of the objects of religion is *not prior* to the practice of that religion itself, and we should not think that the latter need wait on the former to accomplish its epistemic function.

Moreover, as with scientific and mathematical practice, there are derivative forms of understanding located in the religious life that are instrumentally valuable when it comes to existential meaning-making, many of which emerge from sustained religious practice, not theological reflection. Such practices may even be partially constitutive of this epistemic end, insofar as learning to practically navigate religious spaces—both physical and conceptual—may, for some subjects, just be *what it is to find existential meaning*, even if such meaning is not easily expressible in propositional terms. That is, the religious subject, by performing and professing and contemplating, learns how to fluently navigate the religious context—or, to channel Elgin, she learns to wield her religious commitments to further her hermeneutical ends. She may thereby or therein come to "grasp" how an institutional network of religious commitments fits together in a way that provides her with a cognitive, affective, and volitional orientation in reflective (and affective) equilibrium that is as acceptable to her as—or perhaps more acceptable than—any other existential hermeneutical alternative.

In this sense, then, the capacity of a religious tradition to produce existential meaning for subjects committed to the religious enterprise goes far beyond that tradition's ability to produce a theoretical system of propositional candidates for cognitive assent. It represents a cultural vehicle for grappling with and coming to grasp the significance of our individual and collective human experiences and locating them within a larger whole. It allows us to "read meaning" off of our lives and to *orient* ourselves in ways that can make sense of the most fundamental aspects of our existence, even in cases where full propositional belief might be lacking or irrelevant.[8] For this reason, it becomes even more significant for APR to explore the affective, volitional, and embodied aspects of religious practice, especially if we are interested in developing a religious epistemology that recognizes the significance of these aspects for the dynamics of religious understanding.

Tethering religion and "making fit"

Those religious epistemologists who are heavily invested in projects aimed at defending the rationality of MaRTeR-belief might object here that the kind of hermeneutical approach to religious understanding I have sketched out above is not really *epistemic* in the first place, at least not in any sense of concern to analytic epistemology.[9] On the traditional view, knowledge is generally considered to be something "discovered" or "received," not "constructed" or "produced," as the hermeneutical approach might suggest. Indeed, there is a strong inclination in analytic epistemology to associate the cognitive value of our epistemic projects with a strict mind-to-world direction of fit, even on an epistemology according to which acceptance or suspension can reasonably supplant belief in particular contexts. Put in Elgin's terms, we think that, in order to be of any genuine epistemic value, our theological models and the cosmic narrative frameworks in which they find expression must be "tethered" or "hooked up" to reality in some relevant way—and that they must be able to "communicate" that reality to us in ways that serve to increase our knowledge or deepen our understanding of it. And the worry here might be that the hermeneutical notion of *making* existential meaning belies the idea that the primary function of religious frameworks is to "fit" the way things really are.

This discomfort with the hermeneutical approach is exacerbated by my suggestion that APR needs to pay increased attention to the ways the epistemic is fundamentally tied up with and influenced by the sociopolitical and the ethical. As suggested in Chapter 1, the preference in analytic religious epistemology seems to be to try to *divest* religious (and especially theistic) beliefs of their social, political, and practical dimensions—so as to evaluate them solely in their (disembodied and dislocated) "epistemic" aspects as candidates for knowledge. On such a view, accuracy and truth-aptness are prized above all. The parallel metaphysical projects in APR then attempt to figure out which conceptions of the divine are most likely to "correctly" mirror the way things are independent of any particular agent's situatedness or standpoint. Or, alternatively, they take a favored theistic belief (e.g., "God is all-powerful and all-knowing") and try to locate some conceivable model of the divine that, if it were real, would make such a belief an accurate representation of that reality. This, in turn, is entered into the philosopher's log as evidence or justification for the beliefs in question, and the theist can rest a little easier knowing that there is some possible conception of God that, if actual, would make their theistic beliefs rational (assuming, of course, that their beliefs also had that concept or something approximating it as their content).

Now this is not necessarily a complete waste of time as far as it goes, and it is probably a good thing for at least some theistically-inclined members of APR to be involved in these kinds of projects. Many theists today (including many of those outside the academy) are concerned by the possibility that their beliefs are incorrect, inaccurate, or irrational—especially in light of the (sometimes very loud and public) secular challenges to theism that permeate the social discourse. My own preference, as will become even more apparent later on, is for a radically expanded and diversified APR in which the current project of defending the epistemic rationality of theistic belief (which tends to employ a very *narrow* notion of epistemic rationality and a very *broad* notion of theism) plays only a very small part. However, for our purposes here it will be sufficient to show that adopting my approach neither precludes the pursuit of religious epistemology in general nor undermines the currently dominant epistemological approach in particular. Indeed, not only can the hermeneutical approach lay good claim to being considered sufficiently epistemic, it also is commensurate with epistemological projects that favor accuracy over appropriateness (or, alternatively, view accuracy *as* appropriateness)—provided that those pursuing such projects are, at a minimum, a) willing to admit that accuracy as an epistemic value might not be sufficient for judging the appropriateness of religious models and frameworks in *all* epistemic contexts and b) open to the idea that APR's epistemological approach should be (more) responsive to social and moral considerations. Let us thus briefly explore the ways in which religious systems according to the approach I have been recommending may still be considered epistemically valuable, while at the same time showing how and why APR must also go beyond its exclusive business of trying to tether by truth.

There are, quite obviously, various functions that philosophical analyses of religion are intended to serve. One project APR has traditionally pursued (usually via some form of "natural theology") has treated religious traditions as providing competing or complementary *explanatory* frameworks to be placed alongside the scientific theories in cosmology, physics, evolutionary biology, and so on that also purport to provide explanations of the origin and nature of the cosmos, human beings, and other features of the universe. On such an approach, a particular religious framework will be treated as one explanatory hypothesis among others (e.g., those in the natural and social sciences), and its epistemic tether will only be as strong as its ability to successfully compete with or accommodate these other explanatory theories. However, as we have seen in the previous chapter, even scientific theories regularly trade in felicitous falsehoods and non-true idealizations, so it may not be illegitimate for religious narratives and models to do the same, such that truth in the sense of one-to-one correspondence between the models of the religious account and "divine reality" will not be the only relevant factor to take into consideration when evaluating the strength of a religion's tether. For example, we might wonder whether, in some cases, a religious framework is capable of depicting the causal relationships depicted in particular scientific theories in a different (but perhaps compatible) way—one which, perhaps due to its particular form or genre, might actually make certain features of the universe more salient or accessible to us. Therefore, thinking more carefully about exemplification, semiotics, and modelling rather than mere correspondence and accuracy might help us make a bit of headway in some of the rather sclerotic research concerning science and religion.

Of course, even if we extend our gaze beyond the ways in which religious models serve as components of explanatory cosmological paradigms, the idea that religion might employ non-true models or "felicitous falsehoods" should not really be all that controversial, even for many theological realists. This is especially so for those realists of, say, an apophatic or skeptical theist stripe who cleave to the idea that the divine (at least in some respects) necessarily outstrips our ability to conceptualize or speak about it, or who maintain that even philosophical language about God is sometimes, often, or always at least analogical, if not metaphorical or parabolic. On these kinds of approaches, many of our conceptions of and language about God serve as helpful models or metaphors for understanding the divine, but they do not (perhaps even cannot) match up perfectly with the way God "really" is. Still, even if they are strictly speaking not-true, they can help us make epistemic progress with respect to the way we conceptualize and relate to God. Theologians can discuss whether and which particular models are better or more "fitting" than others, given the purported revelations of the tradition in question. Philosophers can think about how to tweak or modify particular models to make better sense of theological "mysteries" or logical conundrums that arise within particular religious frameworks. Practitioners can employ various models to be able to better relate to God in ways that might open them up to religious experiences of a certain kind—even, perhaps, to a kind of "direct" perception of the divine (a purported form of religious experience popular in much of the APR literature), which they may then use as a reference point to develop additional (even if still descriptively inadequate) models to talk about God, as we see in many contemplative and mystical traditions.

In some cases, religious readers or listeners might even be presented with *intentionally* false models of God (and not just in an incidental or inevitable sense). For example, some mystical traditions set paradoxical images of God alongside one another, or introduce various attractive or popular models of the divine and then explicitly negate them.[10] Such practices, in which religious contemplatives encounter not only non-true but also *contradictory* and *incompatible* conceptions of God, are nevertheless taken to serve valuable epistemic and moral functions. For example, they can elicit epistemically valuable emotions like wonder and awe,[11] the cognitive effect of which may kindle an awareness of our cognitive inability to fully comprehend ultimate reality, thereby protecting against theological vices such as cognitive idolatry and promoting intellectual virtues like epistemic humility. Similarly, baffling and ambiguous religious narratives such as the story of Job, which remains a source of bewilderment for many Christian and Jewish practitioners, can also present opportunities for advances in understanding. Such narratives may be starting points, in which we "venture hypotheses and test them to discover whether they make sense" of the symbols and models with which we are confronted (Elgin 2017: 218). Or they may be sources of cognitive disruption that serve to underscore the Socratic point that there is epistemic value in recognizing what we do not know or cannot understand. Ultimately, each of these kinds of cases can be relevant for—or even partially constitutive of—existential meaning-making in a universe that transcends our full comprehension. But they also make clear that viewing truth as the only—or even the ideal—tether falls woefully short of explaining the full epistemic value of such religious models and thereby drastically limits the scope of what we in APR can do with them.

At the same time, just because religious models and the narrative frameworks they occupy are not necessarily tethered via strict correspondence relations, this does not mean they are not reality-responsive. Rather, as we have discussed above, *exemplification* can also bind models, theories, and entire systems to reality. Ian Barbour, for example, proposes that religious models "suggest beliefs which correlate patterns in human experience" (Barbour 1974: 842) and can "serve an 'attention-directing' function, accentuating the patterns which we see in the facts" (901). The models employed by religious traditions can exemplify or make salient aspects of reality that we may be inclined to overlook or ignore by appealing not only to our cognitive faculties but also (and perhaps even primarily) to our sensual, aesthetic, and affective capacities, and their output may evoke or suggest not merely cognitive attitudes about the world but also fundamental ways of feeling and acting and *being oriented in and toward that world*. That is, they can help us better "move about" as embodied, reflective, sensitive creatures in a complex and difficult-to-navigate universe.

Importantly, it is not merely theological concepts, propositions, and narratives that serve exemplary functions in the religious life. Religious rituals and other forms of embodied religious practice also foster understanding via exemplification in ways essential to existential orientation, moral understanding, and human flourishing. Just as artistic expressions like dance can, as Elgin puts it, "deepen understanding by sensitizing us to things we tend to overlook, by undermining stereotypes, by problematizing assumptions we did not even know we were making," religious ritual, too, can exemplify moral properties or "embody views about weighty philosophical [and theological] matters—the relation between mind and body, between autonomy and interdependence, between the ordinary and the extraordinary" (Elgin 2017: 219–20).

Here it is worth noting that such rituals are not simply tethered insofar as the attitudes of the person(s) performing the ritual match up to the world, either by representing it as it really is (as in the case of believing) or by changing it accordingly (as in the case of acting on intentions or desires), though ritual certainly can and regularly does perform these functions in various ways. What is special about some forms of religious ritual, however, is how they are often simultaneously able to *represent* the way we think the world *ought* to be and to *promote* that good *through the very means by which they exemplify*, even in those cases in which we cannot directly change the world to fit our attitudes.[12] Indeed, there is good reason to think that the kind of exemplification involved in these kinds of religious ritual transcends the traditional direction-of-fit binary. Take, for example, Robert Adams' suggestion that ritualized prayer may be a form of *collective symbolic action*—a way of performatively *standing for the good* or *in solidarity* with one another. By "expressing our loyalties symbolically in action," Adams claims, we can actually "*give more reality* to our being for the goods and against the evils [. . .] that we are relatively powerless to accomplish or prevent" (Adams 1997: 10, my emphasis). It can also call participants to move from what Terence Cuneo (2016) calls an "ethics of proximity" toward an "ethic of outwardness," and it can create opportunities for liturgical participants to promote or otherwise "stand for" certain attitudes and ideals (e.g., awe, humility, solidarity, resistance), even if they are not occurrently experiencing them

(Wettstein 2012: 45). We come to understand how to properly interpret the symbolic nature of corporate prayer by both witnessing and engaging in liturgical rituals—by watching others bend their bodies and recite certain words and by ourselves participating in such movements with others. Yet insofar as we witness and participate in a symbolic commitment to the good, we also thereby promote the good, and we cultivate an understanding that extends our prayers beyond the walls of the temple, church, or mosque. Our bodies themselves become symbols for a form of meaning-making that is tethered less by confirmation or checking and more by *transformation* and *becoming*.

The point here is that, in the above cases, "making meaning" neither implies pulling meaning out of thin air, nor simply "making it up" as we go along. The interpretive endeavor involves both *finding* or *discovering* meaning (sometimes through a process of *uncovering* or *recovering*) and *creating* or *promoting* it: it is both receptive *and* constructive. Indeed, being able to "make" meaning in the first place is a cognitive achievement, insofar as one comes to be familiar with a relevant set of symbols and narratives and how they can be meaningfully employed in particular contexts. To be able to understand religious symbols, practices, and narratives "we need to be able to interpret [the relevant] vocabulary or idiom," and this is itself a difficult epistemic task (Elgin 2017: 218). Furthermore, as suggested above, religious frameworks provide a kind of *orientation* by which one can come to understand one's experience and relation to others and the world in ways that ideally serve to enhance world flourishing. But orientation is as much an *epistemic* notion as a practical one. Someone with a compass in the wilderness is in a better position to make their way to the nearest town than their directionless peers, but their practical advantage in this regard depends heavily on the epistemic advantage they enjoy due to their possession of these orienteering tools, as well as their ability to appropriately implement and interpret them.

Of course, not all religious traditions will succeed in promoting flourishing to the same degree if they do so at all, or they may promote forms of insular understanding that are more harmful than beneficial. Exemplification can serve pernicious ends, as when the social realities exemplified in particular religious concepts function to further perpetuate harmful practices and prejudices. Yet like a scientific paradigm that doesn't end up providing the epistemic and practical benefits we expect of it (or doesn't do so as well as some other approach on the table), those religious traditions or movements that fail to promote the ends of existential meaning-making and world flourishing become candidates for reformation or replacement. And should it turn out that such ameliorations are not forthcoming (or do not "stack up" when compared with other, more "secular" meaning-making enterprises), then this may be a reason to leave religious models behind for other forms of meaning-making, as some secularists have suggested. In any case, this is one issue regarding which a discussion between APR and its ontological and ontotheological critics will be necessary, yet in order to be fruitful it must move past its obsession with the strictly realist question centered around MaRTeR.

To summarize, it should be clear by now that the question of religion's actual epistemic value goes far beyond the question of the truth or probability of MaRTeR and is itself a question that can and should be investigated by APR in conversation with its critics. Similarly, although we think it important that religious traditions be tethered to reality in some relevant way, their "rightness" or "fittingness" is not just a matter of their happening to be passively "hooked up" to the facts via a one-to-one relation of correspondence, but rather a matter of actively *making fit*—an activity that requires openness, adaptiveness, and a willingness to make adjustments. As Goodman and Elgin put it: "[F]itting is neither passive nor one-way, but an active process of fitting together; the fit has to be *made*, and the making may involve minor or major adjustments in what is being fitted *into* or what is being fitted *in* or both" (Goodman and Elgin 1988: 158).

The idea of "making fit" is also helpful when it comes to thinking about the history and *dynamism* of religious traditions, another task that is significant for a self-critical religious epistemology. As Janet Soskice notes: "Should we feel inclined to overlook the extent to which doctrinal formulation depends on models, it is useful to be reminded of the many models that either didn't make the grade or, alternatively, enjoyed popularity at one time and were tactfully abandoned at another" (Soskice 1987: 106). It is not merely obduracy, strictness, and severity that explains the "staying power" of religious traditions—nor, might I add, their truth-aptness. Rather, as Nietzsche recognized, their continuity also has to do with their ability to be imaginatively applied and adapted in new circumstances and their flexibility in helping human subjects make meaning anew in the face of renewed or unforeseen existential challenges—not seldomly through the evolution or creation of more fitting models. As we have seen, the cosmic narratives provided by religions and the conceptual models they employ can provide frameworks and vocabularies that serve to both *form* and *inform* the commitments and attitudes of persons, families, and communities—but these frameworks and vocabularies themselves may be equally *transformed* by the changing situations, standpoints, and actions of these social units.

In this sense, although evaluative assessments of religious propositions will always be context-sensitive and perspectival, dependent as they are on the contingent models they employ, this need not mean judgments concerning truth and falsehood will, or even should, just disappear. For example, we can hold up various religious frameworks against each other (or against secular frameworks) and see how they "stack up" with respect to representing the world to us.[13] Likewise, from within particular religious traditions, judgments of correctness can also be made with reference to the models themselves. That is, particular acts of asserting or professing can be checked against or assessed for fit within the current religious model, and particular models may be checked for fittingness with the overall religious framework. Some models may cohere better, some less well. For better or worse, much here depends on who the gatekeepers are for the delineation and preservation of the models in question and the conceptual objects they contain, as well as on the kinds of authority they are able to exercise over other participants—but this is also the case for science and mathematics (and many other epistemic systems). Still, so long as subjects are operating under the constraints of a certain model, they can make felicitous and sincere assertions about "correctness" and "incorrectness" by reference to the model itself, regardless of their doxastic commitments concerning how closely (if at all) the model or the imaginings represented within it resemble some absolute, mind-independent reality.[14]

For their part, infelicitous, incongruent, unfitting, or otherwise "heretical" statements that "rub up against" the orthodox model in a tradition or the introduction of competing models within a framework may be rejected or condemned by the religious community or its authorities, but they may also represent beneficial epistemic frictions that can drive useful model change in the sense discussed previously. Whether coming from without or within,[15] such disruptions may raise questions concerning the adequacy of the model itself and ask epistemic subjects to step *outside* the model to consider how it stands with respect to alternative models. Here, comparing models may require the establishment of a *meta-discourse* from within which such assessment may take place—both to ensure that the parties to the discourse are not talking past each other and to establish the contexts that are relevant for the parties in question (e.g., which persons or groups are included in the conversation and which criteria or ends are relevant for the comparison). And while the likelihood of a religious model's more closely approximating some objective reality than some alternative may be one relevant criterion for the comparison of the two, it need not be the only (or even the primary) one. The motivations for comparing, adopting, rejecting, or transforming models may have as much or more to do with how such models affectively or aesthetically resonate with the participants in the discourse, or how well they allow for the pursuit of shared moral or social goals that the said participants might care about.

In this sense, *desires*, *values*, and *collective aims* may be just as important as beliefs and probability calculations to considerations of appropriateness within or between models, since evaluative assessments of particular objectual and propositional religious concepts may be appropriately driven by factors that go beyond the merely mind-to-world (or even mind-to-model) direction of fit. A particular conception of the divine may, for example, "match up" with the model as it has been historically handed down or traditionally lived out in a particular setting. But it may no longer be up to the task of helping worshippers meaningfully orient themselves in a particular contemporary context. Likewise, when religious communities encounter each other in plural societies, traditions may end up "borrowing" imaginatively from each other, or "syncretistically" merging ideas from one model into another, as with Christianity's adoption of certain pagan ideas and practices, or the Sikh adaptation of the Hindu *Ramayana*. In all these cases, changing practical demands, social concerns, and intersubjective contexts may exercise a profound influence on how religious objects and narratives come to be revised, renewed, or rejected.

A particular model may also be reimagined in light of conflicts concerning social values. In some cases, the relevant values may be internal to the tradition itself. For example, a growing social or theological focus on religious commandments of neighbor-love may lead a religious community to recommend a change in traditional attitudes toward those who violate certain historically-sanctioned sexual taboos, or they may even revise the sexual norms of the tradition.[16] In other cases, a certain value discourse initially external to the tradition may come to shape the imaginative model with which the tradition operates. For example, the proliferation of human rights discourse in the political vocabulary of a society may cause a reshaping of religious thought concerning, e.g., God's relationship to human beings, or how holy war is to be understood, or how to treat members of sects other than one's own—and it may do so in ways that may affect the entire religious framework within which such concepts operate.[17] Similarly, if certain religious models serve to perpetuate harmful stereotypes or contribute to forms of epistemic or social injustice, this may provide participants in the discourse with justified moral or political reasons to call for model change, regardless of any abstract or "value-neutral" arguments that can be given from the ivory tower in their favor.

Unmooring APR: a double task for the future

One might worry here that the introduction of considerations traditionally considered "non-epistemic" into the appropriateness conditions for model change threaten to make the divine (and other superempirical objects or states of affairs) largely a matter of *projection*—of fashioning the divine after our (desired) image, not the other way around. But perhaps this is a feature of the approach, not a bug. As Grace Jantzen has pointed out, the mere fact that our desires and values influence the images of God we develop doesn't entail that such a God does not exist. If anything, she notes, we might expect that "[a religious approach] teaching that human beings are made in the divine image would have exactly that consequence" (Jantzen 1999: 89). Moreover, if we shift our focus from knowledge to understanding in APR, we might come to agree with Jantzen that "what is needed is not an eschewing of projection, but rather a *consciousness and deliberateness* about it, including, crucially, the deliberate projects of those who have largely been excluded" (90, my emphasis).

On such an approach, then, APR inherits a double mission concerning understanding. Its first task is *analytic* and *diagnostic*: APR can explore, evaluate, and interrogate particular, contextual religious models vis-à-vis the kinds of religious understanding they may or not produce when employed or embodied in religious practice. A not insignificant part of this task, however, also involves thinking critically about the performative aspects and perlocutionary effects of the discourse surrounding the models in question and, more meta-philosophically, about the ways they tend to be treated of (or ignored) in the discipline itself. That is, APR needs to develop a *sensibility* for the harmful and/or exclusionary effects that particular models and discourses can and do sometimes have on those groups whose voices have tended to be marginalized or silenced in these discursive arenas, as well as to begin exploring those models and traditions it has traditionally chosen to ignore.

This leads to a second task for APR, which is unabashedly *projective* and *(re)constructive*: Where it diagnoses models and modes of discourse as conceptually inadequate, epistemically harmful, or morally toxic, APR must also think about ways of ameliorating such conceptual shortcomings. One possibility is simply to reject the religious approach altogether. But we might also suggest alternative or novel modes of religious projection that provide beneficial epistemic disruptions and frictions, or we may seek to productively recover or reappropriate particular historical religious ideas in ways that create new opportunities for resonance or religious meaning-making, or some alternative to these.

Indeed, one of the central projects of a contemporary religious epistemology must be to interrogate the models *of* our time with an eye toward developing, as Sally McFague (1987) put it, models *for* our time. In the terms we used above, it is our duty as philosophers and theologians to first tether religious models to *our* collective reality—namely, to locate those models that are sensitive to the realities and lives of those whom they affect, and which are capable of speaking and moving religious subjects, of facilitating the making of meaning and promoting human and non-human flourishing in the contexts in which *we* live.[18] Importantly, this diagnostic and constructive challenge for an APR of the future does not ignore the epistemic but incorporates it as a central component. For example, McFague claims that accepting *"the knowledge that we have the power to destroy ourselves and other forms of life* [. . .] and understanding the changes it implies for our ways of thinking about the world and for relating to others in the world" should make us call into question the usefulness of the ways we have been taught to think about power (McFague 1987: 15–6). Yet to change the ways we think about power also requires us to think about the ways certain idea(l)s of power are expressed in dominant Western monotheistic models of the divine. So, given our knowledge about our own destructive abilities and proclivities, and our diagnostic understanding of dominant Western approaches to God, we need to ask ourselves whether there might not be models that are better tethered to the reality that confronts us than those we have tended to explore in APR. McFague, writing at the height of the Cold War, was worried about a nuclear holocaust. Today, we may be more concerned about global warming and climate change, or about social and political unrest. In both cases, however, our knowledge of these realities, together with our desires, values, and collective aims, calls us to these diagnostic and constructive undertakings.

This dual task also shows us why the bracketing of the debate over MaRTeR in APR and the shift from knowledge to understanding in religious epistemology might be not only beneficial but necessary if APR wants to remain socially relevant. First, as Jantzen puts it, "the 'truth' question asked too insistently and too soon" can distract APR scholars from reflecting critically on the ways dominant religious models in APR have been "used oppressively, to silence the emerging myths that would enable resistance to dominance" (Jantzen 1996: 110). Second, the insistence that that the realism-antirealism question with respect to any particular model be settled before all else—or the restriction of discussion to only those theistic "perfect-being" models traditionally viewed as plausible candidates for religious knowledge—can actually function "as a way of foreclosing [a] creative openness to new possibilities" (Jantzen 1999: 191). That is, focusing too much on the question of realism can preclude the introduction of alternative, potentially transformative religious imaginings that could serve as philosophically productive foils to the dominant models in the literature. Shifting the discussion away from MaRTeR thus makes room for the development or recovery of alternatives that can provide the kinds of beneficial "epistemic frictions" discussed above in a way that can help ensure that understanding goes hand in hand with considerations of epistemic and social justice.[19]

An understanding-centered religious epistemology must therefore also be what José Medina (2013b) calls an *epistemology of resistance*. From the level of theory, such an epistemology must encourage and explore possibilities for the acknowledgement of and engagement with multiple perspectives and imaginings that can present epistemic counterpoints to the dominant models in the interest of achieving a greater degree of reflective objectivity, whether these be internal epistemic frictions within a singular tradition or imaginative dissonances between traditions or approaches. From the level of implementation, such an epistemological approach will attempt to create the conditions for and actively promote a kind of "kaleidoscopic consciousness," one which seeks understanding in reflective and affective equilibrium between the various cognitive-affective forces, "without some forces overpowering others, without some [...] influences becoming unchecked and unbalanced" (Medina 2013b: 50).[20]

This process should be understood as fluid and dynamic, a process constantly open to questioning and revision. As in science, "the method of reflective equilibrium is dialectical and its results are provisional. [...] [N]othing is in principle immune to revision. An account that we can on reflection accept today may be one that we cannot on reflection accept tomorrow" (Elgin 2017: 67, 89). It is also not a matter of an individual merely weighing her cognitive options. It is a *social and interactive process* of imaginative acceptance and disruption, of locating cognitive and affective resonances and dissonances, of continually negotiating and re-negotiating the imaginative territory, as well as interrogating the ends such imaginings are supposed to serve and examining their real-life effects. It is, as Medina puts it, a "transactional traffic between the subjective and the intersubjective as mutually constituting and interdependent domains that have to acknowledge and engage each other and work together toward maintaining some sort of epistemic equilibrium [...]" (Medina 2013b: 50–1).

Conclusion

The alternative epistemological approach I have proposed here maintains that a religious epistemology centered around understanding can, in contrast to its knowledge-centric counterparts as traditionally employed in APR, better show just how religion as a hermeneutical enterprise is epistemically valuable, as well as how we as philosophers of religion can go about exploring and theorizing about religion from within our discipline. This creates room for the possibility championed by many APR scholars that the deliverances of religious practice and doctrine may be epistemically rational, yet it does not make everything contingent on first establishing the truth or probability of MaRTeR. With Medina, I maintain that such an understanding-centered epistemology can and should be a social epistemology of resistance that actively acknowledges and engages multiple voices and perspectives, allowing for productive epistemic frictions to serve as checks and balances in our pursuit of understanding in reflective equilibrium. This is an idea I will turn to repeatedly in this book, because reorienting APR—and ourselves—toward ideas, questions, and models we have traditionally eschewed or ignored *in the interest of epistemic ends* is no easy task, and we need to be reminded over and over again of the importance of not only being passively *open* to epistemic disruption but, as Helen De Cruz (2020) has suggested, to actively *seeking* it out.

Notes

1 Compare Martin Krieger's claim that mathematicians and mathematical physicists explore "just which features of the world are necessary if we are to have the kind of world we do have" (Krieger 2004: 1230).

2 Compare the description of religion by Anthony Pinn as "a hermeneutic by means of which human experience [. . .] is mined for what it says about our response to the deepest existential and ontological challenges we face" (Pinn 2015: 35). Importantly, however, I by no means intend to maintain here that this hermeneutic aspect is *sufficient* for a system of practices' being considered a religion. In line with Schilbrack (2014), for example, I am inclined to think that religions also involve reference to the "superempirical" in some relevant way (so long as 'superempirical' is understood sufficiently broadly), or we might weaken this claim a bit and adopt Nancy Ammerman's condition that there be "a spiritual dimension [to religion] that invokes direct or indirect (institutionalized) connection to something that is 'other than' everyday reality" (Ammerman 2020: 9).

Moreover, I do not desire to reduce all such meaning-making enterprises (e.g., sport, literature, political activity, theater, etc.) to instances of "implicit" religion. At the same time, these activities may share hermeneutical meaning-making features with religion to some degree or other—which could perhaps point us toward points of resonance for productive discourse between religious and secular worldviews (e.g., by making salient certain structural similarities and/or symbolic continuities between them).

3   Note that I am *not* claiming here that all religious traditions in fact aim at human- or world-flourishing, nor that they actually succeed in making existential meaning in this way (or do so to the same degree). This is merely a candidate for *one way among others* that religion may be epistemically valuable apart from its mere alethic value. I take investigations into this and related issues to be one of the additional tasks that APR might tackle. For a somewhat similar approach, albeit one more interested than mine in defending realism and the centrality of belief, see Barbour (1974).

4   As will become clear in subsequent chapters, I do not use the word "imaginative" here to indicate non-veracity but rather to point to a particular way we access certain features of reality.

5   Compare here Paul Ricoeur's related discussion of the "world" of a text (Ricoeur 1995). This is a helpful metaphor, insofar as it also fits with our colloquial reference to the "world" of an author's imagination or of a particular fictional context (e.g., the "worlds" of Tolkien or Harry Potter). A better comparison for a cosmic narrative framework, however, might be the way we use the term 'universe' with regard to comic books or fictional series (e.g., the Marvel and DC "universes," or the "universe" of Star Trek vs. that of Star Wars), in which distinct figures and storylines by various authors are integrated into an overarching narrative context, which itself may branch off into various worlds or "multiverses," as well as admit of "canonical" or "non-canonical" articulations and interpretations.

6   Stump focuses on what she calls "Franciscan knowledge" (which includes most generally knowledge-by-acquaintance and more specifically knowledge of persons), but much of what she discusses could fall under my treatment of understanding and imagination in this book. Indeed, although her explicit topical focus is neither on cosmic narrative frameworks nor on the epistemologies of understanding, her book is infused with a concern for both of these topics. Stump also engages in a form of APR "beyond realism," insofar as she notes that she is "treating the biblical narratives only as stories, not as history or as revelation; and nothing in this project presupposes the truth of belief in God. [. . .] Those people who think there is no God in the actual world can thus accept my conclusions without giving up their atheism" (Stump 2010: 37).

7   On this point see, e.g., Fricker (2007: 2) and Medina (2013b: 82ff.).

8   As I will argue in later chapters, I think such existential meaning-making can be achieved even if the subject's credence with respect to certain fundamental religious

propositions is zero, so long as she imaginatively accepts and is authentically committed to the propositions in some relevant way.

9 There is a tendency in both analytic and phenomenological circles to set up hermeneutical conceptions of understanding in contrast to epistemological notions (see, e.g., Okshevsky 1992). I think this is a mistake, and one of the tasks of bringing APR together with its critics may be to more fruitfully explore the ways in which the traditionally "epistemic" can be understood as "hermeneutic" and vice versa.

10 See, for example, my discussion of Meister Eckhart's seemingly incompatible descriptions of God as pure intellect, on the one hand, and as pure being, on the other—as well as his explicitly contextual and pragmatic approach to theology—in Griffioen (2023b). I take this idea up again in Chapter 9.

11 On this point, see, e.g., Bagger (2007) and Yadav (2016).

12 In this respect, religion may be more like some forms of art and literature than science.

13 Indeed, everything I say here and below with respect to models may be applied to entire religious traditions and sub-traditions themselves, as when agents are engaged in interdenominational or interfaith discourse. However, as I discuss presently, such endeavors will likely require the establishment of a *meta-discursive framework* from which dialogue can successfully take place. This is yet another project which APR may be suitably equipped to take up.

14 I discuss this in more detail in subsequent chapters.

15 Here we may include competing approaches from the same religious tradition, challenges from other religious traditions, as well as atheist and/or secular models. They may vary in degree and kind, making it more or less difficult to establish a relevant meta-discourse. (Note that this may also correspond to scientific theory change: Some challenges to the model require only a tweaking or modification of the current theory. Others may involve replacing the entire theory and/or overthrowing the paradigm within which it arises.)

16 In the Abrahamic traditions, according to which human beings are part of God's natural creation, this often involves a renegotiating of the imaginative space concerning what can be said to be "(un)natural" to the human being—or, in some cases, which qualities, dispositions, and behaviors can be considered consistent with being created in the image of God.

17 For a somewhat dated yet still nuanced discussion of the intersection of sexual norms and human rights discourse in US-American religious contexts, see Olyan and Nussbaum (1998).

18 The "we" here is intentionally ambiguous. McFague, for example, is focused on providing a holistic Christian theology "for an ecological, nuclear age" which encompasses all human and non-human creatures. However, as model-choice is context-sensitive, the scope of "we/our" may be much more restricted than this. In

fact, being explicit about context is one way in which APR scholars who wish to proceed with "business as usual" can continue to do so (i.e., by specifying the limited context within which they are working). Either way, as I discuss further in Chapter 8, it would be helpful if scholars were more explicit about to whom their analyses are *addressed* and more sensitive to those they might *affect*. Far from creating more clustered, specialized cells of discourse, such transparency might instead avert both unnecessary harm and preventable misunderstandings, as well as create opportunities for more pluralistic comparative and communicative projects.

19 Jantzen facetiously asks why so many philosophers of religion are afraid of deferring the truth question in the interest of other epistemic and moral ends, concluding that "few people, even if they believe in a literal God and a literal hell, believe anymore that God would send anyone to that hell for deferring belief, especially if the deferral is for moral reasons" (Jantzen 1996: 110). Indeed, it does seem that if there is a loving God of the MaRTeR persuasion, such a divine being would also have an interest in its rational creatures having morally appropriate attitudes toward and true beliefs about *each other*—attitudes and beliefs that might be precluded or inhibited by some imaginings of that God.

20 Medina formulates these two norms (acknowledgment/engagement and equilibrium) as the two regulative principles of what he calls *epistemological resistance*.

From Reorientation to Reform

Implications for the Discipline

What do the shifts in orientation suggested in the previous chapters (that is, looking metaphysically beyond MaRTeR-style realism and epistemologically beyond propositional knowledge) mean for APR and its future?

First, it is important to note that the approaches I have championed here permit much of APR to continue conducting "business as usual"—at least with respect to its interest in exploring the metaphysical contours and implications of perfect-being theology. However, it recommends that APR scholars do so with a more nuanced and contextualized epistemic outlook. Those involved in this theistic project must be explicit about the fact that their view is not (and likely does not even approximate) the objective "view from nowhere" of pure, impartial, abstract rationality. Instead, they need to come to see themselves as operating with one conceptual model among others and to actively seek out additional perspectives to complement or complicate their own story. This may sound relatively simple (it is not[1]), but the way the discourse in mainstream APR tends to proceed, as well as the relative isolation(ism) of the discipline as discussed above, gives us good reason to think that this is not currently happening as much as it should.

Interestingly, however, when the perfect-being project starts to interrogate itself in the ways suggested, it might find itself moving in a direction closer to that of *analytic theology* (AT), which at the very least is willing to acknowledge that its purposes proceed from a particular creedal perspective and are tradition-specific.[2] Here, an understanding-centered epistemology is especially well-positioned to contribute to what we, channeling Anselm, might call a project of *fides quaerens intellectum*. In this vein, drawing on fourteenth-century Christian theologian Peter Aureoli, James Arcadi discusses AT as form of "declarative theology" concerned with "help[ing] the faithful seek deeper embraces of the articles of faith" or to "imagine better" the things to which one is religiously committed (Arcadi 2017: 50, 40). Importantly, a perspectivally-sensitive search for more objective understandings and better religious imaginings can be declarative in this way without requiring the "collective ambition" of the analytic theological enterprise to be, as Louis Berkhof puts it, "a constant endeavor to see the truth as God sees it" (quoted in Rea 2009: 8). In this sense, I resist Michael Rea's claim that those who challenge the supposition that we can have "access to 'the truth as God sees it'—i.e., absolute, perfectly objective truth" (in the APR-preferred sense described in Chapter 1) will not believe that "any sort of *robust* theology can be developed in the analytic mode" (Rea 2009: 8). Personally, I suspect that no *epistemically adequate and just* theology from the "God's-eye view" can be developed in any mode, but this does not preclude an understanding-centered epistemology of resistance from serving as an important tool in articulating a non-minimalist AT that is both potentially "objective" insofar as it is sensitive and attentive to the plurality of the perspectives of those who make up the tradition in question and "robust," so long as stability and dependability are not used as excuses for inflexibility or intractability. A tradition (or discipline) can be stable yet dynamic, dependable yet pliable—and a central project for an AT that aims to be both epistemically responsible and socially responsive will be to critically discuss the ways in which a particular religious tradition can stay true to its historical and doctrinal roots while at the same time speaking meaningfully to the contemporary faithful.[3]

Of course, the shift to this kind of epistemological approach would also require of AT that it, too, seek out epistemic frictions and resistant imaginings. This can mean taking into account theological approaches that have typically been marginalized in analytic theological contexts (e.g., feminist, queer, or liberation theologies—as well as explicitly non-analytic approaches). It can also involve promoting the development of analytic theologies outside of Western Christianity and actively engaging with those theologies.[4] Indeed, an understanding-centered epistemology of resistance seems much more promising for such theological endeavors than its knowledge-centric counterparts, especially if one thinks (as I am inclined to) that the way forward for systematic theology in the next century is comparative.[5] At the same time, comparative AT, like APR itself, cannot ignore the practical dimensions of religion in its search for understanding, as I will discuss presently.

Still, the AT approach is just one way that current APR scholars may proceed, namely creedally and normatively. But a context-sensitive, understanding-centered religious epistemology need not be confessional in this way. To take just one example, the epistemological approach endorsed here might also lead to a re-orientation in more general epistemologies of interreligious, intrareligious, or religious-secular disagreement—say, by focusing less on individuals' duties to adjust their individual credences or on the aim of seeking cognitive agreement and concentrating instead on the ways in which subjects can establish epistemically valuable self- and other-understandings through friction, resonance, and reflective equilibrium. As Muhammad Legenhausen puts it:

> We miss opportunities for self-understanding and for understanding others when we are focusing exclusively on where we agree and differ in our beliefs, and on debating strategies. Understanding is to be won through resonance, and not merely by the elimination of conflicting beliefs. Indeed, in the absence of resonance misunderstanding can persist despite agreement".
>
> Legenhausen 2013: 38–9

In such an epistemological endeavor, not only cognitive but also *affective* or *aesthetic* resonance will be important—more important, perhaps, than the achievement of straightforward agreement or the elimination of cognitive disagreement.[6] To my knowledge, this has yet to be adequately explored at any great length in contemporary religious epistemology.

Finally, in the shift from knowledge to understanding, APR may find new avenues to more productively engage with the ontological and ontotheological objections discussed in Chapter 1. With respect to the former, by moving largely past the realism–antirealism debate and the insistence that propositional knowledge is the central epistemic aim in the religious and scientific enterprises, the claim of the ontological critic that APR is no better than a "philosophy of fairies" has less bite, since not everything epistemically relevant hangs on answering the question concerning the existence and nature of a perfect being. The more interesting debate here lies not in the question of whether the God of MaRTeR exists or whether the theistic believer is "within her epistemic rights" to believe in such a God, but rather in whether particular religious systems really do perform the hermeneutical functions to which they aspire and, if so, whether or not they do so in ways that better contribute to world-flourishing than purely secular approaches. The answer here might be negative, in which case it is worth thinking about ways in which secular worldviews might (already) perform these hermeneutical tasks in a modern world. In this way, APR may also branch out into what some non-analytic thinkers have called "a-theology," "theological humanism," or "passionate agnosticism."[7] Alternatively, APR may explore resonances and dissonances with concrete secular and scientific perspectives (e.g., the human rights discourse, climate science, or debates around artificial intelligence) with an eye toward how such perspectives may be productively incorporated into or addressed by religious frameworks in ways that allow for the pursuit of common social goals.

The project of adequately addressing the ontotheological objection—namely that modelling God as a "being among beings" commits a grave epistemological, metaphysical, and theological error—will take a bit more work, and to do so we will need to foray a bit more deeply into the role that the *religious imagination* plays in the religious life, as I will do in the following chapters. For now, it will suffice to say that the more "cataphatic-leaning" APR scholar and the more "apophatic-leaning" postmodern theologian may simply be operating with competing models of or approaches to the divine—even if they may ultimately be operating within the same overarching cosmic narrative framework. An analytic religious epistemology of the future, then, must take the postmodern model seriously—especially insofar as the charge is ultimately one of *idolatry*—and think more carefully about the roles that positive *and* negative theology may play in religious understanding, especially when it comes to taking the divine seriously *qua* divine.

In all these ways and many more, it seems that shifting (or, minimally, widening) our epistemological focus to religious understanding may represent a promising way forward for a philosophical theism of the future. However, there are still some lurking worries. I have claimed that belief might be less important in religious contexts than acceptance. Yet many APR scholars either explicitly claim or implicitly insinuate that belief is central to the religious life, either as a key component or an attitude to aspire to, so my claims about its relative dispensability (or the appropriateness of taking it as an ideal) will require a bit more elaboration. In Part Two, then, I will more carefully explore how APR can be not just reoriented but also *reformed* when belief is dethroned as the central attitude in the religious life, especially if we think that religious *practice* enjoys some kind of primacy in that life.

Notes

1 Note that the ordinary philosophical anticipation of objections or engaging in intellectual exchange with critics in print or at a conference is not necessarily the same as actively seeking out epistemic frictions (though it may play a part in such seeking).

2 On the conceptual running together of APR and AT, see Wood (2021), Chapter 1.

3 Indeed, there is no reason to take "robust" to mean only those approaches that point to the truth of MaRTeR or which restrict the robustness of a theory or model to strongly realist views (see, e.g., Boon 2012).

4 Projects in Islamic and Jewish AT and APR are encouragingly on the rise, but although the scholars in these projects tend to refer back to seminal projects in Western Christian AT, I have yet to see much work going in the other direction.

5 On this point, see von Stosch (2009, 2012).

6 Navid Kermani's (2018) *Wonder Beyond Belief: On Christianity* provides one example of how these latter kinds of resonances may productively be explored.

7 For a few examples of extra-APR work already going in this direction, see: Boscaljon (2013); Klemm and Schweiker (2008); Pinn (2015).

Part Two

Reform

4

Beyond the Cognitive

Faith, Commitment, and the Religious Life

Worship of God precedes affirmation of [God's] realness. We praise *before we* prove.

Abraham Heschel, God in Search of Man

Introductory remarks

I argued in previous chapters that, as in science and mathematics, knowledge is not the only epistemic valuable aim in the religious "game" and truth need not always be the driving focus of that game. I therefore suggested that APR should "reorient" (or at least broaden) its gaze from the heavily knowledge-focused epistemologies that drive much of its current work to understanding-centered epistemologies that can perhaps better motivate how the religious life can be of genuine epistemic value beyond merely being "rationally defensible" or constituting "possible knowledge" for some very limited set of religious epistemic agents. In this context, I suggested that we think more carefully about the central role that religious *practice* plays in the religious life—including its epistemic role in contributing to existential meaning-making. If we do so, we might end up viewing classical and contemporary discussions in APR from a somewhat different angle. For example, we might find that some debates, although theoretically interesting, end up obscuring the religious life more than they illuminate it. Or we might discover important and philosophically rich aspects of that life that we have heretofore overlooked or simply taken for granted. So it is, I will suggest, with debates surrounding religious faith, which is the topic of this chapter.

I have already noted a few times that the over-intellectualization of religion in APR sometimes threatens to render the religious life nearly unrecognizable. Not only may APR's approach to religion betray certain Western, post-Enlightenment, even Protestant biases;[1] it more generally tends to overlook what John Cottingham (2005) has called the *primacy of praxis* in the religious life. Unfortunately, APR's intellectualist tendencies bleed heavily (one might say "hemorrhage") into its analyses of religious faith. Although APR scholars are well aware that the religious life involves other significant attitudes and orientations than the merely cognitive, as an object of philosophical scrutiny, they have often treated religious faith as though it were a predominantly intellectual matter—usually by focusing the bulk of their attention on so-called "propositional faith," or *faith that [p]*, as a candidate for rational appraisal (not seldomly as yet another means of trying to defend the epistemic rationality of MaRTeR-style theism against its ontological objectors). A number of these views also treat *belief* (or at least a high degree of subjective certainty) as either a paradigm attitude or ideal cognitive state in a life of religious faith, even if they allow that other attitudes may sometimes be permissible in lieu of belief. (More on this below.) Unfortunately, whether intentional or not, in giving discursive primacy of place to the intellectual aspects of religion, APR has created the impression that religious *cognition* is most fundamental or central to individual subjects (and, seemingly, communities), with everything else in the life of faith being derivative of, posterior to, or built around it.

Now I by no means intend to say that the propositional is of no importance to the religious life. Religions have conceptual content, and this content implicitly or explicitly comes to expression in particular propositions that represent candidates for belief or some other positive cognitive stance. For example, I suggested in the previous chapter that one epistemically valuable dimension of religious traditions has to do with their providing existential meaning and orientation via a kind of cosmic narrative framework. Such narratives contain various worldly and other-worldly characters or objects that act and are acted upon, spiritual and non-spiritual realms or dimensions of reality, continuities or interactions between the natural and supernatural worlds, and so on—and these narrative contents are largely expressed (or at least express*ible*) in propositions, which themselves often imply, entail, or simply give rise to further propositions about, say, the metaphysical nature of that content, how we come to grasp it, and how we ought to act as a result. And many of these propositions are taken by religious authorities and adherents to be central to the traditions in question. I thus concur with sociologist Nancy Ammerman that in our analyses of the religious life it is important to "pay attention to cognitive models" and the kinds of cognitive stances that religious subjects adopt with respect to them, but we should do so with the recognition that such models "are intersubjectively shared and visible in joint patterns of action" and may be more or less cognitively "comprehensive" (Ammerman 2020: 12).

Armed with this insight, it might be worthwhile to put APR's cognitively-loaded cart back *behind* the praxic horse for a while and see what happens if we start our analyses of religious faith from religious *practice*, not propositions. What emerges might ultimately be compatible (perhaps even co-extensive) with some of the theories of propositional faith currently found in the literature, but reorienting our attention in this way might nevertheless help us better see the usefulness—and limits—of those accounts and present alternative ways of arriving at the significance of the propositional. Thus, instead of beginning with religious cognition and then figuring out which (if any) affective and volitional components we need to "add" to get something acceptably "faith-like," it might be interesting to begin with the kind of faith most relevant to religious practice and seeing where we end up with respect to religious cognition.

In this chapter, I will propose just such an approach to religious faith, according to which the volitional and affective aspects of the religious life regain the prominence in APR that they actually enjoy in lived religion. In this way, I hope to show how APR can move beyond the kind of "intellectualism" that has underscored the knowledge-centered epistemologies discussed in Part One of this book and make room for understanding-centered, praxis-focused social epistemologies that can point the discipline in promising new directions and better bring it into conversation with similar movements elsewhere in analytic philosophy, as well as with neighboring disciplines that take religion as an object of investigation.

I should note here that I am not interested in defending the rationality of religious faith in what follows, nor (unless explicitly specified) in exploring how it is that faith is or can be theologically or morally virtuous.[2] Whether any particular case of faith is epistemically warranted, practically rational, or morally virtuous is beyond the scope of my focus here but could represent an interesting future program for APR to pursue. Before setting out my own account, however, it will be helpful to lay the groundwork for this alternative approach to faith—first, by exploring (as the literature tends to do) some uses of the term 'faith' and its cognates in ordinary (English) language to generate a few uses that might be relevant for our analyses and, second, by looking at the deficiences in the way the current debate tends to play out in the analytic philosophical literature.

APR, faith, and faith-locutions

Let us start by examining a few ordinary-language uses of the term "faith" in English as commonly referenced by APR theorists of faith and how these uses have translated into current approaches to faith in APR.[3] Take, for example, the following sentences, in which faith is in some sense ascribed to a subject (S):

(1) S has faith that p.
(2) S has faith in A [to ϕ].
(3) S is faithful to O.
(4) S is a faithful Q.
(5) S is a member of the Q-faith.
(6) S is a person of faith [within Q].

Sentences (1) to (6) each express a different sense or mode of the English word 'faith.' In (1), S is said to have faith with respect to some *proposition* (p). In locutions like (2), on the other hand, the focus of faith is not on a proposition but rather on an *agential object* (A), in whom S is said to have faith, often with respect to A's undertaking some particular action (ϕ). However, whereas the faith-locutions in sentences (1) and (2) are roughly interchangeable with the locutions 'believes that' and 'believes in,' respectively, the adjectival ascription 'faithful' in (3) and (4) displays a kind of *fidelity* or *dedication* to a person, group, or institution that does not seem as immediately reducible to some doxastic (or even sub-doxastic) cognitive state. Sentence (3), which uses 'faithful' as a predicative adjective, designates a prepositional object (O) to which or to whom S is allegiant or devoted. Sentence (4) differs from (3) insofar as 'faithful' is used attributively to modify Q, which picks out some relevant *identity-feature* or *role* instantiated by S, as when we say someone is a "faithful customer" a "faithful Milwaukee Brewers fan" or a "faithful Muslim." Sentence (5), in which 'faith' becomes a countable noun ("a faith," "many faiths"), takes on a more explicitly religious connotation and places the focus on S's membership in some particular tradition (Q), but does not say much of anything about S's involvement in Q beyond mere belonging. At the same time, it does imply the existence of a *community* to which S belongs. Finally, the use of 'faith' in (6) seems more comprehensive than the other senses, insofar as it implies not only belonging as in (5) but also some combination and appropriate incorporation of the senses of faith expressed in (1) to (4). That is, (6) characterizes S as someone whose identity is deeply tied up with the Q-faith to which S belongs.

In keeping with some of the literature,[4] I will call models of faith based on the attitudes expressed by (1) and (2) *propositional faith* and *objectual faith*, respectively. Cases of the type (3) and (4) I will call *devotional faith* (insofar as the subject is devoted or dedicated to something or someone). The nominalized use in (5) can be dubbed *institutional faith* (i.e., belonging to *a* faith, understood as a socially-constructed, institutionalized phenomenon), and the more comprehensive sense in (6) is suitably characterized by the term *global faith*. Given its focus on the intellectual aspects of religion, APR has largely centered its attention on propositional and objectual faith (usually as candidates for rational appraisal),[5] and they have thus generally understood institutional faith as expressed in (5) as being constituted by the central propositions and doctrinal creeds of a religious tradition, with respect to which one could have propositional faith, and/or the objects/agents described in such creeds, in which one could have objectual faith. (For this reason, Robert Audi uses the term "creedal faith" for cases similar to (5).) Global faith, then, is understood, minimally, as the conjunction (and appropriate integration) of propositional and objectual faith with respect to a (creedal) faith.[6] Devotional faith, for its part, is often briefly mentioned and then dropped or glossed over as more-or-less parasitic on, and/ or posterior to, propositional and objectual faith.

Even those APR scholars who have made great strides in exploring the non-doxastic, affective, and practical dimensions of religion, still often tend to center the cognitive in their explorations of religious faith. For example, when Audi speaks of global faith, he claims that, in contrast to character traits that are primarily action-centered, "global faith—as embodied in being a person of religious faith—is, comparatively, though by no means exclusively, *cognitively* centered: an element appropriately developed, and manifested, by *believing* (or otherwise *cognizing* [. . .]) the right kinds of things on the right kinds of grounds" (Audi 2011: 308, my emphases). Although I agree with Audi that being a "person of faith" in the global sense represents an "overall stance in matters that govern important aspects of human life" (Audi 2013: 58), it is still noteworthy that by making of "a faith" in the sense of sentence (5) a propositional and doctrinal notion ("creedal faith"), and by focusing on global faith as cognitively centered, attention is again drawn away from the primacy of praxis in religion, as well as the situated, embodied, and social understanding it generates.[7]

I turn now to how one (perhaps even "the") central contemporary debate concerning religious faith plays out in the literature and the ways in which, even while moving away from the necessity of religious *belief*, APR scholars have remained squarely cognitively-centered in their analyses. Indeed, I think the two camps in this debate, like the proponents and opponents of MaRTeR in Chapter 1, are more or less playing the same intellectual "game," but it is a game that drastically limits what these models of faith can really do for us as philosophers of religion.

Doxasticism vs. non-doxasticism

It would be nearly impossible to touch on every account of religious faith in the philosophical literature. However, faith-theorists in APR tend to stake their claim in one of two camps—namely, *doxasticism*,[8] which claims that belief is necessary for religious faith, and *non-doxasticism*,[9] which denies the doxasticist claim and proposes various "positive cognitive stances" intended to stand in for belief. This debate is usually centered on propositional faith, though the question of belief also arises for objectual faith in theistic contexts, since it seems intuitive to many theorists that to have faith *in* God requires (minimally) believing that God *exists* (and, usually, that God exists as a *person* in whom one could put one's faith). If this is right, then objectual faith would appear to presuppose at least some level of doxastic propositional faith.

Although doxasticism still generally tends to be taken to be taken as the "default" (and "commonsense") position in APR concerning religious faith, with respect to which non-doxasticists target their criticisms, given the relative uptake and discussion of non-doxastic models in recent years, current doxasticists tend to proceed rather defensively, focusing their efforts largely on meeting the challenges to their views raised by non-doxasticists over the past decade. One of the biggest worries raised by the latter is that doxastic accounts of faith do not appear to leave room for *doubt*, whereas non-doxasticists (to my mind, plausibly) maintain that uncertainty not only seems compatible with faith (Howard-Snyder 2019b; McKaughan 2013), it might even play a central role within it (Verbin 2002). A common non-doxasticist strategy is to refer to individuals generally viewed as exemplars or paradigms of religious faith who confessed to being riddled with doxastic doubt—Mother Teresa being one of the prime examples— and noting how we still take their faith to have persevered through such times of uncertainty and anguish (McKaughan 2018).[10]

The objection from doubt against doxasticism is often bound up closely with the idea that faith is in some way *risky* or *precarious* (Bishop 2002, 2007; Buchak 2012, 2017b). This worry expresses the intuition many theorists have that faith involves the *will* in some relevant way (even if this sometimes gets expressed in epistemic terms). For example, we often speak of taking a "leap of faith," in both religious and non-religious contexts. Likewise, the notions in secular discourse of "*taking* something on faith" or "*putting* one's faith in someone" seem to be associated with a certain kind of epistemic and/or practical risk. To put it as John Bishop does, faith appears to involve a kind of *venture*. Yet when we view paradigmatic faith as merely a matter of "holding faith beliefs, and being glad of the truths so held" (Bishop 2007: 105), it is difficult to see how faith risks anything at all from the standpoint of the subjectively certain religious believer.

The non-doxasticist proposal

Proponents of non-doxasticism about faith maintain that their approaches can better account for the compatibility of faith and doubt and the inherent venturesomeness of faith than the "default" doxasticist model. In order to accommodate the former concern, non-doxasticists propose that other attitudes—for example, affirmation, assumption, and above all *acceptance*—may stand in for belief. These are usually combined with or folded into some other attitude or stance, which they then take to be sufficient for faith. In propositional faith, this is often (though by no means exclusively) identified with the attitude of *hope*[11]—which, cognitively speaking, allows that one need only believe that the faith-proposition in question is *possible*, not probable or actual. On this kind of approach, propositional faith that *p* amounts to something like accepting *p* (and acting accordingly) because one hopes that *p* is true. Since we do not hope for things we already believe, uncertainty or doubt seems built into hope. It is likewise venturesome, insofar as one risks disappointment if what one hopes for and has "put one's faith in" does not end up obtaining. With respect to objectual faith, the relevant attitude is often taken to be something like *trust in* or *reliance on* some agent (usually to do something).[12] This, too, seems compatible with doubt, since we tend to think that one can display trust or reliance when one is uncertain (or even if one strongly doubts) that the agent will do as one is entrusting them to do. In such cases, especially when something of importance is at stake, these attitudes can also be very risky.[13]

Importantly, however, on such accounts, even if the propositions in which the non-doxastically faithful turn out to be true, faith will not constitute religious *knowledge* (unless the non-doxasticist is willing to lower the threshold for what counts as knowledge). This may not bother some non-doxasticists (like myself), who are more concerned with understanding than straightforward factual knowledge, but it may be an unwelcome result for those APR scholars who, in line with the tradition, would like not only to defend the rationality of the religiously faithful but also to allow that religious faith, if true, could constitute genuine knowledge. If the non-doxasticist gets around this by allowing that belief can be *compatible* with religious faith, then they will have to give some account of how such doxastic faith remains venturesome. If they deny that belief is compatible, they get the odd result that someone who, by faithfully hoping *that there is a God* and acting accordingly, is opened up to a transformative religious experience causing them to believe this proposition would thereby *lose* their propositional faith, given that their belief is, by their lights, no longer "risky" in the relevant ways. Dropping the risk requirement altogether remains an option, but it will be important to show that the doubt condition does not fall with it.

The doxasticist response

To the challenges by the non-doxasticist that accounts of faith requiring belief cannot accommodate doubt and do not risk anything, doxasticists have responded that their opponents are either simply begging the question against doxasticism or equivocating on the term "faith" (Malcolm and Scott 2023; Mugg 2022). I think there is something to both of these responses.

The claim that faith is "clearly" compatible with doubt by appeal to intuitions about particular examples does seem, in some sense, to simply assume what the non-doxasticist is out to prove, since it is always open to the doxasticist to simply respond, "That's not an objection; that's just my view"—and maintain that Mother Teresa did *not* have propositional faith at those times in which she was in the grip of extreme doubt. It is also open to the doxasticist to appeal to a graded notion of belief, such that, while doubt can *weaken* the status of the belief held by the subject, it need not extinguish it, so long as it remains above a certain threshold. This would also be more compatible with faith's being seen as inherently risky or venturesome, though insisting on the latter condition would likely make faith incompatible with full subjective certainty, even on doxasticist approaches—and this, in turn, might undermine the whole point of doxasticism in the first place.

However, if the doxasticist is willing to weaken their account in such ways, each side of the debate will still have some explaining to do. The doxasticist will have to explain how their view does not just collapse into the non-doxasticist view, especially if they are inclined to significantly lower the threshold for belief or allow for non-belief in particular contexts.[14] The non-doxasticist, for their part, will have to explain why their account is more plausible than a weakened degree-of-belief model. (Perhaps, for example, an appeal to hope is more "faithful" to the kinds of ways people in Mother Teresa's situation are inclined to describe their experience than appeals to mere "weakened belief" or "lowered credence.") Still, so long as the doxasticist wants to accommodate the intuition that faith and doubt are compatible, they are likely to need to modify their theory in ways that make it look increasingly less distinguishable from non-doxasticism—and we might begin to wonder what it really hinges on in this debate in the first place.

Alternatively, if the doxasticist wants to stick to their guns and maintain that doubt actively *undermines* or represents a conceptual *contrast* to faith (e.g., by appealing to the intuition that doubt is a *challenge for* or *test of* faith, not a part of it), then we might, in the words of Jonathan Kvanvig, "end up with the view that faith requires, not merely belief, but (psychological, subjective) certainty" (Kvanvig 2018: 107). And this conception of strong doxastic faith—even if common in some religious circles—is "certain to result in self-deception among those who wish to be people of faith, especially if, as he claims, "uncertainty is rationally unavoidable" (107). Indeed, when it comes to the *dynamics* of faith, a strong doxastic model might have the perlocutionary effect[15] of promoting a quasi-"Pascalian" project of self-deception for those desiring of faith[16]—especially if religious faith is viewed as something to be cultivated or emulated. Put a bit differently, it seems that taking subjective certainty to be paradigmatic of faith might be incompatible with viewing religious faith as a virtue to be cultivated, and a religious community that embraces both is likely to have the effect of motivating individuals grappling with uncertainty or doubt in that community to irrationally "double-down" on their religious beliefs or otherwise engage in irrational projects aimed at acquiring or maintaining religious belief.[17] This might go some way to explaining why faith demonstrates a kind of resilience against counterevidence, but it might be an unwelcome result for those doxasticists who are interested in defending the rationality of religious believers or holding up faith as a virtue.[18] Such doxasticists must either give up or significantly weaken their doxasticism (as suggested above), reject the idea that faith can be a virtue, or show how the dilemma just presented is a false one.

These concerns notwithstanding, I think doxasticists are nevertheless right to point out that there might be an equivocation between the sense in which religious exemplars can be said to persist in their faith in the face of doubt and the sense required for propositional faith. What really seems to makes Mother Teresa an exemplar of faith is that she maintained a strong *faithfulness to her tradition* despite finding herself unable to believe certain central propositions about God. In fact, the way she herself characterized much of her experience indicates that she not only worried that God might not exist, she actually may have gone through long periods of disbelief. If this is right, then if the non-doxasticist really wants to contend unequivocally (and univocally) that she maintained *propositional* faith in the face of her doubt, it might show, as Malcolm and Scott (2023) point out, that "contrary to non-doxasticism [...] faith is compatible with disbelief" (52). For non-doxasticists unwilling to adopt this unpopular position (a version of which I will defend below), they would do better to admit that, even though Mother Teresa might have been incapable of taking up whatever weaker positive cognitive stance they might require for non-doxastic propositional faith, she nevertheless maintained something like what I have called *devotional faith* above, while lacking propositional faith in particular propositions of her faith-tradition. We might even say she exhibited *global* faith despite lacking *local* propositional faith, which would explain why we continue to consider her a "person of great faith."

In this sense, doxasticists like Malcolm and Scott still have a response to most contemporary non-doxasticist views. At least concerning the Mother Teresa case, either non-doxastic propositional religious faith is compatible with disbelief or the non-doxasticist uses different senses of the term "faith" when claiming she continued to have faith in the face of doubt. However, despite elaborating briefly on how being a "person of faith" differs from having propositional faith (53), it is telling about the focus of the analytic faith-discourse that Malcolm and Scott then go on to simply dismiss the Mother Teresa case by claiming they are only interested in the "psychological profile" of faith and *therefore* they are only interested in "faith attitudes," which they equate with propositional and objectual faith. That devotional or global faith might *not* be wholly irrelevant for developing a psychological profile of faith doesn't seem to be something they think worth addressing.

Interestingly, instead of just taking the win against non-doxasticism, with respect to propositional faith, Malcolm and Scott want to show that doxasticism can, in fact, make room for the compatibility of doubt and faith. First, they claim that faith and doubt are compatible insofar as subjects can be "double-minded"— which appears just to mean that belief is context-dependent, such that one "believes that p in one context and doubts it in another" (49). However, they also claim that one can "single-mindedly" have faith that p and doubt that p in a particular context on their "normative" doxasticist account, according to which faith and belief can come apart, but only "in a context that is [...] parasitic on a context in which having faith that p is normally to believe that p" (34). They later specify this to mean that cases of non-believing faith will be "derivative [or] reliant on a background in which believing faith is normal" (35). *What* counts as "normal" here and for *whom* "believing faith" must be normal if someone is to be able to have "beliefless" propositional faith is somewhat unclear. Some of the examples Malcolm and Scott give simply involve a subject's losing a belief they once held yet remaining committed to acting on the relevant proposition. This kind of case, of course, is commensurate with non-doxastic models of faith, so long as the subject doesn't disbelieve the proposition. Later, however, they indicate that their theory basically covers all cases except those "wholly pragmatic" ones in which the subject "does not believe *p*, has never believed it, and is not in a community where it is normal to believe it" (63), so belief's being the "norm" in some community concerned with the relevant proposition(s), also appears sufficient to ground a person's non-doxastic propositional faith. In the end, it seems that, on Malcolm and Scott's normative doxasticism, only these "wholly pragmatic" cases are left over for the non-doxasticist to accommodate. However, allowing such cases, they claim, would make "genuine" propositional faith indistinguishable from *pretense*, a result that they (rightly) assume would worry many non-doxasticists in APR. Therefore, they think, non-doxasticists about faith should just convert to normative doxasticism.

I will take up the philosophical hand-wringing surrounding religious pretense in Chapters 6 and 7. For now, it is sufficient to note that, when doxasticism is modified in ways like those proposed by Malcolm and Scott, the theoretical gap between the doxasticist and the non-doxasticist is, yet again, significantly narrowed—and, yet again, we might wonder what's really at stake in "being right" here.[19] Indeed, if both doxasticists and non-doxasticists agree that faith and doubt are compatible, as well as that our understanding of Mother Teresa's being a "paragon of faith" depends on *more* than merely whether or not she has propositional faith all the way through her "life of faith," then both sides also agree that there is an understanding of faith that outstrips the limited focus on propositional (and, we might add, objectual) faith. And apart from the project that takes as its end the assessment of the epistemic *rationality* of the religiously faithful, there seems to be no principled reason to prefer beginning our analyses—even our "psychological profiles"—with propositional and objectual faith than with whatever it is that makes Mother Teresa (or anyone else for that matter) a celebrated *person of faith*.

Playing the same game?

I have suggested that some of the more nuanced versions of doxasticism and common forms of non-doxasticism are not, perhaps, as far removed from one another as one might initially think—or at least that the differences are of little consequence. In fact, there are a number of things upon which these two camps agree:

A. They tend to agree that *propositional and objectual faith* is where the "really" philosophically interesting stuff is at. And, with few exceptions, when they shift their attention to phenomena like devotional or global faith, it is only to briefly mention their awareness of them or to make them largely parasitic on propositional and objectual faith.
B. They generally affirm that, whether or not faith is compatible with non-doxastic cognitive attitudes or stances, it rules out *disbelief.*
C. They recognize that faith is intimately connected to *acting* on the grounds of that faith, implying that some feature, component, or companion of faith is action-guiding or otherwise linked to motivation.
D. They acknowledge that faith is in some relevant way "sticky," "gritty," or otherwise *resilient* in the face of evidential and practical challenges, and that this fact needs explanation. Faith is not just a matter of a subject's believing, accepting, assuming, or affirming various propositions; the faithful subject is also disposed to resolutely hold on to their faith under threat or when otherwise challenged.
E. They both admit that religious faith is not merely a matter of one's cognitive stance, such that some *non-cognitive feature* is also necessary for such faith—and they often imply that it is this attitude that, at least in part, explains (C) and (D).

What does this mean for APR discourse surrounding faith? (A) means that, yet again, the actual *life of religious faith* is largely ignored. This is not to imply that propositional and objectual faith are not significant to that life, nor that they play no role in devotional or global faith. Quite the opposite. But in neglecting to incorporate the role that religious community and practice plays in even these senses of faith—and in making practice and religious devotion *posterior* to such faith both causally and in terms of importance—APR seems to get things exactly backwards and to ignore those features of the religious life that make it especially epistemically valuable and personally meaningful. In this sense, perhaps an alternative approach is necessary, if only to remind APR scholars of some of the assumptions they are making.

(B) sometimes goes more or less unquestioned because it is simply assumed that disbelief is psychologically incompatible with the attitudes or stances theorists propose to be required for or compatible with religious faith—at least not without a kind of internal irrationality on the part of the faithful subject. This claim is rejected by so-called "religious fictionalists" or "theological instrumentalists," who maintain that "wholly pragmatic" cases of the kind discussed above are both possible and compatible with at least propositional faith (and potentially also objectual faith), insofar as one can view religious propositions as *fictionally* true or false (and the objects of those propositions as existent "within the fiction"). They can therefore choose, for instrumental reasons, to accept and utter such propositions as part of their engagement with and within (what they take to be) religious fictions.[20] Both doxasticists and non-doxasticists, however, tend to see it as a potential objection to any account of faith that the fictionalist might be said to have faith, either because of worries about pretense like those raised above, or because propositional faith would seem to at least require *some* "positive cognitive attitude" toward the proposition(s) in question, whereas disbelief seems to be the paradigmatic case of a "negative cognitive attitude" (Howard-Snyder 2019a: 450).[21] Here again, though, we might wonder whether things would look differently if we shifted our focus to the primacy of praxis in religion, instead of placing all our emphasis on propositional and objectual faith at the outset.

(C) and (E), for their part, usually go hand in hand. Since many doxasticists take a non-motivational approach to belief (that is, belief by itself is not sufficient to motivate action), they need (E) if faith is to be tied at all to action. Even non-doxasticists do not think that a mere "positive cognitive stance" (Howard-Snyder 2013) is generally sufficient to make acceptance of a proposition an instance of propositional faith and that an additional positive conative or affective state is necessary to explain both the cognitive assent and the willingness to act on the proposition (McKaughan and Howard-Snyder 2023). Appeals to (E) are also often generally used to explain (D), namely what it is that makes faith so resilient in the face of evidential or practical challenges. In this sense, (E) does double (or even triple) explanatory duty, explaining what turns a positive cognitive attitude into faith, how that faith can give rise to "faithful" action, and why it exhibits resilience when challenged. Unfortunately, the analysis of this (apparently pretty important!) element of religious faith has not been explored in sufficient depth. As Malcolm and Scott remark, "while many writers on faith have taken a position on the practical and non-cognitive profile of faith, the current state of philosophical debate [. . .] is in the early stages of development" (Malcolm and Scott 2023: 133).

An analysis of faith that takes religious practice as its starting point might be able to make some headway on this "profile" of faith, which is usually just "tacked on" to a theory of faith when the cognitive attitudes can't "cut it" by themselves. I therefore (finally!) want to turn to my own account of religious faith by flipping (A) on its head and assuming that religion is, in the first instance, something we *do*, not first and foremost a mere set of propositions to be cognized—and that recognition of this fact *matters* for our philosophical accounts of religious faith.

Faith and the will: commitment, authenticity, and the religious life

To see what an account of religious faith looks like from this perspective, it will be helpful to return to Cottingham's notion of the *primacy of praxis* and to remind ourselves that, for most people, religious practice and ritualistic or liturgical activity long precedes extended theological reflection or the development of well-worked out doctrinal beliefs. As Abraham Heschel writes, "We *praise* before we *prove*. We respond before we question" (Heschel 1955: 120).

Indeed, some (perhaps many) religiously faithful individuals rarely if ever engage in extended theological reflection. The propositions they affirm (or even "basically believe," in the Plantingan sense) often do not contain the sharper contours or carefully "carved joints" of our concepts in APR and may be rather fuzzy around the edges (though, as we shall see in Chapter 5, they can sometimes be much more concrete and thereby "believable" than those we entertain in philosophy). At the same time, even if the average theist has never asked themself whether God could create a stone so heavy that God Godself could not lift it or considered that affirming certain divine attributes like immutability or omniscience might threaten the possibility that their petitionary prayers are efficacious, most of the religiously faithful have at least some, often a rather deep, grasp of the content of the propositions central to their tradition. And they come to much of this understanding, not (or not just) by theological instruction or catechetical study, but by active, embodied participation in the rituals and activities of the religious community itself. They recite *words* together with others who affirm them; they sing *songs* and listen to *stories*; they engage with the *visuals* of religious art or architecture, the *smells* of ritual incense or foods, the *feels* of the beads of a rosary or the etching of a ceremonial tattoo, the *tastes* of holy meals or consecrated wine, the *kinesthetic* sense of liturgical movement, the *spatial* awareness of religious places—and they simultaneously learn (sometimes for better, sometimes for worse) to *respect* and *trust* religious authorities. This is not only the case for those religious individuals raised from childhood in a particular religious tradition but also for many cases of adult conversion. In most cases, it is participation and increasing involvement with a religious community that one does not initially belong to—as well as the affectively-laden *resonances* that tend to underlie and/or accompany such participation—that pave the way for an individual's conversion to a tradition and acceptance of its propositional content, not the other way around.[22]

In this sense, Cottingham's "primacy of praxis" goes beyond merely attributing causal or temporal priority to religious practice. He proposes that "it is in the very nature of religious understanding that it characteristically stems from practical involvement rather than from intellectual analysis" (Cottingham 2005: 6). There is a kind of "coming-to-grasp" a religion's *meaning* and *significance* that can only really develop in and through the embodied and dynamic engagement in religious practice within a community or social group. Religious subjects "learn by doing." By engaging in religious praxis and communion with others so engaged, practitioners come to *understand* how to physically, emotionally, and conceptually navigate the narrative framework of the tradition in ways that open up the kind of hermeneutical understanding that religion can provide. Meaning-making of this kind is an undertaking of the *whole person*—and, importantly, of the person in *relation to* and *community with* other persons—not just something that happens "in the head" as a matter of believing (or coming to believe) certain things. If APR wants to do justice to this fact—and, we might note, to any models of God that might arise from such religious contexts—it must therefore go further than it has typically been willing to go. Or, as liberation theologian Gustavo Gutiérrez puts it: "Only if we start in the realm of practice will we be able to develop a discourse about God that is authentic and respectful. [. . .] At issue is our entire existence. Acceptance of the word, a turning of the word into life and concrete action: this stands at the beginning of any understanding of the faith" (Gutiérrez 1990: 3, 6). An APR approach centered on religious understanding and the primacy of praxis, then, will need to focus on an approach to religious faith that allows affect and the will to play a more significant role (rather than just characterizing them as "downstream effects" or "accompanying elements" of religious cognition), while at the same time still making room for the conceptual and cognitive aspects of religion, as these elements, too, are obviously indispensable when it comes to both religious understanding and the religious life at large.

I therefore propose that we think of religious faith first and foremost as involving a *practical and social commitment* to a religious community and/or (sub-)tradition, including (among others, and to varying degrees), its rituals, practices, institutions, authorities, concepts, norms, narratives, creeds—and, of course, also its propositions. It is this overarching volitional commitment, I suggest, that is best characterized as the central feature of specifically *religious* faith.[23] On this view, then, it is *devotional* faith that occupies the position of privilege—making religious faith "proper" a matter of faith*fulness*—while propositional and objectual faith represent downstream commitments posterior (and in many cases subordinate) to religious devotion. In this sense, religious faith, properly understood, is fundamentally *practical*, even where it is epistemic. This is not to say that propositional or objectual faith held on epistemic (or other practical) grounds cannot temporally precede or play a causal role in the acquisition of religious faith. Perhaps an individual has a mystical experience or becomes convinced by a cosmological argument and decides that some form of theism must be true, so they convert to a particular religion or seek out a religious community. On my account the propositional faith they acquire from their experience or intellectual endeavors is best characterized as "spiritual" or "theistic"—but not specifically *religious*—until their propositional commitments become in some sense tied up with or even derive their meaning from the practices and persons of that community or tradition.[24]

Thus, instead of proceeding as APR tends to do and explaining sustained religious commitment in terms of propositional and/or objectual faith, my approach analyzes the latter in terms of the former. Of course, the additional (e.g., epistemic) commitments one acquires with respect to religious propositions and concepts and one's overarching commitment to a religious tradition or community will generally mutually support one another, and a threat to the former will often be a threat to the latter, but it need not always be. In many cases, religious commitment can (and does) withstand the loss of belief—and is what carries one through the inevitable fluctuations in one's doxastic confidence over time. Further, while some people may lose their devotion to participating in a religious community because they cease to believe certain propositions they take to be central to their tradition, often things go the other way around. For example, finding out one's religious community has done great harm in the name of their faith, or that religious authorities have abused or exploited vulnerable members of their community—or finding oneself simply unable to worship after a traumatic experience—may first deeply shake one's volitional commitment to one's religious community and *therefore* cause one to question whether one's commitment to the propositions and/or persons central to that tradition might not also be the result of error, deception, or misplaced trust. Alternatively, subjects may remain committed to particular propositions but give up their devotion to the particular community that grounded their commitment to those propositions, in which case their *religious* faith may be greatly weakened, even if, e.g., their *theistic* faith remains—or the focus of their devotional commitment may be reoriented to a different level of description.[25]

As I will discuss in more detail below, a volitionally-centered account of faith that rejects (A) by refocusing attention on commitment and religious engagement can, I think, provide a better link between religious cognition and faithful religious action (as in (C) above), in addition to better explaining faith's resilience (D)—while preserving non-doxasticist intuitions about both the compatibility of faith and doubt and the venturesomeness of faith. With regard to (B), I will follow religious fictionalists in rejecting the no-disbelief constraint on religious faith, but my account will diverge from many forms of fictionalism insofar as it is not motivated by a strict metaphysical anti realism concerning the objects of religious discourse (though it is intended to be compatible with such anti realism, as well as with realist views), nor does it affirm that religious faith need be pursued solely or primarily for instrumental reasons. In this sense, my account will allow that faithful subjects may fall on *all* levels on the doxastic spectrum from belief to non-belief all the way to disbelief. However, this claim will take a bit more defending than I can do in this chapter, and I will spend more time defending the rejection of the no-disbelief constraint in later chapters.

For now, it will suffice to note that rather than beginning with propositional and objectual faith by grounding it in such particular attitudes as, e.g., belief, trust, or hope, and then searching for some non-cognitive feature sufficient to do the "gritty" and resilient motivational work that faith is supposed to do, we instead begin with religious participation and the devotional commitment to a tradition or community that emerges from it, and notice the various kinds of auxiliary propositional and objectual commitments to which this larger "project of committed belonging" gives rise. Of course, as Jonathan Kvanvig remarks, "it would be nice if we were clarifying the more obscure by the less obscure" when it comes to analyzing religious faith (Kvanvig 2018: 24). Therefore, lest we make of "commitment" a mere empty placeholder, as much of analytic philosophy does, it will be important to think a bit more about the nature and forms of commitment and how they might help us better illuminate our models of religious faith rather than making them even more opaque.

The nature of commitment

Rather surprisingly, the notion of "commitment" is left largely unanalyzed in the philosophical literature and is generally treated as a sort of *sui generis* concept needing little clarification. However, as Ruth Chang has rightly noted, commitment is by no means an unambiguous notion. For example, a commitment may be an *event* (e.g., *making* or *acquiring* a commitment to something), or it can represent a diachronic phenomenon persisting over time (e.g., *being committed* to something) (Chang 2013: 79). Some commitments are rationally or morally required by the "given" reasons we (take ourselves to) simply have, while some commitments are in some sense "up to us" to determine (80). Of these latter commitments, some may just arise in the context of our situatedness in the world, but some are chosen, as when we decide to undertake a large project and see it through or to adopt an animal and care for it. Of these chosen commitments, some are explicit, public, and performative, as when a person takes an oath of office. But they can also be made privately, as when one simply resolves to read more novels in the coming year or quietly sets out to work on one's character. Still, not all of the commitments we explicitly undertake have this intentional or promissory aspect to them (79). Many of our most basic and strongly held commitments (e.g., allegiance to family, country, or even a sports team) are not choices we ever decided to make, and these latter forms of commitment need not be reflected upon or called into question, so long as challenges to them do not arise. (For example, one may never consider how strong one's commitment to one's homeland is until one has lived abroad or is considering changing one's citizenship.)

Still, whatever else commitments might be, they are, as Chang points out, essentially *reason-giving*. In being committed to a person, a country, a project, a team, or a cause, the fact of my being committed provides me with independent or strengthened reasons[26] to act in certain ways with respect to the object of my commitment (and with respect to myself in relation to that object). As Chang puts it, "commitments explain why we have the special reasons we might not otherwise have without having made the commitment" (Chang 2013: 80). For this reason, she ultimately characterizes commitment dynamically as an *essentially volitional activity* by which an agent wills a consideration or set of considerations to be reason-giving for her. Commitment involves "the activity of placing your will—your very agency—behind its being a reason" (93). In this sense, commitments are, according to Chang, *stipulative*.[27] That is, in contrast to one's external or "given" reasons, commitments generate *pro tanto* reasons for an agent by a sheer, voluntaristic act or state of willing. This can involve deliberately making a choice to place one's agency behind something, but it may also take the form of implicit willing—of an expression or manifestation of what the agent herself "stands" behind.

Of course, our commitments can change over time, whether via a deliberate act of will (as when one explicitly takes up or renounces a commitment), or simply by "evolving" (or "devolving") as a person's situation, character, and identity changes over the course of her biographical history. Sometimes we may be surprised by what we find ourselves committed to upon reflection.[28] At other times, we may find various commitments conflicting with one another (as when the reasons arising from the commitments to one's family conflict with those from the commitments to one's vocation), in which case the question becomes which commitments will be given more normative and deliberative weight for the agent in a given scenario. In some cases, certain cognitive commitments (which may or may not amount to full belief) may lag behind other commitments we have made, as when a person avowedly committed to combatting racism or sexism finds themselves caught in the grip of the remnants of implicit cognitive commitments to racist or sexist stereotypes.

In terms of normativity, Chang maintains that the voluntaristic reasons willed into existence via commitment are still subservient to one's all-things-considered "given reasons" and cannot change their valence (Chang 2013: 109). For example, joining a hate group does not override one's moral obligation to treat human beings with respect. Likewise, committing oneself to a conspiracy theory does not rationally trump one's overall epistemic reasons for concluding it to be false. At the same time, the form of willing which stipulates that certain considerations will (henceforth or continue to) count as reasons for an agent may give rise to certain downstream effects that *add* to an agent's given reasons. In adopting a child, for example, one acquires new moral or legal obligations as a parent that one did not have prior to making such a commitment. Likewise, being committed to a social or political cause may lead one to act in ways that create expectations and obligations that one cannot simply be "freed from" by renouncing one's commitment. (As Chang puts it, commitments have "exit costs.") Even one's given epistemic reasons may be affected by one's practical commitments, since practically committing ourselves in certain ways may open us up to new experiences and new sources of evidence. Still, where one's given reasons are not sufficient to rationally or morally guide action, Chang maintains, it is permissible for the reasons generated by one's commitment to be the difference-maker.[29]

Commitment and religious faith

There may be different senses of 'commitment' not discussed above. It is commonly held, for example, that beliefs are a species of cognitive commitment, whereas intentions are practical commitments.[30] I do not wish to contest these uses of "commitment"—I even think they can be folded into Chang's account—but I think centering devotional faith by understanding it as a sustained commitment to a religious tradition or community opens a door for a promising approach to religious faith that has been hinted at by several philosophers but never really spelled out because of the assumed priority of the propositional.[31] I will explore some of the advantages of this account below, but a few clarifications and qualifications are in order before we proceed.

First, the kind of commitment I am envisioning with respect to devotional faith need not be deliberately chosen and can be a matter of the orientation of one's will over time. Religious commitment can be something one grows up with, something one "falls into," or something that one deliberately decides to undertake by which religious considerations become reasons for engagement, action, and reasoning—and it can sometimes provide candidates for attitudes philosophers have proposed to be central to propositional and objectual faith, like belief, hope, trust, or reliance. But instead of understanding local cases of propositional and objectual faith as primary and taking such attitudes as their defining elements, on this approach it is an agent's *commitment* to particular religious propositions and objects (including divine and human persons) that really makes them faithful in these respects, where this commitment is either partially constitutive of or entailed by their overall religious commitment. (And note that each of the above attitudes either involves or is compatible with such commitment.)

Second, not just any act of reason-giving willing will do. Faith also requires a central *affective* component.[32] As hinted at above, I think "full-blown" or "authentic" religious faith is a kind of commitment that involves the *whole person* and is expressive in some way of their "core" self (or, on accounts that emphasize the multiplicity of the self, of one of their central identities)—e.g., of their fundamental desires, overall life orientation, narrative identity, etc. Put a bit differently, it is not only a matter of a person's giving religious considerations heavier normative weight in their theoretical or practical reasoning but also of their affectively *standing behind* or *identifying with* those commitments in some relevant way. Authentic faith, on the account I am developing here, is expressive of what a person would be religiously disposed to do or affirm given opportunity and absent constraint by or interference from external forces with which they do not centrally identify.[33] It is also a *reflective* notion, at least minimally in the sense that, for those persons capable of reflecting on their commitments, the commitment in question would be endorsed were the person to reflect on it. Overall, then, we can say that *authentic religious faith* involves a sincere commitment to a religious community and/or (sub)tradition that is in some relevant way expressive of a central aspect of a person's identity and which they would, given certain reflective capacities and absent impinging external constraints, endorse upon reflection. Likewise, *global faith*—or the faith exhibited by someone who is not only a member of *a* faith but also said to be a person *of* faith—is best understood as involving a strong constellation of well-integrated, authentic propositional, objectual, institutional, and practical commitments stemming from their overarching devotional commitment.[34]

The incorporation of an authenticity criterion into the commitment model of faith (hereafter 'CF') makes room for the possibility of insincerity, self-deception, and other forms of "bad faith." It also reminds us that we are perfectly able to commit ourselves to ends that we don't really endorse.[35] It thus allows us to differentiate between cases in which a person's committing themself to religious participation and/or affirmation is largely a heteronomous matter—or perhaps simply a matter of purely strategic reasoning—and those cases in which the commitment represents something the person themself can get behind and will for themself, independent of those factors that constrain their will in ways they would not otherwise endorse. Consider, for example, a woman raised in the Muslim faith, who has largely deconverted and no longer practices at home, but whose parents remain devout. We can imagine that, when visiting her parents, she may commit herself temporarily to dressing in *hijab*, avoiding foods that are *haram*, going to mosque with her parents. She may recite the *Shahada* during daily prayer or affirm aloud and act in accordance with relevant religious propositions.[36] Further, she may have various (morally or prudentially appropriate) reasons for so doing—e.g., respect for her parents and her upbringing, a sense of childhood nostalgia, or perhaps merely a desire not to create conflict. But her religious commitment in this case is not authentic, even if her prudential reasons for so committing (for example, being a good daughter) are. This may be because she no longer takes these actions themselves to be expressive of who she currently is (or as something with which she can centrally identify), or because she would not endorse such commitment were she not visiting her parents, or both. Something similar may be said for someone living in a theocracy who only commits themselves to the state religion because of fear of punishment or political retribution.[37]

The authenticity criterion as formulated above also permits that there can be persons of faith who have never reflected on their religious commitments, either because they are not capable of such reflection or because the necessity of reflection has simply never arisen. As noted above, I make no claims about the rationality of such faith. For those who think rational faith must be more robustly reflective, such persons as just described might be excluded. However, I am not yet prepared to make any such claims about said persons' rationality with respect to their faith, though I suspect that a satisfactory account can be given of how they, too, may said to be rational in their non-reflective faith. Significant for our purposes is the point that non-reflective faith of these kinds can be considered cases of *full-blooded* faith on my account, and not merely instances of "proto-faith," "quasi-faith" or "faith-like" behavior. This may be an important point when it comes to considering the faith of children, those suffering from dementia, or the severely cognitively disabled. It may even create interesting avenues for the development of accounts concerning the idea of a religious community's collectively "calling" the non-faithful into the faith (e.g., through baptism or initiation) or "holding" the already-faithful in the faith (e.g., in the case of comatose patients or those suffering from dementia, mental illness, or other temporarily or permanently reflection-undermining conditions) in a sense similar to Hilde Lindemann's (2014) account of calling or holding someone in(to) personhood.

Finally, the authenticity criterion also allows for the possibility that someone may count as religiously faithful, even if their actions are constrained or coerced in such a way as to prevent or limit them from exercising or living out their faith, so long as they remain committed to doing so absent those constraints. This allows, for example, that someone who is bedridden and cannot attend religious services or partake in religious ritual can still be considered a person of global faith. Likewise, those who are imprisoned or religiously persecuted for their faiths may still be considered faithful if forced under duress to refrain from practicing their religion—or even to renounce it. Certainly, the line between faithful commitment and deconversion or apostasy will be fuzzy in many cases, but this is exactly as we should expect, since most challenges to faith directly threaten one's commitment and can cause one to call one's own sincerity into question.[38]

Indeed, CF as a model of religious faith is clearly compatible with the intuitive idea that faith can be a matter of *degree*, as opposed to an all-or-nothing phenomenon. In fact, I think CF is best understood as a relative or comparative notion, as there is a variety of ways in which a person's commitments can—and usually do—wax and wane, grow and shrink, and vary in strength and depth, as the person herself and her circumstances change. In a quantitative sense, one may simply be committed to, e.g., doing more or fewer things as required by or consistent with the religious tradition in question. In a more qualitative sense, one's commitments may be carried out with more or less affective enthusiasm. Moreover, with respect to authenticity, the degree to which one's commitments are expressive of one's central identity may change over time, and one may endorse them to greater and lesser degrees at different times and in different contexts. As Audi notes, a person's overall constellation of commitments can be more or less pervasive in their psychology or central to their life. It can exhibit more or less *stability* (i.e., "resistance to erosion or extirpation" over time), and it can vary with respect to "the degree to which, like a deep root that nourishes a whole tree, the religious elements in question—the cognitive, attitudinal, and behavioral commitments—control cognition, emotion, and action and are important in the person's sense of identity" (Audi 2013: 100–1).[39]

Theoretical advantages of the commitment model

Shifting APR's attention to authentic commitment understood in this way can productively reorient theoretical discussions of faith around the more volitional senses of the term, as expressed in what I have above called *devotional faith*. When we adopt this kind of theoretical approach to religious faith, we can see how CF might have significant advantages over alternative approaches that matter for the reformation of APR as a discipline.

CF makes religious faith recognizable

First and foremost, CF makes religious faith recognizable from the standpoint of religion understood as a social phenomenon and therefore makes for a good approach for a discipline purporting to be a philosophy of *religion*.

To begin with, CF makes room for the primacy of religious praxis by not over-privileging the propositional and cognitive aspects of religion from the outset and making room for commitments to embodied ritual, devotional practice, corporate worship, and the like to acquire the significance in philosophical theory that they already enjoy in the actual lives of the religiously faithful. Certainly, all or most religions are likely to contain central conceptual and propositional elements that define the contours of its cosmic narrative framework. At the same time, how "creedal" faith is supposed to be and how important it is to assent to, affirm, or even believe the propositions central to some faith will vary by tradition and context. Still, in contrast to many analyses in APR, CF does not give the appearance of simply assuming that the propositional and conceptual aspects of a religion are easily divorceable from the practical and social aspects of religion, nor that the former are clearly of more religious (or philosophical) significance than the latter.

Additionally, CF highlights the essentially *relational* and *social* nature of religious faith that many accounts of faith in APR tend to obscure or ignore. Faith is not a solely individual phenomenon, even if it is attributable *to* individuals. It involves communal, corporate, and collective activity and, as will be discussed further in the next chapter, a shared religious imagination. CF accounts for this aspect of the religious life, since the relevant kind of devotional faith concerns, most basically, an overarching commitment to a historically- and culturally-situated religious *community*, where 'community' may be understood as narrowly or broadly as demanded by context. Thus, we may speak of the commitments that arise from belonging to one's local temple or mosque, or we might refer to affinity and affiliation with a larger sect or denomination, dedicated membership in an overarching institution like "the Roman Catholic Church," or identification with a particular religion writ large (e.g., Sikhism). One may even have a much more theological or eschatological understanding of that community—as when Christians speak about baptism as entrance into the "community of the faithful" or the Church as "the body of Christ."[40]

This ability to make religion recognizable might also enable APR to better bring itself into dialogue with neighboring disciplines in the social sciences, who likewise study religion as a social phenomenon and create opportunities for valuable interdisciplinary resonances and research. It also lends itself well to engagement with comparative theology, as well as more public-facing endeavors such as interfaith dialogue or joint action in pluralistic civic contexts.

CF is explanatorily valuable

CF is likewise valuable from a philosophical standpoint insofar as it takes faith—even propositional faith—"out of the head" and recasts it as a matter of the *whole person* (including their socio-cultural-historical situatedness)—and it does so by recovering the role of the *will* in the life of religious faith. That is, instead of focusing its attention predominantly on an individual's cognitive attitudes toward the intellectual content of a tradition and then "tacking on" a non-cognitive attitude or stance sufficient to motivate action and explain faith's resilience, it puts commitment at the heart of religious faith, a stance that is fundamentally volitional and, especially in the case of authentic commitment, affectively loaded. By bringing these more "agential" features of faith back into focus, CF does not need the "auxiliary attitudes" of cognitive-centered theories to explain how faith can exercise as much motivational and normative force as it does in the lives of religious individuals.

Remember the points of agreement between doxasticists and non-doxasticists discussed above. We saw that no theory of propositional or objectual faith can be *wholly* cognitive, insofar as the theorists in question want to hold on to both faith's ability to motivate action (C) and its "stickiness" in the face of epistemic and practical challenges (D).[41] They therefore need to add to their accounts some non-cognitive feature of faith (E) that explains both faith's connection to action and its resilience—and a stance that is inherently volitional and reason-giving seems like a promising candidate for such a feature. Our commitments, both religious and non-religious, can and often do persist in the face of both counter-evidence and lagging motivation. They matter to us; we care about them; in many cases, we have internalized the values that are associated with the kind of commitments in question. So it should come as no surprise that faith is both motivational and "sticky."

Moreover, the notion of commitment allows us to take an explicitly *diachronic* approach to religious faith and can thereby show us how faith is commensurable both with significant periods of doubt and even with actions or decisions that, absent the commitment, might not otherwise be comprehensible from the standpoint of an observer (or even, perhaps, of the faithful subject themself). As Laura Buchak has pointed out, commitment makes a *difference* when it comes to faith—one, I would add, that a mere positive cognitive or conative stance (or even their conjunction) might not: "Faith allows an individual to make choices that are integrated over time, even if these choices sometimes seem irrational from her current [synchronic] perspective" (Buchak 2017a: 125).[42]

Commitment can thus explain why religious faith can withstand "not only [. . .] *cognitive* troughs, occasions when new counterevidence threatens faith, but also *conative* troughs, periods of emotional flagging, tiredness, fatigue, dryness, dullness, weariness, drabness, cold, emptiness, and a dimming of desire" (Howard-Snyder and McKaughan 2022: 311)—as well as how someone can "remain a person of faith despite a [long] walk on the bottom of the cognitive [and, we should add, affective] barrel" (322). As I will discuss in later chapters, it is precisely the fact that one can find oneself "on the bottom of this barrel" while remaining committed to one's tradition that I think religious faith—even of a sincere and authentic kind—is compatible with disbelief, as well as belief, but we will need something like commitment (and not just some conjunctive "positive cognitive and conative stance") to make sense of this fact.

CF's compatibility with epistemic doubt and affective malaise also demonstrates its ability to be understood as a *venture*. Even in cases where religious faith is accompanied by strong belief, hope, or trust, an account that does not make room for commitment is missing exactly that aspect of faith that makes it venturesome. This is so in both a wider and a narrower sense. In the narrower sense, CF is venturesome insofar as it allows for the possibility of going beyond the evidence, acting on hope, (en)trusting where one is uncertain, and so on. In the wider (and perhaps more significant) sense, as a matter of the will as opposed to the mere intellect, CF locates religious faith in the realm of the *practical*, where—for fallible beings like us who are unable to perfectly foresee the future or to comprehend the ways in which the actions to which our commitments give rise will play out—always involves risk. Indeed, not only is religious commitment venturesome in this respect, it places the faithful agent squarely in the domain of the *social and intersubjective*, for religious commitments gain much of their significance from the fact that they are shared, transmitted, and collectively negotiated in spaces of communal action. Commitment is that which turns the individual from a solipsistic believer or passive experiencer into a *political agent* in the world who acts for reasons and is responsible to others. Understood thusly, religious faith is less a matter of being in cognitive agreement with like-minded believers and much more about being volitionally oriented *outwardly*—toward socially-directed action *with* and *with respect to* similarly committed others.[43] It also dictates how one is to be oriented toward those who are *not* like-minded or similarly committed.[44] And insofar as it is political in this sense, religious faith is essentially a risky matter.

CF widens the scope of faith and reforms the discourse

The CF model I have proposed is, I think, commensurable with many of the accounts of faith out there in the APR literature, but it goes beyond them in ways many faith-theorists might not be comfortable with. I see this as a feature of my view, not a bug—both because this book endeavors in some sense to play the role of "disruptive gadfly" in APR debates that are becoming somewhat sclerotic (maybe even necrotic) and because I want to cast a wider net with respect to faith, making it more inclusive and, I think, more commensurate with what we find in everyday religious communities (including those outside Western Christianity). CF does this in a few ways.

First, insofar as CF is grounded in a *practical and social commitment*, even where it is (also) epistemic, it is fundamentally a pragmatic account, though as I hope to show in later chapters, not necessarily a (merely) instrumentalist one—and as such it should make us think more about the role of *non-epistemic* (e.g., practical, aesthetic, social, intersubjective) considerations in ways that go deeper than merely trying to defend propositional and objectual faith from secular charges of wishful thinking.

Second, although religious commitment in a devotional sense may be explicitly chosen, as in cases of taking religious vows, joining a new religious community, or converting to a different faith, it may simply be an "unconscious and non-deliberate decision" (Chang 2013: 79) or even something one never decided upon at all but which nevertheless expresses one's identity and the reasons one wills to be authoritative in the context of one's own existential narrative.[45] (In fact, this latter form of CF might be the most common.)

Third, since faith understood as commitment need not be rational or even occurrently reflective in order to be present, CF permits instances of faith that may be inauthentic or irrational ("bad faith," "insincere faith," etc.). Moreover, it can also allow those without fully developed rational or reflective capacities, as well as those who have lost such capacities, to potentially count among the religiously faithful in ways other accounts might not.

Fourth, since religious faith according to CF is compatible with subjects' occupying all positions on the doxastic spectrum, it is compatible with both doxasticist and non-doxasticist accounts of faith, as well as with fictionalist accounts—though unlike the first two, it rejects the no-disbelief constraint, and unlike the third, it suggests neither an error-theoretic anti realism nor a purely instrumentalist approach. It is compatible, too, with attitudes often taken to be central to religious faith like hope, trust, and reliance, but it does not take any one of these as necessary for faith. In fact, CF opens up the possibility that faith need not be positively valenced at all. That is, just as faith might be compatible with disbelief, it might also be compatible with affectively dark nights of the soul—or the commitment might be so internalized that it remains a core aspect of one's identity, even though one wishes it were not.[46]

CF presents new opportunities for APR

Finally, construing faith from the perspective of the primacy of religious practice and community shows both the ways in which *fides quaerens intellectum* is the state in which most religious practitioners find themselves and how devotional faith can itself give rise to the kind of conceptual and propositional understanding necessary to make existential meaning within the context of a particular faith. That is, in most cases religious understanding begins with practice and the formation over time of a commitment to a community and its traditions, not with a rational consideration of propositions or a careful weighing of the evidence. We may be discursively introduced to the relevant conceptual content, told what it means, and so on, but we only begin to really *understand* it (and the role it plays) when we encounter or are involved in the practices of the religious community.

Taking religious faith "out of the head" by focusing on CF, devotional faith, and religious practice in community can both allow APR to better understand religion itself (both on its own and in collaboration with neighboring fields) and to think more carefully about the ways in which religious practice gives rise to a deeper understanding of just what is at stake in the religious life. Not only is a religious tradition "an amalgamation of many thoughtful people's work, evidence-gathering, and thinking" (Buchak 2022: 754), it is also full of social and embodied ritual practices that have historically *oriented* and *informed* these "thoughtful people's" thinking—and which today help thoughtful and less thoughtful religious practitioners alike orient themselves toward the features of reality that make up the central content of that tradition's narratives and better *understand* its meaning for their lives. Therefore, developing a more comprehensive account of how religious practice "fleshes out" the content of propositional faith and the kinds of epistemic attitudes to which it can give rise could be immensely valuable, even for a traditional religious epistemology. Ultimately, CF allows an APR concerned with the kind of understanding discussed in previous chapters to come to better grasp religious practice and corporate worship itself and how it allows its practitioners to continue to make existential meaning and pursue wisdom in the face of various challenges. Put a bit differently, orienting ourselves toward faith understood on the CF model can allow us think more about the ways in which devotional (and global) faith is relevant to making existential meaning and how such meaning can be valuable *beyond* questions of metaphysical realism or the mere possibility of religious knowledge.

Conclusion

In this chapter, I have argued that when we shift our vantage point from the heavily intellectualist approach traditionally championed by APR, which tends to center the propositional and the cognitive, to an approach informed by the primacy of praxis and the volitional and affective aspects of religion, we can recover a model of religious faith that does justice to actual lived religion on the ground. By centering our models of faith on authentic religious commitment, understood as a matter of willing religious considerations to be reasons for one in ways expressive of one's core identity and orientation in and toward the world, we can begin to develop an approach that can better make sense of the role of the *vita activa* and not just the *vita cognitiva* in religious understanding.[47]

Of course, this is not to maintain that the cognitive and propositional play no significant role in the religious life. In thinking about sincere religious faith understood as authentic commitment, it will be important to say something about the ways in which religiously faithful individuals may be committed to the fundamental propositions of the traditions to which they belong in ways that are conducive to approaching religion from the perspective of understanding and the primacy of praxis. As we have seen, I am in agreement with many contemporary "non-doxasticists" that religious faith need not involve belief. However, I have already gone further than most non-doxasticists in proposing the more controversial thesis that religious faith is compatible not only with the doxastic attitudes of belief in the sense of positive certainty and nonbelief in the sense of uncertainty (including agnosticism, or suspension of belief), but also with *disbelief* in the sense of negative certainty or a credence of zero, even if faith of this latter kind may be rare. This claim needs more defending, and in the following chapters I will attempt to show how faith can be doxastically permissive in these ways. In Chapter 5 I will argue that, instead of focusing on religious *belief* as the central cognitive attitude in religious faith, philosophers and theologians would do better to focus on another essential feature of the cognitive religious life, namely that of the religious *imagination*. In so doing, I think APR scholars can actually better make sense of the ways the cognitive and the practical are fundamentally intertwined in the religious life. In Chapters 6 and 7, then, I will suggest that a global religious faith at the intersection of the propositional and the practical manifests itself most appropriately as a kind of "earnest make-believe"—one that does not require credence but is nevertheless wholly compatible with religious authenticity and which can result in epistemically productive hermeneutical understanding of the kind discussed in Chapter 3. In fact, I will claim that such forms of religious make-believe can transform "mere" faith into something like a *living religiosity*.

Notes

1   See, e.g., Arnal and McCutcheon (2013), Seligman et al. (2008), Stringer (1996). I also find the term that is the topic of this chapter, namely 'faith', troubling in this respect. Add to this concern that many of the "faith-locutions" discussed in Section 4.2, when translated into languages other than English, do not yield locutions involving clear cognates of 'faith'-words in those languages. This makes any analysis of religious faith fraught from the beginning and, I submit, rather artificial, whichever way we look at it. I will continue to use the term in this chapter, so as to be able to remain conversant with the extant APR literature, but as the reader will see, faith on my account ends up being largely co-extensive with something like "religious devotion." This is not unintentional, as it is meant to be applicable to contexts and traditions outside of (Western Protestant) Christianity, even where the term 'faith' is not. Still, as we will see in Chapter 7, I think there may be an additional kind of "religiosity" that goes *beyond* "mere" faith and (from the standpoint of any particular religion) is *preferable* to it.

2   For a few promising approaches to these questions, see, e.g., Buchak (2022); Jackson (2023); Jeffrey (2017); McKaughan and Howard-Snyder (2023).

3   Importantly, for reasons like those raised in note 1 above, I do not think that models of religious faith need be strictly beholden to their usages in English (or ordinary language in general). However, I do find that it can be a helpful way of easing into an analysis of a topic, and since many of the faith-models in APR take their inspiration from these kinds of uses, I will follow them (for now) in their approach.

4   APR scholars have used different labels for these various senses. For example, while in agreement on propositional and global faith, Robert Audi (2013) and Daniel Howard-Snyder (2016) differ in their labels of models based on sentence-type (2). Audi speaks here of *attitudinal faith*, whereas Howard-Snyder employs my preferred term of *objectual faith*. Audi calls faithfulness in the senses of (3) and (4) *allegiant faith*, which—although it picks out the loyalty- or fidelity-aspect of such sentences—fails to capture the sense I think most apt for the religious case, namely that of devotion, dedication, or (as I shall argue) commitment. Audi further employs the term *creedal faith* for cases like (5), but as I discuss in note 7 below, I think a broader term is warranted.

5   It is often assumed that objectual faith—when understood as faith *in* a person—either presupposes or is reducible to a form of propositional faith (minimally insofar as one thinks that for a subject to have faith *in* a person they must be willing to accept that there *is* such a person). I spell out my rejection of this assumption in Griffioen (2022).

6   Audi, for example, claims that "a good case can be made for understanding global faith wholly in terms of the other three kinds [propositional, attitudinal/objectual, creedal/institutional]" (Audi 2013: 62).

7   I therefore prefer the term "institutional" rather than "creedal" here—first, because religious faiths may be more or less creedal (or perhaps not creedal at all, insofar as a creed implies an institutionally formalized and propositionalized central theology) and, second, because much of what makes up any particular religious faith (even a creedal one) goes far beyond its propositional and conceptual creedal content. As an institutionalized socio-cultural phenomenon, the contours of a religious faith are also (and perhaps even primarily) marked by its institutionally-approved and socially-encoded rites, norms, taboos, physical spaces, embodied practices, aesthetic expressions, and so on. Of course, as Kelli Potter (2013) notes, the twin problems of heterodoxy and heteropraxis with respect to identifying what makes up "a" particular religious (sub-)tradition or faith will still loom large in any of these discussions.

8   See, e.g., Plantinga (2000), Swinburne (2007), Mugg (2022), and Malcolm and Scott (2023) for some different versions and ways of defending doxasticism.

9   See, e.g., Audi (2013), Howard-Snyder (2016), Buchak (2017b), Kvanvig (2018), and McKaughan and Howard-Snyder (2023) for just a few of the various non-doxastic accounts on the market.

10 In many mystical traditions, including the Carmelite tradition of Teresa of Avila and John of the Cross, the so-called "dark night of the soul," or the sustained experience of divine hiddenness, is considered a significant *part* of the journey of faith that only occurs *after* one has made significant spiritual progress. It is thus somewhat ironic that, despite the title of his article, McKaughan (2018) only places Mother Teresa in "the" mystical tradition insofar as she is said to have had strong religious experiences early on in her life.

11 Muyskens (1979) and Pojman (1991) are commonly cited in this context, though Muyskens actually distinguishes hope from faith, the latter of which he equates with a doxasticist model. His claim is that a religion of hope is ultimately superior to a religion of faith-*qua*-belief. Pojman, for his part, although explicitly equating faith with hope in some passages, ultimately appears to view faith as a kind of commitment or acceptance, one which hope *or* belief is sufficient to ground, depending on what the subject takes to be evidentially warranted.

12 See, e.g., Swinburne's (2007) account of "Lutheran faith," as well as McKaughan (2013, 2016) and McKaughan and Howard-Snyder (2023) for a few accounts that incorporate trust or reliance as a central element.

13 Of course, there may be a distinction between trusting and *entrusting*, only the latter of which does not involve belief. Moreover, one may think that both involve a *vulnerability to betrayal*, which might seem incongruent with the omnibenevolent God proposed in most APR circles. For more on these aspects of trust, see, e.g., Hieronymi (2008).

14 Malcom and Scott (2023), for example, present a "normative" doxasticist account, which I discuss in further detail presently.

15 Perlocutionary effects are, according to J. L. Austin, those effects "we bring about or
   achieve *by* saying something," i.e., the intended or unintended aims or byproducts of
   a locutionary act (Austin 1962: 109). See also my discussion of religious make-
   believe vs. religious belief in Chapter 7 below, as well as my discussion in Chapter 8
   on the perlocutionary effects of APR's theodical discourse.

16 I do not think Pascal himself endorsed self-deception with respect to his (in)famous
   wager, but he is sometimes read in this way.

17 For a more extended discussion of the dynamics of self-deception understood as a
   diachronic phenomenon, see Griffioen (2010).

18 Given that the charge of many of religion's ontological objectors (see Chapter 1)
   hangs on a charge of self-deceptive irrationality, the religious apologist will need to
   be very careful concerning the kind of doxasticism they propose.

19 Malcolm and Scott themselves seem to think that, in contrast to their position,
   non-doxasticism entails that faith centrally involves *bullshit*, since it appears to flout
   the belief norm ("BN") of affirmation that one should only affirm those things that
   one believes. However, given that typically the bullshitter differs from the
   straightforward liar in not *caring* about whether what they affirm is true or false, it is
   unclear why this should follow from non-doxasticism. That is, it does not follow
   from the fact that one neither believes nor disbelieves *p* that one has no concern
   whatsoever for the truth of *p* or that it makes no difference to the individual whether
   or not *p* is the case. Moreover, as we have seen in Chapter 2, flouting BN appears to
   be part of what good science regularly does, insofar as it operates on models and
   employs propositions it does not take to be true in pursuit of greater understanding.
   So perhaps BN is not as watertight as some might think. In any case, it's not entirely
   clear to me how Malcolm and Scott think the beliefless "faithful" allowed by their
   own normative doxasticism, even if "abnormal" or "parasitic" on belief contexts, are
   not subject to similar charges of bullshit (or even pretense, if belief is heavily
   normed in their community).

20 For various forms of fictionalism/instrumentalism/naturalism concerning religion,
   see, e.g., Deng (2015); Le Poidevin (1996, 2019); Jay (2014); Wettstein (2012).

21 Importantly, however, as Howard-Snyder (2019a) points out, much hangs on the
   nuances of the non-doxasticist theory in question. In this and the chapters that
   follow, I will try to show non-doxasticists that they need not fear disbelief (or
   pretense) as much as they do.

22 On this point, see Lewis Rambo: "[R]eligious action regularized, sustained, and
   intentional is fundamental to the conversion experience. Ritual fosters the necessary
   orientation, the readiness of mind and soul to have a conversion experience, and it
   consolidates conversion after the initial experience" (Rambo 1993: 114).

23 I leave open whether or not my account can be extended to non-religious forms of
   faith. There is a tendency in the literature to want to make one's account of religious

faith a species of faith more generally—where, say, religious propositional faith just means "regular faith" with "religious" content. However, it does not seem all that implausible to think that religious traditions (and similar phenomena) might demand *more* of a subject with respect to their faith than, say, the mere psychological conditions provided by a non-religious analysis of faith. On this point, see Malcolm and Scott (2023: 4). At the same time, we may think—at least as regards institutional and ideological contexts (e.g., sports team affiliation, political orientation, academic pedigree, etc.)—this way of framing the faith-context captures something that a more myopic focus on propositional or objectual faith doesn't.

24 This means, for example, that neither Hayy ibn Yaqzan nor the *philosophicus autodidactus* has properly *religious* faith, even if they may, by reason or revelation, come to a form of non-religious propositional theistic faith. It may also correspond to the intuition of some Christian and Sufi mystics that true union with God means going *beyond* both social morality and religious faith as one transcends (and, for those oppressed by such social structures, are "liberated from") the limits and confines of the contingent and conventional, and aligning oneself with the wholly necessary and yet most genuinely free divine will.

25 In the latter kinds of cases, one might, e.g., still identify as a committed "Protestant Christian" but no longer as a committed "member of the Southern Baptist Church." With respect to the former kinds of cases and the possibility that deconversion due to religious trauma could be rational, whether or not one's religion is true, see Panchuk (2018).

26 There are likely many cases in which there is an overlap between the reasons a commitment provides and the reasons one would have without the commitment, as when both moral demands and religious commitments recommend giving to the poor. However, even here the fact of one's having (or having made) the commitment seems to give these reasons more *pro tanto* normative weight. For example, it might be the case that I (always) have a moral reason to refrain from causing unnecessary harm to other persons. Yet it seems that causing unnecessary harm to a spouse or partner or child to whom one is committed is especially bad or blameworthy. Commitment may also be the kind of thing that makes the consideration of whether it is permissible to rescue one's partner over an equidistant and similarly-easy-to-save stranger "one thought too many" (see Williams 1981).

27 Chang calls commitment "the practical analogue of stipulating the meaning of a word" (Chang 2013: 93).

28 That is, it seems possible to be unaware or self-deceived about our commitments.

29 If this is right (as I am inclined to think it is), then a view of faith as authentic commitment makes no claims on whether or not it is morally or rationally permissible for one to be religiously committed in such a way. This is a further discussion for APR to conduct with its ontological and ontotheological critics.

However, it is important to note that such a discussion must go beyond whether it is merely *epistemically* rational to be thusly committed. Given its volitional nature, considerations of practical rationality and moral permissibility must also be part of this discussion.

30 See, for example, Audi (2013: 9).

31 See, for starters, Buchak (2022), Kvanvig (2013, 2018), and McKaughan (2016).

32 This may be implied by Chang's discussion of placing one's very agency behind something, but it is worth specifying here some of the features of this "placement" that are especially relevant for religious faith.

33 This formulation allows that certain psychological states may count as "external forces" in the relevant sense—e.g., if perceived as alien to the agent's will or as something with which she does not centrally identify. However, it also does not rule out cases in which an agent's commitment is, in fact, causally determined by some external factor, so long as the agent identifies her will with those forces or takes them to be commensurate with her central attitudes or projects, similar to Harry Frankfurt's (1971) example of the unwilling and willing addicts.

34 On this last point, see also Kvanvig (2013, 2018).

35 On this point, see, e.g., Wallace (2001).

36 I am grateful to Ali Hasan for this example.

37 I leave open here whether someone who commits themselves to a religion only or primarily out of fear of eternal punishment or damnation can be said to have authentic religious faith in the sense specified above. Many theorists of faith demand that it usually involves at least some positively-valenced attitude toward its object(s), such that persons committed out of fear might not count as authentically faithful, or at least count as less sincerely faithful than their more positively-oriented religious counterparts. At the same time, I agree with Malcolm and Scott (2023) that "faith is not indefatigably positive: it may endure even when positive attitudes about the object or content of faith are in abeyance" (144)—and I think CF can account for this. While negatively-valenced religious attitudes of lament, complaint, or protest may, in some cases, undermine instances of local propositional or objectual faith, they need not thereby annihilate a person's devotional, or even their global, faith. How much loss of local faith a person's global faith can endure will depend significantly on their particular psychology, situation, and social context.

38 For a moving and difficult depiction of this ambiguity, see Shūsaku Endō's 1966 novel, *Silence*.

39 The question of how strong, deep, wide-ranging, pervasive, stable, well-integrated, etc. a religious commitment or set of commitments must be to cross the threshold for its counting as religious faith at all will depend largely on context and on the question we are concerned with answering. The relevant factors for us to say that some particular act or assertion of an agent represents an act, expression, or instance

of religious faith may not be the same as those we are interested in when evaluating a person's life narrative (or some extended segment of it), or when thinking about whether someone is or was a "person of faith."

40 An individual's religious commitment might also vary, depending on the level of description in question. Thus, someone might consider themselves a "good Christian" but a "bad Catholic"—or vice versa. Likewise, one might find oneself more committed to one's more immediate religious community and their practices, rituals, and concerns—even if heterodox—and less to the particular denomination or sect to which that community officially belongs.

41 Note that on doxasticist accounts, even if belief is sometimes sufficient to motivate action, it is unlikely to be able to explain its own resilience in cases of faith, so the theory in question still cannot be wholly cognitive.

42 I am quite sympathetic to Buchak's account of propositional faith, though she is more interested than I in examining when propositional faith can be rational, and I tend to find her limitations on which propositions are candidates for faith too restrictive. That being said, the fact that she takes time to extensively consider the role that faith traditions play with respect to propositional faith and vice versa (see Buchak 2022) is certainly a welcome addition to the literature.

43 The idea of religious faith as outward-looking holds much promise for future treatments of faith. Kvanvig notes this feature of religious faith in passing when he claims that because faith looks outward, it provides a better counter-balance for the self-deprecating tendencies of humility than mere self-trust, which is inward-looking (Kvanvig 2018: 153). Cuneo also discusses the importance of liturgy in cultivating an "ethic of outwardness" over an "ethic of proximity" (Cuneo 2016: 25ff.). However, a more detailed treatment of the ways in which religious faith is outward-looking remains to be undertaken.

44 When approached from this perspective, we see that the problem of religious disagreement is not merely—or perhaps even primarily—an epistemological problem.

45 On religious commitment in the context of existential narratives and the dependence of the overall rationality of faith on "the attitudes appropriate to 'keeping the faith', in the sense of being a person of that faith," see Audi (2013: 89–92).

46 For a few challenges to the "positivity theory" surrounding faith in the literature, see Malcolm and Scott (2023).

47 On this point, see also Chapter 9.

5

Beyond the Doxastic

Recovering the Role of Imagination in Religion

*By those who consider a balanced repose the end of culture, the imagination
must necessarily be regarded as the one faculty before all others to be
suppressed. "Are there not facts?" say they. "Why forsake them for fancies? Is
there not that which, may be known? Why forsake it for inventions? What
God hath made, into that let man inquire."*

*We answer: To inquire into what God has made is the main function
of the imagination. It is aroused by facts, is nourished by facts; seeks for
higher and yet higher laws in those facts; but refuses to regard science
as the sole interpreter of nature, or the laws of science as the only region
of discovery.*

George MacDonald, "The Imagination"

Introduction

In previous chapters, I proposed three ways in which an analytic philosophy of
religion (APR) for our times could productively reorient itself, especially with
regard to its ability to engage in more fruitful dialogue with its ontological and
ontotheological critics. First, I proposed that APR would do well to look beyond
the rather unhelpful and intractable debates concerning whether belief expressive
of a very particular kind of robust theistic realism could amount to religious
knowledge. Second, drawing on analogies with mathematics and the natural
sciences, I suggested that APR should expand its epistemological approach from
a largely knowledge-centered epistemology focused on defending the rationality
of metaphysically robust theistic belief toward an epistemology centered on
existential hermeneutical understanding. Finally, I explored what a model of

faith might look like when we take seriously the primacy of praxis suggested by an understanding-centered epistemology, and I proposed that authentic commitment is of central importance to understanding religious faith as both an individual and a social phenomenon. However, in so doing I went even further than most scholars in APR by proposing that religiously committed subjects located *anywhere* on the doxastic spectrum (e.g., from full belief to non-belief all the way down to disbelief[1]) may nevertheless be able to exhibit genuine faith, even in a local propositional sense.

In this chapter, I want to further motivate the plausibility of approaching the religious life as doxastically permissive in the ways I have suggested, even with respect to its conceptual and propositional content. Ultimately, I will suggest that the cognitive side of religious faith, even where it is doxastic, is one that requires a high degree of *imaginative acceptance*—and that it is this feature that cognitively and conceptually unites authentically committed religious practitioners under the banner of faith. In the chapters that follow, I will go even further and suggest that religion often (appropriately) involves a kind of *earnest make-believe* in which imaginative acceptance takes center stage, uniting the propositional and the practical in the religious life.

Imagining the religious

It will therefore be important to look in some detail at a dimension of the religious life that I have heretofore left largely unexplored, even if it was implicitly presupposed in my discussion of the significance of religious models in Chapter 3, namely that of the *religious imagination*—or, to reframe it in more dynamic terms, of the *activity of religious imagining* in the life of faith.[2] In this section, I want to explore religious imagining in a bit more detail and to show how, when paired with commitment of the kind discussed in Chapter 4, it features centrally in propositional faith (as well as in some forms of objectual faith) in a doxastically permissive way.

There are long and extended debates in the philosophical and psychological literature about the taxonomy of the imagination—for example, whether imagining always involves representation, or whether imaginative representation, where present, is best construed as propositional, sensory,[3] or some hybrid of the two.[4] There is a further discussion concerning whether our imaginings are restricted by our judgments about what is possible, or whether the imagination can be extended to the realm of what we take to be impossible.[5] In what follows,

I will take a very broad approach to imagining, according to which imaginative representations may be sensory or propositional,[6] but which also allows that imaginings need not be representational. I will also allow that we are also able to imagine states of affairs we take to be metaphysically or causally impossible.[7] This more pluralistic approach to imagining allows that one may imaginatively entertain concepts or models of the divine and the propositions that are taken to concern or constitute them, where such imaginings need not amount to "images before the mind's eye" to count as imaginings (though they may be like this), and where one may think such imaginings, strictly speaking, are not possible in reality. It will also allow for important modes of embodied religious imagining (e.g., kinesthetic feelings or spiritual "inklings") that do not have a straightforward object or strong representational content. Still, not much hangs on this for the commitment model of religious faith. If it turns out that we have good reason to reject this rather expansive approach to imagining or to focus on one mode of imagining over others, this will merely limit the scope of what can count as a candidate for certain kinds of commitment generally considered to fall under the "cognitive" dimension of religion. This, too, can be a task for an APR of the future, in conversation with contemporary work in philosophy of mind, cognitive psychology, neuroscience, narrative theology, and even (or perhaps especially) literature and media studies.

It is also worth noting here that although in ordinary language we tend to set imagination in contrast to reality, this opposition is misleading: First, imagination appears to be crucial to action-planning and forming intentions, to bringing states of affairs into being that we desire to actualize, and so on.[8] If this is right, then imagination appears central to our ability to exercise our practical agency in the real world. Second, even in simply conceptualizing the world we live in, we often represent things to ourselves imaginatively that we take to exist or believe to be true. We imagine being at home when we are away, or that a certain (existing) person is present when they are absent; we can rightly imagine the earth as traveling in an elliptical motion around the sun, just as we can correctly imagine a water molecule as having ten protons. Even our imaginative representations of objects and scenarios we take to be false, fanciful, or fictional involve many imaginative representations of things we take to be true (Walton 1990: 13). Subjects can also imagine things whose existence they are unsure about, like ghosts, extraterrestrial humanoid species, or the Higgs-Boson particle.

Put a bit differently, not only is imagining compatible with disbelief, agnosticism, or uncertainty regarding the existence of its objects, it is also wholly compatible with belief. In some cases, imagining may even be *necessary* for us to represent things and states of affairs that are not immediately present to us but which we believe to be the case. What is especially important for our purposes is that, where doxastic imaginings (or imaginings also believed to obtain in reality) do represent, what is represented is generally something *absent* or otherwise immediately *inaccessible*. For this reason, Jean-Paul Sartre claimed that imagining as a "positional act" can take four forms:

> It can posit the object as *nonexistent*, or as *absent*, or as *existing elsewhere*; it can also 'neutralize' itself, which is to say *not posit its object as existent*. Two of these acts are negations; the fourth corresponds to a suspension or neutralization of the thesis. The third, which is positive, assumes an implicit negation of the natural and present existence of the object. These positional acts—this remark is crucial—are not superimposed on the image after it is constituted: the positional act is *constitutive* of the image consciousness.
>
> Sartre [1940] 2004: 12–3, my emphases

Sartre's point here is not about the unreality of the things we imagine but rather that the phenomenology of imagining involves the objects presented to the imagination being *negated* or *suspended* in some sort of way, usually because what is imagined is in some sense directly unavailable to the imagining subject. This may involve the object's being represented as unreal, absent, or existing differently from how it is represented. But Sartre's most interesting insight here is that the object may simply be presented to consciousness without its being posited as existing at all. That is, in contrast to both representing something as unreal and to perceiving something as existing, in imagination the question of existence is often merely suspended, as the imagining subject attends to other salient features of that which is imagined.[9]

Whereas Sartre focuses more on the *way* the imagination both posits and negates the objects represented, Garrett Green (1989) centers his attention on the *kinds* of inaccessibility certain objects of the imagination can exhibit with respect to the imagining subject, such that an act of imagining is required to conceptualize them. First, Green notes, some things and states of affairs we represent imaginatively are *temporally* inaccessible to us, as with many of our representations of past and future states of affairs.[10] Second, things may be *spatially* inaccessible to us. This is true not only of the cases of absent friends and faraway places, but also sometimes with respect to very large or small objects, such as supergalaxies or nanoparticles, whose size restricts our ability to directly perceive them.[11] However, Green argues, inaccessibility in time and/or space is not the only reason some things may demand an exercise of imagination. There may also be objects that, if they existed, would be *logically* inaccessible to us, insofar as they would be "*in principle* [. . .] not subject to direct observation," even if they may be imagined in spatial or temporal terms (Green 1989: 64–5). Here we might include such objects as abstract mathematical or logical entities, perhaps some kinds of fictional worlds, and divine beings, personages, and realms—at least insofar as superempirical realities are taken to be in some sense transcendent or, by their very nature, not wholly perceivable or graspable by the human senses.[12]

What APR often overlooks in its narrow focus on the rationality of the doxastic attitudes of the religiously faithful is that getting purportedly transcendent religious objects of discourse cognitively off the ground in the first place and orienting oneself with respect to them requires a feat of imagination, regardless of where on the doxastic spectrum one finds oneself. In this sense, sincere engagement with religious concepts and the propositions into which they enter requires a significant degree of imaginative activity, even (or perhaps especially) for those who *believe* those concepts correspond to reality.[13] Engaging with concepts like "God," "the Transcendent," "Ultimate Reality," "the beatific vision," and so on—and being able to understand and meaningfully utter sentences like "The Holy Spirit proceeds from the Father and the Son" or "the *abiku* is born to die"—require a significant exercise of imagination and, in some cases, take us to the very limits of what we as finite human subjects can represent to ourselves, even where they serve an explanatory function. Likewise, regardless of whether any particular Scriptural story is true or not, to understand the whole of the history of the world as a kind of "cosmic narrative"—one featuring, for example, the interaction of natural and supernatural agents, a struggle between good and evil, and an eschatological resolution—requires an imaginative narrative understanding that goes beyond mere claims about certain historical or empirical "facts." That is, not only do most central religious stories relate events set apart from the contemporary faithful in time and space, such stories are themselves mythical narrative constructs that place purported happenings and persons (whether actual or not) in relation to other significant events and ideas in ways relevant and meaningful to the religious community. They may thus be as much creative as re-creative, as much constructed as re-constructive. Indeed, the religious narratives encoded in many oral and written traditions—the stories that become narrative *paradigms* for religious communities—tend to be those that incite the imagination in ways that allow them to both preserve continuity with the remote past and find application in a contemporary world.[14]

In all these ways, the imagination is no stranger to the religious life. If anything, it appears a crucial part of it. Religious identity and commitment arise out of a dynamic engagement with realities and realms represented as occupying a space outside that of the wholly empirical or natural, as well as with the ways such realities and realms are related to human beings and the natural world. For this reason, theologian David Brown concludes that "the imagination is absolutely integral to the flourishing of any religion" (Brown 2008: 366).[15] Similarly, Grace Jantzen writes: "Far from being a threat to religion, as those might fear whose chief preoccupation is the rational justification of beliefs, the imagination is central to its very possibility" (Jantzen 1999: 95). If Brown and Jantzen are right (as I think they are), then not only does an engaged, understanding-centered philosophy of *religion* need to think more closely about the role the imagination plays in the religious life, it also need not fear that doing so will somehow undermine its commitment to tethering its models to reality in some relevant way. If anything, taking the cognitive activity of imagining more seriously can help APR be more explicit about its projects—and its projections.

The social dimension of the imagination

Expanding our attention to the religious imagination further opens up space for taking seriously the fact emphasized by the commitment model of faith proposed in Chapter 4 that religious individuals are located within a *historical, social, and institutional environment* that provide them with much of the context for and content of their religious imaginings. As José Medina notes, the ability to imagine is necessary for both individual and group identity:

> Imagination is not a luxury or a privilege, but a necessity. Individuals as well as groups cannot have any sort of identity and agency without the capacity to imagine themselves, their worlds, and those who inhabit them. To have an identity and to be the subject of meaningful experience requires the imagination.
>
> Medina 2013b: 268

Something similar may be said for religious identity and experience. The most fundamental aspects of the religious life and religious belonging cannot be investigated independently of the "*shared modes of representing and relating, which are prior to and independent of particular beliefs and affects*" (Medina 2013b: 269) and which, in the religious case, both undergird and operate on the ways individuals conceive of and relate to the divine and other superempirical beings or realms.

As Medina points out, however, such shared imaginings are not "reducible to a mere list of specific cognitive commitments and affective reactions" (269). Instead, they are often imperceptibly or unconsciously internalized by subjects in their environment and can ultimately come to saturate the entire cognitive and affective dimensions of their experience. In fact, as we have seen in previous chapters, not only can the social imagination influence what we believe, it can sometimes operate on our motivations *despite* our beliefs (Fricker 2007: 15). This can be a bad thing, as when someone who has freed themselves from certain prejudicial beliefs still finds their patterns of judgment influenced by biases grounded in or informed by pernicious social imaginings. But it can also be a powerful tool for giving agents ways to construct meaning and to construe the world in a differently-toned religious hue, even if they cannot (in the moment) bring themselves to believe that such images correspond one-to-one with reality.

From a social and institutional standpoint, then, the religious imagination can function both harmfully and beneficially. For example, there are many social religious imaginings that exhibit harmful patriarchal and racial stereotypes, but which are so deeply embedded in our religious (and other cultural) practices, concepts, and speech that we often fail to detect the ways they inform our individual ideas and interactions. Such imaginings may seem innocent, even appropriate, to many religious adherents, especially insofar as they go largely unreflected. But these socially and institutionally embedded "default imaginings" can also exercise a negative influence on individuals' patterns of judgment, feeling, and action, even among those most sincerely committed to "unbiased" and "neutral" reasoning. On the flip side of this, some religious imaginings can provide (and have historically provided) individuals and communities with meaningful models for thinking about liberation and resistance, about transcendence and fluidity, about the possibility of hope and redemption in a perpetually messy world of suffering and evil—and such imaginings can operate positively on individuals and groups, even if such models are not taken to enjoy the kind of "utter objective" truth that one would supposedly discover if one were somehow able to occupy the view from nowhere.

Take the example of the monarchical, patriarchal model of God in Christianity, on which God is a divine king, lord, and/or father, the world is the "realm" or "domain" over which *he* rules, and the religiously faithful are God's dutiful "subjects" or "children." There is, of course, Scriptural and historical support for such a model, and it is one profoundly entrenched in Christian thought, language, worship, and art. Indeed, its deeply entrenched historical roots may provide both theological and psychological reasons for many people's desire to continue to promote such imaginings and the propositions in which they prominently feature. Yet such imaginings have also proven their capacity to exact non-negligible harm. For example, the patriarchal metaphor is often paired with stereotypically male characteristics of anger, strictness, punishment, jealousy, and vengefulness—and while the idea of God as angry or jealous may not be unapt in all scenarios, the imaginative picture of God as angry *father* or jealous *husband* has been employed historically to justify familial and spousal abuse by men and continues to be used to promote misogyny and abuse to this day (Barr 2021; Du Mez 2020). Likewise, the imagining of the world as God's "realm"—as "an alien other over against God," over which the sovereign divinity rules triumphantly from a distance—is, as Sally McFague has suggested, both powerful and dangerous. On the one hand, the picture of God draws us in: "It makes us feel good about God and about ourselves. It inspires strong emotions of awe, gratitude, and trust toward God and, in ourselves, engenders a satisfying swing from abject guilt to joyous relief" (McFague 1987: 64). At the same time, whether we view the God-King's power as manifested in domination or benevolence, it implicitly removes an important degree of responsibility from human beings without us realizing it: "The king as dominating sovereign encourages attitudes of militarism and destruction; the king as benevolent patriarch encourages attitudes of passivity and escape from responsibility" (McFague 1987: 69). And in a world under such immediate threats as war, poverty, and climate change, neither of these models may be up to the task of construing God's relation to the world in a way that can deliver us from the evils of our own making.

Moreover, when we think about the ways construing God as *male* undergirds theological claims about who, in the first instance, is "really" made *imaginem dei*—or when we reflect not only on the role that the racialization of God as a *white* male played in nineteenth-century antebellum American Christianity but also on how acutely it informs many American Christian imaginings even today[16]—we must consider it a task of APR to pose the question of whether these and other contingent religious imaginings may do more overall harm than good (both within the discipline and outside it) and what we should do about it. Consider here, for example, the nearly universal use of masculine pronouns for God in the APR literature. If there is good reason to think that language which codes God (solely) as masculine/male (or perhaps which genders God at all) is problematic or causes harm, then that would presumably speak against our using (solely) masculine language with respect to God in APR.

Of course, the task of exploring social religious imaginings need not be limited to merely diagnostic or evaluative undertakings of those used (and abused) by mainstream APR. It can also be (re)constructive, projective, and even playful—exploring, analyzing, and itself proposing imaginative disruptions (or "resistant imaginings," as Medina calls them) that can serve as beneficial epistemic frictions or foils for those religious imaginings that tend to go unreflected and whose consequences thereby remain relatively unexamined. Thus, we need not replace all distant, patriarchal models of God with embodied, maternal (or even gender-neutral "parental") ones, as some feminist theologians have implied—but nevertheless recovering or reappropriating historical models of God as laboring and birthing creation from a plenitude, as opposed to nothingness,[17] or as feeding, nurturing and protecting us, instead of reigning sovereign over us,[18] can give us tools for rethinking the classical attributes and activities of God as typically construed in mainstream APR.

Similarly, intentionally constructed projections and the development of new models can help us see what more traditional models might cause us to overlook. For example, Serene Jones proposes the model of a woman undergoing pregnancy loss as a way of better understanding the Christian Trinity:

> Theologians like Moltmann and Luther have urged us to affirm that on the cross, God takes [Christ's] death into the depths of Godself. The Trinity thus holds it. First person holds the Second, in its death, united with it by the power of the Spirit. But how can the living Godhead hold death within it? The tradition has told us that at this point in the story, our language breaks down, and we must simply ponder the cross and its mysteries. Perhaps the tradition is right, but perhaps its imaginative resources have been limited by the morphological imaginations of its mostly male theologians. Perhaps what we find in this space of silence is the image of the woman who, in the grips of a stillbirth, has death inside her and yet does not die.
>
> Jones 2001: 242

Jones asks the reader to "consider the power of this as an image for the Trinity"—a model of God that can, perhaps, shake us out of an imaginative complacency limited by dominant theological imaginings toward the possibility that, as I have proposed elsewhere, the Trinity might be no more mysterious or contradictory than human biology itself (Griffioen 2023d: 70). In this sense, even if a particular model itself is not wholly adequate or up to the task of capturing *all* of what God is (what model could?)—or even if the model is straightforwardly *false*—it can point us to aspects of the divine our own models are not equipped to handle and may have even actively occluded.

An alternative kind of re-imagining involves exploring imaginings of God less familiar in APR circles, either as a supplement (or even complement) to what we already find in the discipline or as a way of opening APR up to different ways of *doing* philosophy of religion. For example, in his article on the concept of the Hindu Divine Mother, Mikel Burley explains how the Hindu Divine Mother, especially in the form of Kālī, embodies "painful, distressing and terrible aspects as well as pleasant or joyous aspects of life or the world"—a "fusion of contrasting qualities" who stands in stark contrast "to the all-loving or omnibenevolent god who has been the cynosure of much Western philosophy of religion" (Burley 2022: S5). He further notes how difficult it would be to "take traditional natural theological arguments [. . .] of the sort that have been a mainstay of Western philosophy of religion and adapt them for the purpose of defending the rationality of belief in the Hindu Divine Mother," since doing so would likely "involve abstracting away from many or most of the distinctive characteristics that make the Divine Mother the deity that she is" (S6). Citing his own desire to be faithful to the primacy of praxis in religious understanding, he chooses to frame his approach "in terms of *making sense* or *bringing out the intelligibility* rather than *showing the rationality* of a religious belief or religious commitment," in order to avoid the implication that "coming to hold a religious belief or commitment, and hence also coming to live a religious life, is a process in which intellectual factors play a more pivotal role than they commonly in fact do" (S6).

Shifting APR's focus from (merely) justified belief to imaginative acceptance can therefore provide an alternative way to approach religion and religious traditions that can open the door for philosophers of religion in the analytic tradition (and their interlocutors) to move past unhelpful debates over the rationality of the kind of metaphysically robust theistic realism discussed in Chapter 1 and toward a more productive epistemology of understanding as discussed in Chapters 2 and 3. A further upshot of the shift in focus from straightforward belief to imaginative acceptance is that it allows APR to continue to explore how propositional faith may still in some sense be "in the head" without sacrificing the role of affect and the will in propositional faith, as discussed in Chapter 4. That is, concentrating on the imagination can provide a framework within which APR can undertake its cognitive (and even cognitivist[19]) analyses, while focusing on acceptance requires an examination of how such imaginative attitudes may also be intimately tied to affect, volition, and socio-historical situatedness. We might say it attaches the "head" (previously implicitly treated as a sort of "disembodied intellect," floating free of the messiness and constraints of context and corporeality) to a *body* located in space, time, and a community that *feels* and *acts* and, importantly, *undergoes transformation*. In this respect, APR can make room for the varying levels of doxastic commitment exhibited by religious practitioners—and their fluctuations and changes over time—without sacrificing either its love for the cognitive aspects of religion or the primacy of praxis.[20]

Transformative imagining: the case of Isabella

To see just a few of the powerful effects that religious imagining(s) can have on collective and individual thought and behavior, it might be helpful to turn to a historical example taken from Joy Bostic's (2013) groundbreaking work on 19th-century African American female mysticism and to consider the shift in conceptions of God by a particular enslaved black woman known as Isabella. Bostic notes that the God as commonly (re)presented by slaveholders in the South to their slaves "was white and male and had ordained the subjugation of certain segments of humanity within a hierarchal set of social relationships. He was cruel and vengeful and would severely punish anyone who did not conform to the hierarchal structure he established" (Bostic 2013: 77). Indeed, to use Medina's language, the prevailing social imagining of God perpetuated by their enslavers would come to so deeply *permeate* the cognitive and affective dimensions of the lives of enslaved women and men as to bring about the latter's own imaginative identification of the divine with those very enslavers. In Isabella's case, Bostic writes, "[her] mind was so completely *colonized* that she saw her white male master as an all-seeing, all-knowing god" (81, my emphasis). She sought his praise, even as he demeaned and defiled her, and she came to feel such profound guilt and fear of retribution for her actions, even in private, that she would implicate both herself and others in wrongdoing.

However, despite this "colonization" of her imagination by the institution of slavery, the resulting identification with her slave master/god, and the subsequent alienation from her own community, Isabella was able to recover a contrasting imagining of God—one instilled in her by her mother—which enabled her to begin to feel the tension between "the internalized belief that slavery was morally right and slaves were inferior to their masters" and "the sensibilities instilled within her as a child that abuse and violence against black bodies is unjust" (81–2). This God was a compassionate witness to suffering who listened to prayer and who would be with her even in the midst of the radically inhumane structures of enslavement (72). As Isabella's ideas about her political and moral reality expanded, Bostic argues, she began to recover "African American female ways of knowing, rituals, and the God-talk of her African-derived habitus," and she began to rediscover the spiritual practices of prayer she had been taught by her mother. This combination of reimagining the divine and recovering concrete acts of religious devotion provided Isabella with ways of understanding and addressing her own suffering, ultimately leading her to realize that "her mind [and, we may add, her imagination] did not have to be held captive by the slave master" (82).

Ultimately, Isabella arrived at what Bostic identifies as a divinity "consistent with the God of West African tradition that is understood to be both transcendent and immanent"—a God who both "occupies the totality of all that is and is near enough to see her and help her when she is in trouble" (92). The God of this religious imagining not only stood as a divine witness and judge to Isabella's suffering and the suffering of those around her, He was also simultaneously a *liberating power* who could deliver her from her oppression and who, in the personage of Jesus, represented a dear friend and companion in her suffering. She thereby came to be able to enter into a perceived relationship with God "characterized by love and mutuality rather than fear and violence" (92). This spiritual journey culminated in Isabella's declaration in 1843, on the occasion of Pentecost, that she would no longer be called by her slave name, adopting instead her chosen name, *Sojourner Truth*, and thereby being transformed (or "reborn") into a new *self*—as Bostic puts it, "a radical Subject who claims the authority to define who she is and her place in the world" (93).

In the liberating transformation of the enslaved Isabella into the activist Sojourner Truth, we can see how the various religious imaginings provided by social, cultural, and familial communities and institutions can both trap one intellectually and volitionally in harmful and oppressive structures and provide the means for epistemic and personal liberation. We can also see why restricting the discussion of the cognitive dimension of this story to the *rationality* of Isabella's particular *beliefs* concerning the existence and nature of the divine not only fails to take into account the complexity and depth of Isabella's cognitive life, it also ignores the ways in which that cognitive life was inextricably bound up with her embodied and emotional life, her spiritual practice, and the social conditions of oppression in which she found herself. It may not be the case that

Isabella ever explicitly *believed* her master to be an actual god, but the emotions evinced by the constant imaginative association of God with an omniscient, omnipotent, sovereign master and the psycho-physical trauma endured at the hands of her own master may have been enough to do the motivational work of a full-blown belief-desire pair grounded in fear and the need for self-preservation. At the same time, Isabella's transformation over time into Sojourner Truth went hand in hand with her growing ability to *accept* and eventually *foster* through prayer an imaginative conception of the divine that resisted the dominant (and domineering) model of God-as-white-slave-master. This is not a matter of Isabella's merely having "changed her mind" on the basis of new evidence or "adjusted her credences" due to an updating of implicit or explicit probability calculations, and neither can it be explained without making recourse to her social situation and the conditions of her oppression, to her epistemic *and* non-epistemic ends, and (most fundamentally) to the participation of her own *will* in her imaginative reclaiming and reconstruction of the God that empowered and undergirded her own spiritual self-awakening.

This spiritual journey led Isabella to come to a new way of understanding the cosmic Christian narrative, as well as to a transformed understanding of her place in that story—namely, as a passionate, truth-seeking spiritual *sojourner*, desiring of God and beloved by Jesus. It also represents a gradual (but by no means passive) overthrowing of a deeply-rooted, morally harmful, and theologically inappropriate model. Indeed, although the model of God-as-slave-master may strike us as obviously (and perniciously) false today, it is worth taking note of the continuities between this model and the traditional scholastic list of divine attributes in Western Latin Christendom (here: omnipresence, omniscience, and omnipotence), as well as the influence of antebellum American Calvinism and its emphasis on divine wrath and the wretchedness of the human being. Isabella's act of imaginative resistance—one enabled by the mutually reinforcing chains of imagining and action on the part of her mother and others in her enslaved community[21]—involved the liberation of her mind from the oppressive slave-master model of God that had heretofore colonized her imagination and the replacement of that model with a morally righteous, spiritually edifying, and theologically sophisticated God, one who remains deeply Christian and Trinitarian, while simultaneously bearing strong family resemblances to the divinity of her non-Christian ancestors.

Indeed, through her daily spiritual practice of prayer, Isabella was able to imaginatively exchange God's anger and wrath for God's mercy and justice—and to reshape the omnipresence, omniscience, and omnipotence of the vengeful slave-master God into a "far-near" God[22] who not only permeates all of creation but who also intimately knows, stands with, and has the power to deliver the oppressed. The suffering and striving ("sojourning") individual participates in a mutual relationship of love with this transcendent-immanent God via the mediation and friendship of Jesus Christ, and in so doing, is changed and redeemed. In her resistant and courageous re-imagining of God, Isabella is transformed into just such a "Sojourner," who in her search for Truth ends up exemplifying a love of wisdom—a *philo-sophia*—that seeks understanding in the service of justice. In analyzing Isabella's journey, then, we *must* look beyond belief. True, Isabella's beliefs are by no means irrelevant to our analysis of her transformation, but if APR wants to really be able to do epistemic, moral, and interpretive justice to religious figures and "epistemic heroes"[23] like Sojourner Truth, it will need to look beyond its obsession with the rationality of religious belief. And it is my contention that exploring the various dimensions of the religious imagination in more detail is a very good place to start this journey.

Conclusion

By shifting APR's discussion of the cognitive aspects of religion from doxastic credence to *imaginative acceptance*, or a willingness to act in ways commensurate with imagined religious worlds, one can see how it is that agents can be committed to propositions without necessarily believing them—and how religiously committed subjects may imaginatively represent certain realities and entities, the contours of which are roughly drawn by religious models provided in the service of making existential meaning within a particular cosmic narrative framework. Such subjects may, as Jonathan Cohen puts it, "have or adopt a policy of deeming, positing, or postulating" certain model-relevant propositions—of "including [those propositions] among their premises for deciding what to do or think in a particular context," regardless of whether or not they have a tendency to feel those propositions to be true when considering whether or not those propositions obtain (Cohen 1992: 4). The imagination is indispensable here, insofar as it provides the vehicle for the relevant propositional candidates for acceptance, even where that acceptance is fully doxastic. Moreover, if imagining allows us to represent things outside the realm of what we take to be possible, then such a view could open up the realm of propositional faith even to those who take certain religious propositions or even perhaps the idea of God itself to be, strictly speaking, *impossible*. As long as such imaginative acceptance represents something one genuinely stands behind—that is, so long as the affirmation of such propositions is something with which one identifies and would reflectively endorse absent external constraints—it can also rise to the level of authentic commitment necessary for the kind of faith we have been discussing. If I am right, it would seem that the commitment model from the last chapter is compatible not only with the view that there is no possible world in which the God as described by the tradition exists but also with a spectrum of odd but not necessarily incoherent claims ranging from "I hope that it is possible that God exists" to "I'm not sure whether God possibly exists" to "Maybe God is not a possible being" to "I believe God is impossible, but I hope I'm wrong."[24]

As noted, this represents a more doxastically permissive approach to faith, propositional or otherwise, than that of even most non-doxasticists, who tend to maintain that for a subject to instantiate non-doxastic propositional faith, she must believe p to be epistemically possible *and* neither believe nor disbelieve p (Palmqvist 2021: 4). Importantly, however, doxastic permissiveness of this kind by no means makes faith and its ideal, genuine *religiosity*, easier to achieve or come by than less doxastically permissive accounts. Commitment is difficult work—and religious faith, too, must be carefully nurtured and cultivated. This goes beyond just weighing the evidence for and against particular propositions or considering possible defeaters. Religion may be a means by which our imaginations are easily excited, but the kinds of things it asks us to conceive also push us up against the limits of what we can imaginatively grasp, let alone take as a candidate for belief—and some of the things it asks us to imagine meet with significant imaginative resistance.[25] In this sense, an authentic commitment to religious imaginings often takes significant effort to maintain, even when accompanied by whatever level of confidence or feelings of certainty might be necessary for belief in the reality of the objects of those imaginings.

Similarly, my assertion that the cognitive aspect of religious faith essentially involves imagination and is compatible with a wide range of doxastic attitudes is *not* tantamount to maintaining that subjects somehow thereby relinquish their epistemic obligations and responsibilities with respect to the propositions in question. Nor is it to say that truth is or ought to be of no concern to persons of faith (or for our evaluations with respect to their rationality). But it *is* to say that faith—even propositional faith—is not *solely*, or perhaps even primarily, a matter of the outcomes of these epistemic considerations, even when it comes to considering the rationality of faith. Practical rationality, aesthetic sensibilities, and lived religious experience have important roles to play here as well. In other words, even when thinking about propositional faith, we cannot (and should not) divest it of its role in religious practice and the overall religious life.

Additionally, as we saw in Chapters 2 and 3, truth is not the only value of relevance in our epistemic considerations, especially when we focus on endeavors of understanding over knowledge. *Faith seeking understanding* may sometimes take the form of a search for evidence and the attempt to contour one's beliefs accordingly, but it can also be pursued in less strictly discursive or intellectualist ways. Insofar as the life of faith centrally involves not only the intellectual and reflective capacities of epistemic agents but also (and more centrally) the affective and aesthetic sensibilities of human persons, as well as the ritualistic and spontaneous movements of human bodies within architectural and natural spaces, a *living* faith in the service of understanding is, I think, best characterized as a kind of imaginative and embodied *play*—one which both seeks and constructs meaning through dynamic, interactive, embodied intercourse between the historical and the contemporary, between repetition and innovation, between passive reception and active projection. Yet this kind of play, I will argue, is by no means trivial or un-serious. It is a kind of play concerned with existential meaning-making, and as such it is a deeply serious form of play, one which I will call *earnest make-believe*. Such an approach to the religious life fundamentally goes "beyond the doxastic"—and perhaps, as I will suggest, beyond *faith* itself—without requiring APR (or anyone else for that matter) to give up the importance of those things to which the religiously faithful commit themselves. It is to a discussion of this approach I now turn.

Notes

1   I remain relatively neutral with respect to the ways these categories are divided up, since I think most accounts of beliefs, credences, and the relationships between them are compatible with the account of faith I have given here. Moreover, as I will discuss in Chapter 7, I think the division of religiously committed practitioners into "believers," "non-believers," and "disbelievers" is a relatively artificial one, as well as heavily context-dependent, as Lebens (2021) suggests. (Lebens himself is one of the few philosophers I am aware of besides myself who appears to reject the no-disbelief constraint on religious faith.) For my purposes here, however, I take belief that p to involve a degree of certainty or confidence with respect to p above some context-sensitive, relevantly high threshold, together with a disposition to feel that p when

explicitly considering whether p in the relevant context. (On this latter phenomenological condition, see Alston 1996 and Cohen 1992.) I take disbelief to involve a similarly context-sensitive credence of zero with respect to p (or a credence that falls below some carefully-defined minimal threshold), where the phenomenological aspect involves a disposition to feel that not-p (or, minimally, to wholly lack the feeling that p) when considering whether p. Non-belief, then, represents all attitudes on the doxastic spectrum between the two poles of belief and disbelief with respect to p. This may involve active suspension of belief, as in agnosticism, but it need not—though in the context of religious faith it requires that the subject be minimally acquainted with the proposition p and have some attitude toward it. (That is, when I speak here of non-belief that p I am not talking about subjects who are ignorant of p, have no epistemic access to p or p-relevant considerations, or have otherwise never considered p.)

2   I generally prefer to speak of *acts of imagining* or *imaginings* over referring to *the imagination*, as the latter appears to presuppose some special faculty or capacity for imagining. I take no position here on the plausibility or usefulness of representing the imagination as a distinct faculty, and when I speak here of "the" imagination, I do not mean to imply the existence of such a faculty. Moreover, when I later speak of *the religious imagination*, I am generally referring to a set of individual, collective, and/or social imaginings or imaginative models, not to some special capacity of the subject to represent things in a religious way.

3   Some sources use the term "imagistic." I prefer "sensory" in order to underscore that the representative imaginings in question a) may be literally (and not just metaphorically) somatic in the way they are experienced and b) need not be visual in nature. See also note 6 below.

4   For some of the various approaches to imagining and the imagination, see, e.g., Gallagher (2005); Kind (2016, 2020, 2023); Kind and Kung (2016); Langland-Hassan (2020); Liao and Gendler (2020); Medina (2013a); Rucińska and Gallagher (2021); Van Leeuwen (2011).

5   See, e.g., Gendler and Hawthorne (2002); Levin (2011); Nichols (2006); Priest (2016).

6   As noted, when imaginings are understood as "imagistic" or "sensory," this need not be associated with visual imagery, despite this being the dominant modality under discussion in the literature. I see no reason to exclude auditory, tactile, kinesthetic, or even olfactory and gustatory imaginings from such objectual imaginings, particularly in the religious realm. Indeed, if we are to understand the significance of the kinds of religious imaginings discussed in this and the following chapters, it will be important to take these other forms of embodied sensory imaginings seriously. (For more on the importance of sensory imaginings and experiences to historical Christianity and the failure in the scholarship to take them seriously, see, e.g., Bynum 1988, as well as Van Dyke 2022.)

7   I am less inclined to think we can imagine the logically impossible, though I am, somewhat ironically, open to the possibility.

8   See, e.g., Currie and Ravenscroft (2002); Gendler and Kovakovich (2006).

9   Sartre is often unfortunately overlooked or dismissed by analytic philosophers, especially APR scholars. I do agree with Sartre's critics that there is reason to balk at his claims that imaginings cannot be a source of knowledge or a direct cause of feeling. Still, I think there is a more charitable way of reading these claims that are consistent with what I say here—especially when we shift from knowledge-centered to understanding-centered epistemologies. Unfortunately, these arguments must remain for another time.

10 For an overview of some of the literature in cognitive neuroscience of the relationship between memory, imagination, and consideration of future events, see Gaesser (2013). Whether first-personal memory is best classified as imaginative and/or is structurally parallel to future projection is controversial. For one treatment of this topic, see Debus (2016).

11 Some such objects may be *indirectly* perceivable, e.g., through a microscope or telescope. But such items as "the Higgs-Boson particle" or "the universe" may only be representable through models or other imaginative structures (or, alternatively, through something like "negative representation"—via the denial of particular concrete imaginings). Here, the line between spatial and logical inaccessibility may become somewhat blurred. Still, the connection to the representation of images of the divine should be apparent.

12 There is, of course, the question of whether God could be directly perceived in certain forms of religious experience, as some philosophers (e.g., Alston 1993) have proposed. If so—and on the assumption that this could count as a kind of "cognitive grasping" of the divine—then, at least so long as the subject is undergoing such an experience, there might be cognizings of the divine that do not involve occurrent imaginings. However, even if such cognizings are possible, it is unclear whether they could provide a subject with any sort of stable *concept* or *model* of God without the involvement of the imagination. I leave a more nuanced discussion of this question for a later date, but for a detailed discussion of the challenges to the perceptual model of religious experience, see Griffioen (2021b).

13 If Joshua Myers is right, some sensorial imaginings might even achieve the status of what he calls *imaginative beliefs* or "states that are imaginative in format and doxastic in attitude" (Myers 2024: 22). Whether one state with two aspects (imaginative format/doxastically-graded attitude) or two states (imagining + degree of belief) provide a better explanation for the phenomenon I am describing can remain open for our purposes here, but it would be a worthwhile project to think further about these questions in light of my claims here.

14 Compare David Brown's more prescriptive suggestion that "what [. . .] we need in our own day [. . .] is a similar imaginative capacity to maintain continuities, while yet

accepting the need to envisage very different worlds and applications" (Brown 2007: 94–5).

15 As with my own approach, Brown claims it is a mistake to set up imagination and ontology as opposing forces. "Rather than playing imagination and ontology off against one another," he writes, "they should be seen as generating similar challenges and similar problems" (Brown 2008: 288).

16 Compare the backlash against Harmonia Rosales who reimagined Michelangelo's "Creation of Adam" with both God and the first created human being portrayed as black women (Blackmon, 2017).

17 See, for example, Meister Eckhart's model of the "overflowing" Divine who, in its "fullness" of being, births all of creation in a single divine act of divine illumination. Of course, Eckhart is careful to "balance out" models of plenitude with contrasting metaphors of God as emptiness (e.g, God as "desert," "abyss," or "darkness"). For more on these motifs, see Griffioen (2023a, 2023b).

18 In his prayer to St. Paul, Anselm compares Jesus to a mother hen who "gathers her chickens under her wings," warming, comforting, and reviving them. Julian of Norwich uses the God-as-mother motif repeatedly in her *Revelations of Divine Love*, appealing also to the (not altogether uncommon) medieval comparison of lactation and breastfeeding, the blood and water that flows from Jesus' side wound, and the philosopher "suckling" at the "teat" of Divine Wisdom.

19 The semantics of such an approach will need to be more fully worked out, but we can imagine them operating similarly to fictionalist accounts of religious language, albeit without the insinuation that assertions in the target language are false or refer necessarily to non-existent objects and states of affairs. For the germs of such a theory, see Griffioen (2016). For a defense of the claim that hermeneutic fictionalism is compatible with metaphysical realism, see Jay (2011). A perhaps more promising alternative might incorporate a form of inferential expressivism, similar to that developed by Incurvati and Schlöder (2019).

20 The shift to the imagination also makes room for the possibility that religious credence in most contexts is not to be identified with factual belief, as Neil Van Leeuwen (2014, 2017) suggests, though I do not take any position on this particular debate here. Like my approach in Chapters 6 and 7, he compares religious credence to make-believe, suggesting that both are "practical setting dependent" (2014: 706). However, although this comes close to what I say about the contextual nature of religious imaginative acceptance, I think Van Leeuwen sometimes fails to appreciate the ways in which the practical setting may encompass one's whole life (even if this will be, for many religiously faithful, the ideal and not the norm). Neil Levy (2017) presents a nice contrast here in his discussions of the ways in which theological credences may guide behavior *across* practical settings, as well as the ways in which non-religious factual beliefs may also be practical-setting dependent without threatening their status as factual beliefs.

21 On the importance of *chained action*, or "the interconnected and mutually influencing actions that become chained in social networks and sometimes in social movements," to the social impact of "epistemic heroes" like Sojourner Truth, see Medina (2013b: 225ff.).

22 The notion of a "far-near" God is prevalent in much Christian mysticism and made explicit in such medieval authors as Marguerite Porete and Henry Suso.

23 See Medina (2013b: 186–7).

24 Many thanks to Greg Landini for saying such bizarre—but, to my mind, not necessarily incoherent—things to me on occasion.

25 On imaginative resistance, see Gendler (2000); Moran (1994); Walton (2006).

6

Beyond the Indicative

The "Ultimate Horizons" of Pretend Play

*A picture held us captive. And we couldn't get outside it, for it lay in our
language, and language seemed only to repeat it to us inexorably.*

Ludwig Wittgenstein, *Philosophical Investigations* (§115).

Introduction

In his 2016 book on the philosophy of liturgy in the Eastern Orthodox tradition,
Terence Cuneo explores some of the concrete ways in which the imagination is
relevant to the religious life. For example, he explains how liturgical participation
can be analogous to imaginative immersion in narrative literature, and he
proposes that the "liturgical script" calls for both a destabilization and
reunification of the individual's narrative self-conception, similar to the ways I
have discussed friction and resonance in previous chapters. However, Cuneo
thinks that liturgical reenactment performs a different function than merely
reading a novel or acting out a play. Not only do Eastern Orthodox liturgical
scripts call for imaginative immersion and the acceptance of certain propositions,
he claims, it also "belongs to the essence of this activity that the assembled
commit themselves to ethical and religious ideals of various sorts" in so
immersing and accepting (Cuneo 2016: 103). Inspired by Orthodox theologian
Alexander Schmemann, he argues that liturgical participation of this kind is best
construed as a response to a divine invitation to transform the world and one's
own self by way of repetitive, affirmative faith-constituting acts of commitment.

In addition to the affective and moral transformation that can result from
such participation, Cuneo maintains that liturgical practice is also *epistemically*
valuable, insofar as it provides what he calls "ritual knowledge." Such knowledge,
he claims, has less to do with "being in [some] type of doxastic state with respect

to propositions about God as with conducting oneself in certain ways with respect to God that count as engaging God, and knowing how to conduct oneself in those ways" (Cuneo 2016: 165). Indeed, what Cuneo has in mind with the term "ritual knowledge" sounds much more like what I have characterized in earlier chapters as a form of *understanding*, rather than straightforward justified true belief. Put in these terms, we might propose that imaginative ritual participation contributes to a kind of understanding that assists in fulfilling the overarching hermeneutical task of meaning-making that belongs to the religious life.

At the same time, Cuneo also repeatedly asserts that such activities as make-believe or pretense "have almost no place in the liturgy" (Cuneo 2016: 78) and that "among the responses *not* ordinarily called for by the liturgical script [. . .] is that of engaging in make-believe behavior" (92). He goes so far as to aver that "we have decisive reason to reject an account of liturgical reenactment according to which it consists in make-believe behavior. For if it did, then liturgical reenactment could not be normatively transformative" (104). He appears to think the imaginative liturgical activities through which subjects are called to play certain "target roles"[1] could not aim "to transform the self by way of committing oneself to certain ethical and religious ideals" if they were merely a matter of make-believe. Cuneo is not alone in his skepticism about pretense and make-believe. For example, although sympathetic to the idea of religious make-believe, Natalja Deng writes: "Clearly, much of the comfort religion ordinarily provides is lost when belief is replaced with make-believe," and "the nature of religious practice is fundamentally altered when one treats it as make-believe" (Deng 2015: 202–3). She thinks that "other things of value may be gained" by adopting a make-believe approach to religion, such that religious participation "can still be interesting and emotionally satisfying for those so inclined" (202), but it seems that, for Deng, there is little overlap between the worship of the make-believer and that of the "true believer."

Finlay Malcolm (2018), in his discussion of whether fictionalists[2] can have faith, takes the concerns regarding words like "pretense," "make-believe," and "play" in APR and turns them into a potential worry for non-doxasticist accounts of faith:

> What guides the intuition that fictionalists do not have faith? Well, for one thing, fictionalists are engaged in a pretence. [. . . .] If we grant that the fictionalists, who are engaged in a form of pretence, can actually concurrently have faith, then perhaps non-doxastic faith in general also involves pretence. After all, if you

> don't believe something but merely act as if you do, how can you avoid the claim
> that you are *merely* pretending? If advocates of [non-doxastic theories] can show
> how their belief-less faith is different from the position of the fictionalist, they
> may be able to show how their faith is *genuine* and not *merely* a form of pretence.
>
> Malcolm 2018: 224–5, my emphases

In this passage, religious fictionalism is conceptually tied to a form of pretense, and the purported "challenge" for APR theorists who want their accounts of faith to be more doxastically permissive than doxasticist views (according to which belief is a necessary feature of propositional faith) is how to escape the charge that this makes religious faith a matter of pretense.

Perhaps it is due to my work in philosophy of sport and engagement with theories of games and play, but I have always found the resistance in APR to words like "pretense," "make-believe," and "play" a bit odd, even if not altogether unsurprising. I suspect that much of the resistance to speaking of these kinds of activities with respect to the religious life has to do with a fear of *maligning* and/ or *trivializing* religious practitioners in a way that would do a disservice to the ingenuousness and seriousness of the religious enterprise. On the one hand, the worry might go, if a significant portion of religious participation were to involve any robust form of pretense, it might mean that religious practitioners regularly engage in fake, dissimulative, or even outright deceptive behavior. On the other hand, if it involved make-believe or play, it could suggest such practitioners do not really take their religion seriously after all—or, alternatively, that religious practice is itself "silly" or not something to be taken seriously. Given the relatively defensive stance of APR and its religious allies against its loudest and most militant "cultured despisers," the not-so-new, anti-religious atheists[3]—who, it must be admitted, have not seldomly attributed devious, dishonest, or immature motivations to religious adherents—it should not be surprising that philosophers of religion might feel a sense of obligation to demonstrate that religion is, in fact, a *very* sincere and *very* serious business, one that trades in rational belief, not make-believe.

At the same time, in my experience, a related *intra*-religious concern also looms large in these discussions,[4] namely the assumption that someone engaging in religious make-believe amounts to a kind of religious "freeloader"—someone who tries to get all the "benefits" of religious practice without the "costs" that accompany belief, or who otherwise "cheapens" the earnestness of those self-designated "true believers" who practice their religion with "great solemnity," and who take doxastic faith to be normative, or at least ideal, for the tradition. Here, it is sometimes hard to know exactly why we should be worried. In some religious communities, where the faith-ideal is (I think, troublingly[5]) understood as involving certitude, I suppose it may involve a concern for the spiritual or soteriological well-being of the person who they take to be engaged in religious practice without the requisite degree of belief. Of course, such a view seems to assume a) that believers don't make-believe and b) that religious make-believe is somehow inferior to religious belief—both assumptions that I will challenge in what follows.

However, in conversation with those who tend to voice the intra-religious objection, the worry is less often phrased in terms of a concern for the well-being of the make-believing practitioner in question and more about a perceived "unfairness" or "disrespect" on their part toward the doxastically committed. Here, the problem for the believer is not that a critic of religion is accusing *them* of being (consciously or unconsciously) engaged in a kind of insincerity or self-deception, but more that *they themselves* are potentially being "defrauded" or "made a mockery of" by their non-believing, "pseudo-religious" comrades who (they assume), in not possessing the requisite strength of belief, cannot be considered appropriately sincere. Again, the objection arises from the assumption that "true believers" have no need of (and do not engage in) religious make-believe, paired with concerns about being somehow "hoodwinked" or their "good faith" being "exploited." Ultimately, then, the overarching worry seems to be that the non-believing religious make-believer is *insincere* and/or *irreverent*—someone engaging in a kind of deceptive or careless religious "play" that desecrates what is supposed to be most solemn, serious, and holy. It is thus perhaps not so difficult to see how APR scholars—especially those who think that the ideal kind of faith is *believing* faith[6]—might balk at the idea of taking religious make-believe seriously.

It is also worth noting here that some of the moral and theological panic surrounding the possibility of religious fraud that tends to accompany the epistemic panic in APR is very much a cultural matter. For example, among white Protestant and Catholic Christians in the US and the UK (where APR and its downstream pastoral effects[7] are quite prominent), there are deeply embedded historical narratives involving religious marginality and persecution that still inform contemporary narratives of religious believers as victims (Bruner 2021). Both nations also have a long and storied history of spiritual(ist) experimentalism and religious charlatanerie. It is, then, perhaps no surprise that a very particular understanding of sincerity is often placed at the heart of religiosity in these contexts (McCrary 2022).[8] These histories also inform a legal context in which the concept of "sincerely held religious belief" plays a central role. (In the US, for example, demonstrating religious sincerity is important for questions concerning who can claim exemptions from such policies as the military draft, vaccine mandates, or anti-discrimination law, or when an individual's religious freedom has been violated.) However, to appeal to another, equally "American-inflected" value—namely, that of individual *privacy*—it is difficult to see how a person's doxastic conviction at a particular time or lack thereof is really anybody's "business" unless it somehow makes a significant moral, theological, or practical difference.[9]

My goal is therefore to make the case that we have reason to reject moral objections concerning deception as well as theological objections concerning irreverence—and to argue that, from a practical standpoint, not only is religious make-believe[10] compatible with various doxastic constitutions and constellations, it actually goes hand-in-hand with what we find in religious practice at its "highest and holiest." However, in order to be able to motivate these claims, I will have to do some significant conceptual ground-clearing. Therefore, in this chapter I want to explore in more detail the concepts of pretense, play, and make-believe that seem to cause APR scholars such discomfort. Once we have a working understanding of make-believe in play (no pun intended), I will go on to show that it need be neither deceptive nor frivolous. This will allow me to explore more thoroughly the concerns about religious make-believe in Chapter 7.

Pretense, play, and make-believe

The term "make-believe" is commonly associated with both *pretense* and *play*—and, more specifically, with the pretend play of *children*. Indeed, because pretense and play go so naturally together in children, scholars have a tendency to focus on *pretend play* as a singular unit of meaning. Importantly, however, these two phenomena can and do come apart. And because much of the hand-wringing over religious make-believe appears to stem from concerns APR scholars have about the purportedly dissimulative aspect of pretense, on the one hand, and the supposedly non-serious aspect of play, on the other, it will be instructive to briefly explore each of these ideas on their own before we combine them to explore make-believe in more detail.

To begin with, play can clearly occur without pretense. Athletes playing baseball, grandmasters playing chess, or college students playing beer pong do not need to pretend to engage in the games they are playing, even if they may sometimes use various forms of strategic deception to mislead their opponents.[11] Likewise, when my toddler repeatedly stacks her blocks, knocks them down, laughs hysterically, and then stacks them up again, she is clearly playing with them, but she does not seem to be pretending in any straightforward sense. She simply wants to be engaged in the activity of alternately stacking and knocking down blocks. Similarly, a subject can pretend without playing. Take, for example, the teenager who, despite not finding it funny, laughs at a mean joke made by their peers, or the junior scholar who, despite finding it demeaning, pretends not to be insulted after being patronizingly called "young lady" by a senior colleague. Neither appears to be playing, but they are certainly engaging in forms of pretense.

What distinguishes pretense from play appears to have to do with both the *positional stance* adopted by the subject toward the content and framework of the activity and the *attitude* with which they pursue that activity. When one pretends, one takes up an *as-if stance*, wittingly presenting an aspect of oneself or the world (to oneself, to another, and/or with others) in a way that contrasts with how one normally takes it to be or operate. Play, for its part, has what Bernard Suits (1977) calls an *autotelic* aspect. A playful activity is one engaged in for its own sake or, at least in part, for the satisfaction of participating in the very activity itself. In formal play, we may call this a *lusory attitude*, which for our purposes can be understood as the acceptance of a stipulated imaginative or game-like framework (and the relevant rules, structures, and boundaries of that framework) *just so that* the activity made possible by such acceptance can occur.[12]

What makes my daughter's block-stacking-and-knocking-over activity play is that it is simply *fun*. She stacks and knocks over the blocks again and again because she *enjoys* the activity of doing so, not because she is trying to become an expert stacker or acquiring the skills to be a demolitionist. But neither is it pretense: She does not (yet!) represent the blocks to herself (or anyone else) *as* an office building or act *as if* she were Godzilla. The peer-pressured teenager and the resigned junior scholar, on the other hand, *do* wittingly present themselves to others in ways that diverge from how they would normally react. But unlike my daughter, they do so for purely *instrumental* reasons. The teenager might be desperately trying to fit in with her more popular peers. The junior scholar might be wary of upsetting someone with institutional power over her—or, as is perhaps more commensurate with many women's experience in academia, she might simply be tired and want to get on with her life by pretending not to be bothered by microaggressions. They do not, we may conjecture, participate in such pretense for its own sake, nor intrinsically value the activity of taking up this particular *as-if* stance. (Our everyday lives are full of instrumental pretense of this kind.)

In pretend play, then, both the *as-if* stance and the lusory attitude are present. The children taking up the imaginative stance of behaving as if the floor is hot lava do so because imagining the living room is "dangerous" in this way and hopping from chair to sofa and back again is fun. Further, they impose and accept certain limitations and constraints (e.g., not touching the floor, only considering furniture "safe"), just so this fun "hot lava activity" may take place. Similarly, the Star Trek enthusiast engaged in cosplay at a convention enjoys, values, or finds meaningful the activity of thinking and acting as if they were a character from a beloved fiction with others who are similarly pretending—and this is a large part of why they choose to pretend in this manner and on this occasion. Some serious role-playing cosplayers might accept quite strict limitations concerning not breaking character while engaging with similarly serious players, while for others the requirements to remain in character may be looser. But whatever the case, in contrast to instrumental pretense, *playful pretense* is, at least in some relevant sense, engaged in for the sake of the *as-if* activity itself or for the meaningfulness inherent in particular form or act of pretending.[13]

Of course, the lines between instrumental and autotelic pretense will be blurry in some cases, and it does not seem implausible to think that many pretense activities are of a "mixed" sort: the pretender engages in them in part to engage in the activity itself but also in part for an additional reason or for some further end. For example, what makes cosplay *play* is the fact that people dress up and pretend to be characters from their favorite books, films, or series, just for the enjoyment of enacting those characters themselves in an imaginative context structured by a particular fiction with others who similarly enjoy such activities. But it can also be a means of socializing with friends, getting followers on social media, finding acceptance within a community, or expressing normally suppressed aspects of their personalities—and some or all of these aims may also be instrumental reasons for those pursuing such pretense. Alternatively, they may simply provide causal or historical explanations as to why the subject has come to enjoy participating in the activity for its own sake in the first place, whether or not they are aware of this fact.[14] For my purposes here, to count as play an activity must be centrally pursued for intrinsic reasons or because one intrinsically values that activity, even if it is also simultaneously pursued for the sake of something else. Put a bit differently, the activity is not *fungible* for some other, equally (or more) effective activity. How "much" autotelicity an activity will require to count as play will be largely context-dependent, but I think the idea that many activities fluctuate between being autotelic and instrumental or can have aspects of both at once should not strike us as all that controversial.[15]

So how does make-believe fit into this schema? Providing a strict set of necessary and sufficient conditions will be difficult, but on the (rather intuitive) view I am operating with here, make-believe is roughly synonymous with *pretend play*. Cases in which pretense and play come apart will therefore not count as cases of make-believe. In general, then, I take make-believe to usually display the following characteristics:[16]

- *Volitionality*: Make-believe is volitional in at least two fundamental ways. First, it involves a *willful* enactment of imagination by the make-believing subject (hereafter MBS)—often via a projection onto one or more "props," which can include the MBS themself and/or agents, objects, or states of affairs independent of the MBS. Second, the MBS *tries to experience* the world as it is imaginatively enacted by *allowing* the imaginative context (at least temporarily) to guide and constrain their behavior.
- *Subjunctivity*: The *stance* of the MBS and the *mode* of the activity within the imaginative context of the make-believe (e.g., in the make-believe "world" or "paracosm") involves thought, feeling, and action in the subjunctive (as opposed to indicative) mood; make-believe involves an MBS's adopting a *could-be* or *as-if* attitude toward the world or some aspect of it.
- *Structure*: What it is (in)appropriate for the MBS to say or do in the make-believe-world is set by the *limits* of the imagined context, even where the boundaries of what is permissible within that context may be flexible or imprecisely defined.
- *Awareness*: There is a *divergence* between what is imaginatively enacted and the way the MBS tends to experience the world when not engaged in the make-believe, and the MBS is a *witting* participant in the imaginative enactment of this divergence.
- *Immersion*: make-believe is a *participatory* activity, often involving an MBS's becoming *immersed* or *absorbed* in the enactment of imagination.
- *Autotelicity*: The MBS is, to a large extent, driven by the goal or desire of *the enacting of the particular imagining itself*. That is, the propositions that help frame the relevant imaginative context and constrain behavior within it are accepted precisely so the make-believe in question and the concomitant experience of and action within the make-believe world can occur, and/or the make-believe is a non-fungible,[17] constitutive part of a larger play

activity, such that to engage in the make-believe just *is* part of what it means to be engaged in that form of play.

Moreover, although make-believe may be a "solitary" or "private" activity in the sense that it may have a special meaning for only one MBS or otherwise go "unshared" with others, it has an implicit *potential for sharedness*. In other words, it is something that, in principle, could be shared with, communicated to, or engaged in by others. We may also thus add to the list:

- *Communicability*: make-believe establishes a context that could be (and often is) *shared* with others who are similarly make-believing. Further, groups of MBSs can *collectively contribute* to the construction and enaction of a shared imaginative context in ways that go beyond the mere additive conjunction of individual instances of make-believe.[18]

That make-believe is witting and volitional in the first sense, together with its structural features and subjunctive mood, points to its being a form of pretense, while its being volitional in the second sense, as well as immersive and autotelic, gestures at its fundamentally playful nature; its communicability points to a further, social aspect sometimes overlooked in philosophical treatments of make-believe. For our purposes here, we may thus provisionally define make-believe as consisting of *those activities in which one or more subjects wittingly engage in a communicable, participatory, and non-fungible enactment of structured imagination, adopting an as-if stance toward various objects and settings within the imaginative context and willingly committing themselves (at least temporarily) to letting their actions and experiences be guided and constrained by the contours and rules of the imaginative context, where that context diverges in some relevant way from the way those subjects would (or do) otherwise experience the world.*

This is certainly a mouthful (and I do not suggest trying to recite it in one breath), but I think that, even if it might not cover all cases we are pretheoretically inclined to call make-believe, this more nuanced understanding of make-believe puts us in a better position to think more carefully about the potential deceptiveness and/or frivolity of make-believe activities.

Make-believe, deception, and frivolity

Worries about make-believe's being deceptive are generally driven by concerns about its connection to *pretense*—since the MBS wittingly undertakes an activity that presents her or the world in a way that diverges from the way she normally takes reality to operate. Concerns regarding its non-seriousness or triviality, on the other hand, usually have to do with the perceived lack of seriousness associated with make-believe's *playful* character. Let us take each of these worries in turn.

Make-believe and deception

Interestingly, while the charge that make-believe is deceptive has to do with its being a form of pretense, it may turn out that it is precisely make-believe's *playfulness* that usually precludes its actually being so. An act of deception, we may say, involves an agent, A, intentionally attempting to bring it about through something they say or do that another agent, B, comes to believe some proposition (or set of propositions), p, which A, at the time of the deception, takes to be false. If B comes to believe p on the basis of A's deceptive act, then we may say that A has successfully deceived B into believing p. Therefore, it would seem that for pretense to be deceptive, it must be both *instrumental* and undertaken for the purpose of *persuasion*. That is, A must pretend intentionally *in order to* achieve some further end A cares about, where the success of A's act relies on their pretense being *convincing* to others who are not themselves pretending.[19]

Although pretense in the context of make-believe is an intentional activity which involves A wittingly presenting herself and/or the world as other than she normally takes or experiences them to be or to operate, the content of A's intention when make-believing is not generally to cause B or any other agent outside the play-context to believe her. A is make-believing, not trying to make anyone else believe. Now certainly, there are playful contexts that do involve *intra*-lusory deception. For example, strategic deception is common in game-contexts (think here of head-fakes in basketball or bluffing in poker), though it is less commonly a constitutive and non-fungible part or aspect of those games and serves a solely instrumental purpose within the game of helping one achieve what Suits (1978) calls the "lusory goal" (usually: the winning of the game by adhering to the rules). Such cases of deceptive pretense are unlikely to constitute make-believe in the sense specified above, since one does not engage in the pretense itself for its own sake but rather for the sake of the lusory goal, and the deceptive activity itself is not pursued autotelically. In other cases, deception may be a central component of an activity of make-believe, as with some murder-mystery role-playing games. However, yet again the deception here is *intra*-lusory, such that by willingly entering into the play-context players voluntarily make themselves possible targets (and likewise potential agents) of such deception. Thus, even if there is constitutive, non-fungible deceptive pretense involved, it is of the kind that all players accept and must tolerate within the play-context if they wish to be engaged in the form of play itself.

Still, one might object that some forms of playful pretense might be *unintentionally* deceptive, insofar as they could mistakenly cause an *extra*-lusory witness to the pretense to acquire a false belief, either about the make-believer herself or about the way the world is. In such cases, although the MBS is not engaged in an intentional act of deception, they might be considered reckless or negligent, if their make-believe leads to those not involved in the make-believe to have false beliefs that turn out to be pernicious or harmful. That is, make-believe can, in some cases, be "deceptively misleading" without the make-believer being engaged in an intentional act of deception, and an MBS might thereby be considered culpable for her carelessness with respect to the truth, even if she did not intend to deceive others by her make-believe. It is indeed true that make-believers must, at least in some contexts, be careful with their make-believe, especially where a failure to do so could result in harm to others. Make-believing there is a fire when one is in a crowded theater or that one has a bomb in one's shoe when at the airport has the potential to do real harm, even if one is only "playing." Something similar might be said of "locker-room talk" and other purportedly "playful" (yet demonstrably harmful) ways of speaking and behaving: Even if not intended as serious, the appeal to playfulness does not always exculpate.

For now, however, it is sufficient to note that make-believe is not *inherently* deceptive, even if it may sometimes be (harmlessly or harmfully) misleading, and that its playful aspects are part of what precludes its being so. However, as we've seen above, the features of make-believe that make it playful also make it appear less than serious. So what are we to say about the nature of play? Is there always some aspect of *nonseriousness* to it? Should we always be inclined to doubt the sincerity or earnestness of someone's action if that action is also best characterized as a form of *play*?

Make-believe and frivolity

It may help to think, first, about a few of the reasons we tend to classify play as nonserious. To begin with, the play of children often strikes us as frivolous, given the lightheartedness with which it is often engaged, the ease with which it can be given up, and the flexibility it tends to display in its ability to easily accommodate changing contexts.[20] Since make-believe is often associated with the pretend play of children, then, it is not surprising that we should think of the playful aspect of make-believe as a similarly "flippant" enterprise. Relatedly, when someone takes make-believe "too" seriously—when a child screams in abject horror as an adult "squishes" their imaginary friend by sitting on the chair they the latter is "occupying" or when an adult LARPer sleeps in costume with their sword at-ready—we might suspect that they have run together imagination and reality. Make-believe, we think, when taken too seriously, commits a kind of ontological category mistake. Finally, there is a strong tendency—especially in contemporary neoliberal contexts—to equate seriousness with things like efficiency, productivity, and output. Given its non-instrumental flavor, play tends to belie these values and therefore is often classified as trivial, unimportant, or otherwise non-serious.

However, one need only look at baseball fans to see that play (as well as the rituals that accompany it) can be a matter of great seriousness—and *not* because they have confused reality and make-believe. A fan may be fully aware that the so-called "rally cap" (i.e., wearing one's baseball cap inside out when one's team is behind) has no special metaphysical "power" to change a team's fate, and yet failing to engage earnestly in such practices when they are called for in the context of the game can represent an important failure to respect the game and its practices—a failure to take it seriously *enough*. Likewise, for those who themselves are playing, there is often a sense of "flow" and "absorption" that "wraps one up" in the play context in a way that feels deeply serious (Csikszentmihalyi 2013). Thus, as Johan Huizinga put it in his famous work, *Homo Ludens,* "the consciousness of play being 'only a pretend' does not by any means prevent it from proceeding with the utmost seriousness, with [...] a devotion that passes into rapture and, temporarily at least, completely abolishes that troublesome 'only' feeling" (Huizinga 1949: 8).

In a much overlooked essay, Kurt Riezler (1941) aptly noted the relevant difference between saying that someone is playing and that they are *merely* playing. He suggests it is neither the non-instrumentality of play nor the awareness of a play context's being somehow "outside" the ordinary that makes it nonserious. Although an activity's "detachment" from the demands of reality outside the play framework might be part of what makes it playful, it is ultimately a lack of *devotion* to the play context that makes it nonserious or "merely" playful. Where play is wholly free and unconstrained, perhaps, it might be thought to be unserious, but the constraints imposed by most human play demand a kind of seriousness that even the child recognizes. Indeed, as Ananda Coomaraswamy

(1942) wrote in response to Riezler, "We do not play *carelessly* [. . .]. Play implies *order* [. . .] but the whole point of the game is that we are not playing only to win, but playing a *part*, determined by our own nature, and that our only concern is to play *well*, regardless of the result, which we can not foresee" (551, my emphasis).

Riezler goes even further in his approach to the seriousness of play. In the voice of an interlocutor, he (rather "playfully") suggests that perhaps the problem is less with the playing individual herself and more with the person who applies the qualifier "merely" to someone's play, thereby suggesting a kind of "deficiency" regarding play in comparison with ordinary life:

> At last, so the argument runs, you seem to discover the shortcomings of a thesis that takes for granted the seriousness of ordinary life. In starting from the "merely" you presuppose a standard of seriousness that may be only the standard of the kind of society that thinks in terms of means and ends, in terms of business. It may be that the "merely" is only a habit of speaking. There need not be an absolute "merely" in playing as such—no deficiency. If there is deficiency it may be a deficiency not in play but in the man who utters the "merely" and thus shows that he can not rid himself of his puny sort of seriousness. Your start from the "merely" distorts the story of play.
>
> Riezler 1941: 512

The suggestion here is that the application of the "merely" itself might be *misleading*. We would do better, Riezler thinks, to consider more carefully the ways in which much play is often not *merely* play, "and not only because the result of the play is connected by agreement with means and ends in ordinary life, such as money or honor, but in itself, by its *inherent seriousness*, which is not the seriousness of the real world or ordinary life" (513, my emphasis). He suggests that we show a lack of seriousness when we "merely" relate an object or activity—whether in play or in our ordinary lives—to other objects or activities by understanding it as just one thing among others "in the endless finiteness of [our] chains of means and ends" (517). However, often when we are wholly engaged and absorbed in an activity, "something else appears" that goes beyond "the 'real world' or ordinary life with all its endless chains of aspects, causes, means, in which every step is finite and none the last" (515). This "something else [which] can be grasped with your senses but not put into words," Riezler calls an "ultimate horizon"—a whole that transcends the conjunction of its parts, a *Gestalt*. "Whenever an ultimate horizon grips the whole of our being," he writes, "our concern with whatever it is is really real concern," and it is this that "lets both our play and ordinary life be serious" (517).[21]

Given these considerations, we might thus be able to distinguish at least three ways in which play can be understood as "serious," "sincere," or otherwise "earnest":

Non-trifling seriousness

First, and most basically, there is the sense of seriousness that distinguishes the player (e.g., of a game) from the kind of "quasi-player" that Suits (1978) calls a "trifler" (44ff.). A game-player who is "trifling" goes through the motions of the game and follows the rules but shows little concern for the lusory goal (i.e., does not compete to win). In the case of non-game play (as with much make-believe), we might say the trifler abides by the constraints of the play-context with little concern for the activity itself. In some cases, the trifler might enjoy the various parts of the activity—say, of playing a role or doing something specific with her body, as called for in the play-context, but the activity itself is relatively fungible; it could just as well be something else, as far as she is concerned. Such instances might still count as "playing," but not playing *seriously*. The make-believe of young children might sometimes be like this. It does not so much matter whether the child is pretending to bake a cake or change Bunny's diaper or ride the bus, and one of these activities may quickly morph into the other. What matters here is the fact that *some* imagining or another is being enacted, not necessarily *which* one is enacted.[22]

In other cases, the trifling may come about insofar as one only abides by the constraints of the play for extra-lusory instrumental reasons. In such cases, we might cease to call the activity 'play' in the first place, as its seriousness is related solely to, as Riezler put it, "the endless finiteness of [. . .] chains of means and ends" and ceases to be autotelic in any meaningful sense. This latter attitude may display a kind of seriousness, but it is not of the kind that takes the play itself seriously. As with the playful trifler, the activity in question could be swapped out for some other, more efficient (play or non-play) activity, so long as it would be useful in achieving the end in question.[23]

The "serious" player, on the other hand, cares about the playful activity itself that is being undertaken, as well as the specific moves that must be made within that context to count as being engaged in that kind of play. They are concerned, say, not just with making the "right" moves on the chessboard, but with playing (and potentially) winning at a *game of chess*. They care about being in the reenactment of *this* battle in *this* war and playing the *particular* role they are assigned within that reenactment to the best of their ability. They care that they are engaging in Star Trek cosplay and not Star Wars. And so on.[24]

Regard for the "spirit" of the activity

A second form of seriousness might be what we call regard for the "spirit" of the game or play. This may be similar to (or, in some cases, even part of) being a non-trifler, but it involves the epistemic aspect of being able to properly *discern* the significance of the play-activity in question and its relevant components. A player who plays with regard for the spirit of the activity has some sense of what kind of play would constitute an undermining of the atmosphere the play-context ideally creates. This is why, in some sports, an umpire is given the latitude to rule against players who, although acting within the "letter of the law" as set out by the rules, thereby contravene the "spirit" of the game, or to make certain exceptions for violations of rules that do not undermine it (Griffioen 2015; Russell 1999).

When players show regard for the spirit of the activity, they exhibit a seriousness that goes beyond merely allowing themselves to be constrained by the play-context for the sake of undertaking the play activity itself. There is an aspect of *reverence* for the play-context that both displays a keen *understanding* of the nature of the activity itself and a *respect* for what makes that activity what it is and not something else. Those who adopt this kind of stance toward play are the opposite of triflers, but importantly not all non-triflers will show this kind of serious regard.

Existential earnestness

Finally, there is a more profound sense in which play can be deeply serious that corresponds to Riezler's invocation of the "ultimate horizon" mentioned above. This occurs when the play in question involves reference "to the whole of your world, to an ultimate horizon bordering this whole" (Riezler 1941: 517). Put a bit differently, when play takes on *existential* significance—when it turns into a kind of "frame" or "lens" for seeing the world and one's place in it, and when one devotes or commits oneself to this way of framing things—it becomes *earnest* in a way that goes beyond both "ordinary" life and "ordinary" play.

One way this kind of earnestness can come about is when the play itself "reveals" a kind of significance to the player that points to a sort of "transcendence" or "beyondness" of the mundane world, as is common among both athletes and artists. Here, experiences of utter absorption or "flow" may give way to feelings of awe and wonder, of simultaneous agency and automaticity, of full control and loss of ego (Csikszentmihalyi 1975). Another complementary form this earnestness might take is in the creation of what Tanya Luhrmann calls a *paracosm*, or a "private-but-shared imagined world sufficiently rich in detail that people become engaged in the stories and can return to them again and again, exploring them from different angles, reliving different moments, recasting the scenes as if they were there, even adding new chapters to the story" (Luhrmann 2020: 27). A paracosm is thus a communal way of imaginatively approaching the world or some aspect of it in the subjunctive mode that can "grip the private imagination so powerfully that [. . .] they kindle the sense that they are true" (27).

Such play-contexts create a space in which earnest players can autotelically act and experience themselves, their agency, and their very *being* in ways quite out of the ordinary—and they can do so, not (just) as an "existential balm"[25] but in a way that allows them to experience themselves as *human* in the most profound sense of the word. This can be temporary, or it can be something longer-lasting—a momentary experience or a more habituated *practice*. Certainly, cases of such existential earnestness threaten to explode the ordinary distinction between play and non-play (though, importantly, not between play and work), but our confusion with respect to classifying such activities may, as Riezler pointed out, have more to do with our obsession with instrumentality, productivity, and other post-Industrialist values with which we operate, rather than pointing to an actual metaphysical or conceptual problem. To put it in more Wittgensteinian terms, we may be held captive by a rather neoliberal picture of play that we simply haven't thus far been able to shake. In fact, when we cease being afraid of terms like pretense, play, and make-believe, we may discover that some of our worries about religious make-believe are really *pseudo-problems* that require significantly less concern than even the philosophical defender of theism in APR might have thought.

Notes

1   For Cuneo, "target roles" are those in which "one acts the part of being some way for the purpose of being that way, becoming like or identifying with that which one imitates" (Cuneo 2016: 78). This is contrasted with "pretense roles," since "one doesn't pretend to be that way; rather, in acting in that way, one thereby aspires to be that way" (78). Yet it is unclear why one cannot assume a target role by pretending, nor why one cannot "aspire to be" the way that one pretends to be.
2   I should note here again that the view I am putting forward here is not necessarily to be identified with fictionalism as often discussed in the APR literature, even if it does

share many of the features of such views. (Of course, much depends on how exactly 'fictionalism' is to be understood.) In any case, as in previous chapters, I do not assume here that the committed religious non-believer must believe the target language is false, nor do I think they need be committed to religious practice for purely instrumental reasons (as will become clear presently).

3   See Chapter 1, n.1 above.

4   I do not commonly find this attitude in print, but it has been voiced in several philosophical conversations and Q&A sessions concerning the subject when I have raised the specter of make-believe in the context of religious faith. I also take it that part of Malcolm's "challenge" to the non-doxasticist concerning its indiscernibility from pretense rests on this kind of idea.

5   I take up my concerns with belief's being normative for a tradition below. See also the discussion of strong doxasticism in Chapter 4.

6   This characterization also applies to those proponents of non-doxastic models who take non-doxastic faith-attitudes to be theologically and epistemically *permissible* but nevertheless view sincere (rational) belief as the cognitive religious *ideal*.

7   For more on the "downstream pastoral effects" of APR, see Chapter 8.

8   My own account of faith as *authentic* commitment might reflect this influence as well, despite my attempt to divorce sincerity from belief.

9   One might object here that it makes an *epistemic* difference. But it is hard to see why any particular religious practitioner should care about such a difference unless it plays out in the religious community in a way that makes adopting one doxastic stance over another preferable.

10 In what follows, I will refer to the nominative and adjectival 'make-*believe*', as opposed to 'make-belief', to emphasize the dynamic nature of the activity in question, and I will further hyphenate the verb (e.g., 'to make-believe', 'make-believing', 'making-believe', etc.) to distinguish that activity from anything like 'causing' or 'creating' belief (i.e., from *making* [someone] believe).

11 On this subject, see Kathleen Pearson's (1973) seminal piece on strategic vs. definitional deception in sporting contexts. Whether strategic deception in games always involves pretense (and whether beer pong ever involves strategic deception!) is an interesting issue for future exploration. For our purposes, it will suffice to note that pretense need not be a constitutive feature of such play activities.

12 I have adapted this concept from Suits' work. Since Suits was primarily interested in *game*-playing, he limited the lusory attitude to "the acceptance of constitutive rules [of a game] just so the activity made possible by such acceptance can occur" (Suits 1978: 40), where a game is an activity whose rules prohibit more efficient in favor of less efficient means in the pursuit of some (relatively arbitrary "prelusory") goal. I have broadened this definition a bit to include forms of formal imaginative play we might not be pretheoretically inclined to call "games."

13 As Schmid (2009) has noted, autotelicity can be understood in various ways. For our purposes here, I will use it to mean that the activity is either valued intrinsically by the person pursuing it or minimally is pursued for intrinsic reasons. Moreover, I do not mean to say (as some theorists seem to imply) that any activity pursued for its own sake is necessarily playful. However, I do think that when pretense is autotelic, it is reasonable to call it a form of play and not of, say, mere aesthetic appreciation (even it does sometimes involve aspects of the latter).

14 This is to say, not all functional, psychological, or historical reasons are instrumental reasons *for* an agent—reasons she would in some sense identify with (if not endorse) when made aware of them.

15 This has been one of the most sustained objections against Suits' insistence that professional athletes do not really "play" the games by which they earn their wages. It also reflects the concerns my students often have that to engage in an activity "because you enjoy it" has an air of instrumentality to it. (You do it *in order to* gain enjoyment from it, they insist.) What matters for me is that *engaging in the activity itself* is an important part of the agent's motivation or reasons for why she undertakes it.

16 I have adapted and revised some of these characteristics from the work of various scholars, including Lebens (2020), Lillard (2002), Luhrmann (2020), Mitchell (2007), Seligman (2010), Suits (1978), and Walton (1990).

17 Note: To say that the activity is non-fungible does not mean it is not contingent.

18 I should note here that make-believe's communicability does not mean that everything about it or all experiences from within it are expressible in language. It merely maintains that, in most cases, make-believe involves practices and structures that can be taught, transmitted, and/or engaged in collectively.

19 Of course, not all instrumental pretense need be deceptive. One can pretend instrumentally *with* others who are similarly pretending, or one may pretend instrumentally without having any effect on other people whatsoever. What seems to be crucial here is the idea of someone's pretending *to* others *in order to* get them to believe that the pretender is *not* pretending. (This rules out, for example, that actors in plays or films deceive their audiences. They might even be said to pretend *with*, not *to*, their audiences, but that is a consideration for another occasion.)

20 Though it is worth noting here that children's play is not seldomly also taken extremely seriously by the children engaging in it, even when the child has not confused imagination and reality. Many toddlers, my own included, require that a particular form of play proceed in just such-and-such an order with such-and-such props representing particular non-present objects—and a failure on the part of, say, a parent to be guided by the exact structure of the play-context in question can lead to *very* upset little people!

21 The similarity to theologian Paul Tillich's notion of faith as *ultimate concern* here is likely no coincidence. Riezler was largely responsible for Tillich's being appointed

professor of philosophy and sociology in Frankfurt in 1929, where they also gave seminars together. After being removed from their positions by the NS-regime, they also both emigrated to New York (Tillich in 1933 and Riezler in 1938), where Tillich taught at Union Theological Seminary and Riezler at the New School.

22 But again, see note 20 above.

23 There are, however, interesting questions here when it comes to "going through the motions" in the context of communicating, learning, and practicing *how* to engage in a certain playful activity. Both coaches and players may go through certain moves (sometimes over and over again) without trying to win, where it is clear the goal is to get a potential player to better understand the game and learn how to play (well). This kind of "trifling" (if it can even be called such) is usually deeply serious and immensely important for learning how to engage seriously in the play activity itself. I take this idea up again in the next chapter.

24 I take up another kind of Suitsian "quasi-player," the *spoilsport*, in the Interlude between parts below.

25 On games as existential balms, see Nguyen (2020: 20–1).

7

Beyond Faith

Make-Believe and the Religious Life

*The Platonic identification of play and holiness does not defile the latter
by calling it play, rather it exalts the concept of play to the highest regions
of the spirit.*

Johan Huizinga, *Homo Ludens*

Might as well make believe I love you. / For, to tell the truth, I do.

Oscar Hammerstein & Jerome Kern, *Showboat*

Introduction

Building on the insights of Chapter 6, in this chapter I want to argue that authentic, committed engagement with and within a religious tradition often involves what Rachel Wagner calls a kind of *earnest play*. To "play in earnest" in religion is, as Wagner puts it, "to say yes to the world" of a religious tradition (Wagner 2014: 204)—or, in the "Suitsian" language introduced above, to imaginatively accept and commit oneself to it just so that the activity of existential meaning-making arising within that "paracosm" can take place. In fact, I will go further and argue that religion at its "highest and holiest" involves a kind of *dynamic make-believing* embodying all three kinds of serious play discussed in the previous chapter, by means of which one strives to see and experience the world as *imbued with existential meaning* from within a particular imaginative cosmic narrative framework or "paracosm." In this spirit, I will propose that the most exemplary form of religious practice involves both willingly adopting a *non-frivolous lusory attitude* toward a particular cosmic narrative framework and taking up an *imaginative as-if stance* toward the central propositions, practices, objects, stories, and general constraints of that framework.

Such an approach stands in stark contrast to the trepidation with which APR has traditionally approached the possibility that religious practice involves anything resembling pretense or play, let alone make-believe, which combines the two. However, as we saw in Chapter 6, the moral worry about make-believe's purported deceptiveness and the theological worry concerning its irreverence not only presuppose that religious make-believe and religious belief are *incompatible*, they assume that the latter is a *preferable* stance to the former (if not the ideal stance in the life of faith). Although in Chapters 4 and 5 I motivated the claim that belief is neither necessary nor sufficient for religious faith, and I took a maximally doxastically permissive approach to such faith by placing the religious imagination at the center of the cognitive religious life, I have not yet established that belief is *not* always (let alone usually) preferable to its alternatives in the life of authentic religious faith. Thus, the idea that that religion at its "highest and holiest" involves *religious make-believe* (hereafter RMB), but not necessarily religious belief (hereafter RB), needs some defending.

In order to motivate the need for RMB in the sphere of religion, I will begin with a reminder concerning the heterodoxy of religious participants within a tradition and the dynamism of the religious life, and I will point to research indicating that the act of religious "believing" might not always be of the same sort as the "believing" we engage in with respect to other, more mundane beliefs. I will then draw on work by Samuel Lebens to give some reason to think that the ideal of the religious life both *demands* and can better be *understood* by reference to RMB, not (merely) RB. This approach will show that RMB and RB are not necessarily at odds with each other, but it will also motivate the idea that they sometimes come apart in ways that are important for the authentic religious life. I will then address the moral and theological concerns raised above, and I will give a few reasons why I think RMB might, in many cases, even be *preferable* to RB by itself in ordinary religious practice.

"Make-Believing" About Believers? Fictional Religious Subjects in APR

Before I proceed, there is a rather large "make-believe" elephant in the room that I have up until now largely ignored. In Chapter 1, I alluded to the idea that the so-called "religious believer" whose belief is so strongly defended by APR scholars might himself be a "socially constructed fiction." In Chapter 2, however, I suggested that some such fictions can be theoretically useful, and in Chapters 3 and 4 I followed much of the APR literature in talking about religiously committed "believers," "non-believers," and "disbelievers." I do, in fact, think that this way of conceptually dividing up the cognitive religious landscape can help us refine some of our philosophical approaches to the nature and normativity of religious faith. At the same time, I worry about the fiction of the relatively "doxastically-fixed" religious subject, who may sometimes fall (further) into doubt, but for whom it is assumed that the ideal state in terms of their faith (even if not necessarily their rationality) would be belief. This not only descriptively fails to reflect the radical cognitive heterogeneity of many religious communities and the ability of their differently-credenced practitioners to successfully engage in shared religious practices and linguistic exchanges, I think it also sets implicit normative standards for religious subjects that are more likely than their alternatives to promote rather than prevent self-deception and intellectual vice. If this is right, then we need to proceed carefully.

We must not forget, as APR scholars often seem to do, that individual religious adherents are not static, unchanging figures. Individual belief—especially when it comes to belief in transcendent realms or supernatural beings—waxes and wanes with the vicissitudes of everyday life. Today's "true believer" is tomorrow's "fictionalist" and vice versa. Many of the earnestly faithful have days, weeks, or even years where it is difficult to take such ideas as of an all-knowing, all-powerful, all-loving God seriously, while the most committed naturalist may find herself strongly pulled toward ideas of metaphysical transcendence in certain contexts. Indeed, religious commitment turns out to be cognitively difficult in a way that goes beyond just aligning one's beliefs with the evidence at hand. For example, in the preface to her book, *How God Becomes Real*, anthropologist Tanya Luhrmann (2020) diagnoses one aspect of this problem in her own field, noting that "most theories of religion begin by treating belief in an invisible other both as taken for granted and as a cognitive mistake. [. . .] Then these theories go on to explain why apparently foolish beliefs can be held by sensible people" (ix). Despite the fact that APR scholars are usually less interested than their religious studies counterparts in providing actual theories of religion and more interested in how RB might be neither "foolish" nor a cognitive mistake, their way of proceeding is roughly the same: (a) RB is taken for granted and treated more or less like any other belief, and (b) it is thought to be in some way more fundamental than or prior to religious practice.

Regarding (a), Luhrmann draws on both important philosophical work by Neil Van Leeuwen (2014) and her own years of research on (and within) religious communities around the world, arguing that people's religious commitments to supernatural entities and realms seem to operate *differently* than their beliefs about the ordinary world:

> People may talk as if the gods are straightforwardly real, but they don't act that way—not in the Bible Belt, not in medieval England, not in Fiji, and not among the Nuer. People [instead] behave as if making invisible others real enough to impact one's life in a positive way takes *effort*, as if one has to *learn to think in certain way* and—in consequence—to *behave as if* invisible others are not real in the way that ordinary objects are real. They seem to treat gods and spirits with *different ontological attitudes* than they do things of the everyday world.
>
> Luhrmann 2020: 12–3, my emphases

Regarding (b), Luhrmann denies both that RB is a static given and that it is somehow prior to religious practice. How might our understanding of religion look different, she asks, "if, rather than presuming that people worship because they believe, we ask instead whether people believe because they worship" (x)? Luhrmann's emphasis on religious "doing" and the ways in which prayer, ritual, and worship help *make* religious concepts "real" for people, thereby allowing them to feel "that these gods and spirits matter in the here and now" (xi), parallels my emphasis in previous chapters on what John Cottingham (2005) calls "the primacy of praxis" in religion. This framing allows her as an anthropologist to better analyze the ways in which religious subjects' cognitive attitudes need (and receive) constant bolstering, given the demands the ordinary world places on us—and gives her a path to explore why, although religious practitioners recognize and assert that it is good to trust in or pray to God, they still study for the upcoming test, take shelter in a storm, or lock their doors when they go out.

Still, even if it should turn out that RB is *not* qualitatively different from our mundane beliefs about the world—or, alternatively, that RB is just one species among a variety of value-laden, identity-conferring, fidelity-demanding commitments that lead us to respond in qualitatively different ways than to "mundane" beliefs—Luhrmann's insight that the cognitive element in religion is neither static nor a prior given still stands, as does her observation that cognitive religious commitment takes a significant *effort* on the part of the religious subject that goes beyond just responsiveness to arguments or evidence. Gods, spirits, and transcendental realms need to be *made real* for religious practitioners. To appeal to a notion occasionally employed by the poet Robert Frost, sometimes it is difficult to believe in God, so instead we have to believe God *in* (Abel 1978).

Given the dynamism of actual religious subjects, as well as the very real difficulty of sustaining belief in God, there might be more room for RMB than one might have thought at first glance. Indeed, when we emphasize the primacy of praxis in the religious life, we may find that RMB is less a deviation from the norm and much more the way ordinary religion tends to proceed.[1] Still, that might not address the nagging worry that RMB is morally or theologically problematic—or at least not preferable to non-make-believe activity. It is therefore worth spelling out in a bit more detail what I take RMB to involve and why I don't think it falls prey to concerns about either deception or irreverence.

Religious make-believe: the "highest and holiest" kind of religious engagement?

In the final chapter of Samuel Lebens' groundbreaking monograph in Analytic Theology, *The Principles of Judaism* (2020), he proposes that Orthodox Judaism requires *faith* from its adherents—where faith, as on my account in Chapter 4, is distinct from, though generally compatible with, belief. However, he also claims that, as opposed to mere (or even devoutly sincere) *frumkeit*—which amounts to something like the sincere acceptance of the general theological tenets of the Jewish faith and commitment to keeping the commands of the Torah[2]— Jewish *religiosity* requires an extra "ingredient," namely one involving *striving to be holy.* Lebens claims that "holiness—or, at least one species of it—emerges when people behold the world, and everything in it, through the attitude of awe" (Lebens 2020: 286). Importantly, however, someone can be a person of authentically committed devotional faith with respect to the Orthodox Jewish tradition—and can even fully believe the central propositions of that tradition—without being in a "sufficiently absorbing" state to achieve the attitude characteristic of genuine religiosity, namely that which allows the person to really *experience the content* of the relevant propositions (and the concepts involved therein), as well as their own *positionality* with respect to that content. Striving for holiness, Lebens maintains, involves more than commitment to, or even commitment-to-plus-belief-in, the relevant propositions. It requires additionally engaging that "species of imagination" which enables us to "try to experience the world, and [our] place in it, as if [these propositions] were true" (288). In other words, genuine religiosity involves *imaginative make-believe.* In this sense, Lebens maintains that although "mere faith, or even belief, isn't enough to make a person holy [. . .], making-believe that God exists, to wit, trying to experience the world as a world in which God is your God, *is* an ingredient for real religiosity; an ingredient for inculcating the right posture and attitude towards the world" (289).

Implicit in Lebens' approach, I think, we can locate the volitionality, subjunctivity, awareness, and participatory features of make-believe I set out in the previous chapter, since one *tries* to experience the world and one's positionality within it *as if* something were the case that, even if one believes it to be true, is not generally as "present" or "attended to" as when actively *immersing* oneself in the particular imaginative context enacted in the make-believe. It will also inevitably exhibit a particular structure, insofar as "trying to experience" will involve one's actions being willingly *guided and constrained* by the accepted narrative paracosm in question (in this case, Orthodox Judaism). Moreover, although Lebens tends to talk here about individuals, he is careful to note that "holiness is a package deal" involving the priest, the place, God, and the people (283). In this sense, RMB is not just *communicable*, it is *communal*. And when it is collectively enacted "in a magical moment of joint attention, when all of the pieces fit together, in that moment, holiness emerges collectively" (283).

This "emergence" of mutual holiness in the interdependent "dance" of the various parties involved also indicates that Lebens' account is able to accommodate the feature of autotelicity, making his approach to religiosity not just a matter of as-if pretense but also of *play* (and thus of what I define as make-believe). Although the command of *striving* to be holy might lend RMB an air of the instrumental, as I read Lebens one does not make-believe *in order to become holy*. Rather, the "striving" and the "becoming" are not distinct activities. One willingly enters into the paracosm that pre- and proscribes particular actions, specifies certain rituals, and constrains the concepts and propositions to be imagined, *just so that* this activity of striving, of religiously make-believing, can occur. And when one does so, one both *makes* things holy and is simultaneously *made* holy by those things: "If you view the commandments with awe, then they will become holy, and they, in turn, will make you holy" (283).

For our purposes here, it is not crucial that we take holiness or awe as spelled out by Lebens to be central features of religiosity in general, since they may be particular to Orthodox Judaism. (Whether, for example, generating awe or a "sense of a the sacred" is a central function of RMB can be a matter for APR scholars to explore more thoroughly in the future.) It will suffice to note that, on his account, make-believing is *fully compatible* with believing. At the same time, transforming mere RB into RMB—bringing one's belief from the background to attend actively to it and trying to experience its content—requires significant feats of imagination. As Lebens puts it: "You might *believe* that you're a creature of God. But it takes more to *attend* to this, and to *see yourself* in the moment, through the prism of your belief, as a creature of God. Attentive seeing as engages the imagination" (288).

However, although RB and RMB are compatible in this way, RMB as sketched out by Lebens also appears eminently compatible with levels of doxastic certainty that don't meet the threshold of belief. Like me, he also rejects the "no-disbelief" constraint on faith put forward by many non-doxasticists (Lebens 2021). Moreover, he argues (and I agree) that there are some crucial instances tying the propositional to the practical and social in which religiosity can demand, even of particular religious believers, make-believing things that they take to be *false*, especially when such make-believe can be *corrective* in nature. He compares an ordinary case in which make-believing the members of one's audience are wearing silly hats helps assuage one's public-speaking fears with the injunction in Judaism to regard oneself *as if* one had been a slave and come out of Egypt:

> *As if.* The task isn't to believe; the task is to make-believe. If you walk around [. . .] experiencing yourself *as* personally liberated by God, and you see all other people in the world suffering forms of modern-day slavery as comrades who you can empathize with because you were once where they were; if that's the posture you have towards the world, then you'll be well on your way to being holy.
>
> Lebens 2020: 292

Thus, even though believing and make-believing are not incompatible, there are cases in which they importantly come apart. It would probably be counterproductive if you really *believed* everyone in the audience was wearing silly hats, and it would be straightforwardly absurd to believe that you *really* had been a slave in Egypt. But, as Lebens notes, "To make-believe that *p*, whilst knowing it to be false, is not always irrational, and needn't ever fall into the epistemic vice of self-deception" (293). Indeed, he suggests that perhaps certain religious narratives are just "an invitation to view the world—without deceiving ourselves or anybody else (since we're sophisticated beings who can look at one world in multiple ways)—through the prism of that story" (293).

I will address the question of (self-)deception presently. What is important for our purposes here is Leben's insight that, in make-believing, a life of strict religious adherence or even authentic commitment to a religious tradition can go far beyond doxastic status—and even beyond *faith* itself—to become a *living religiosity.* Insofar as one is able to foreground one's religious commitments, attend to them, and make them present to oneself in religiously circumscribed activities of make-believe, one does not (or not just) *believe in God* but rather *believes God in* via a dynamic enactment of the imagination in which one willingly immerses oneself. Moreover, in this realm, sometimes the individual who does *not* believe the content of the make-believe is in a better epistemic and practical position than one who does.

What is especially interesting about this approach is that one can, in some sense, make the divine *more real* to oneself precisely by moving *away* from the indicative and *into* the subjunctive mode of imagining, contemplating, and experiencing it in the as-if mode.[3] To adapt and expand upon an example from Lebens (2020: 290), if I want to really *attend* religiously to vague theistic concepts like God (a concept which requires the use of the imagination to even get off the ground[4])—that is, if I want to make this idea *real* for myself in thought and worship—one of the best ways to do so is to deliberately immerse myself in the enactment of an *imaginative* world in which God is not just the distant "First Cause" or *primum movens*, but is also *my* God, a being who is close to me and is always breathing life into everything, including myself, from the inside. This world is contrary, perhaps, to the way I tend to view it when I am, say, shopping for groceries, changing a poopy diaper, writing a paper, or even entertaining "sanitized" propositions like "God exists" or "God is omnipotent" while examining yet another philosophical argument for theism. It might even be a *false* world, at least in the sense that the God of my tradition is not a physical being and thus cannot be "close to" or "inside of," let alone "breathe into," anything. Yet it allows me, perhaps by way of certain prayers or bodily rituals, to enter into and be guided by an imaginative context in which I can better take seriously religious propositions I *want* or *need* to be committed to in the context of my tradition, or which might even be *true*, like "every breath is God's gift."

Given the dynamism and variability of the religious life discussed above, RMB of this sort is perhaps not the kind of stance I (or any "average Jo") can sustain constantly. Perhaps for most of the religiously faithful it is only a fleeting experience, and the best we can do is, as Lebens puts it, simply to "strive for moments of religiosity" (Lebens 2020: 290). Even so, understanding the central role of make-believe in making possible such moments can help us see, yet again, why the emphasis in APR on RB and its rationality—as well as the ways it tends to divorce the epistemic from the affective, practical, and social—is fundamentally misguided. (We might even have a better chance of understanding religion by looking to the philosophy of sport and games, where discussions of play and make-believe have real currency, than by looking to analytic philosophy of religion!)

Further, such analysis also provides a useful explanation for the observations of scholars like Luhrman (2020) and Van Leeuwen (2014, 2023) that RB doesn't always behave like ordinary factual belief—that, to loosely paraphrase the famous *hadith*, one should "have faith but still tie up one's camel."[5] It's not that religious adherents are manifestly *irrational*. It's just that make-believe of the requisite kind is *hard to sustain*, and the demands of ordinary life often push explicit religious commitments into the background. Regardless of whether and what one believes, being able to continually foreground the make-believe central to religiosity in a way sufficient to enter a longstanding frame of mind in which one's experience of the world is more often than not "saturated" with the divine is intensely difficult. We might think of it as the gift (or, perhaps, burden) of the saint or prophet—or maybe even the (often unattainable) "end" or "goal" of the mystic's spiritual journey. However, most of us simply don't have the time or privilege, let alone the sheer psychological *flexibility*, to open ourselves up to sustained transformation in this way. In this sense, the saint is rather like an elite athlete—naturally gifted with skills or powers in RMB that many of us lack, yet also able to cultivate those abilities to reach the highest heights of experience and virtue—and to lead, mentor, or serve as exemplars to others in the pursuit of their own spiritual excellence.

All these benefits of the RMB-approach notwithstanding, my suspicion that the subjunctive has, in some sense, more power than the indicative in the religious realm might still cause those who view RB as the optimal cognitive attitude in that realm to suspect that religious practice in the form of make-believe is harmfully misleading, theologically irreverent, or epistemically and/or religiously suboptimal. Therefore, to further support my claim that the religious at its highest and holiest centrally involves RMB, I want to explicitly address these concerns and suggest that not only are they unfounded, there is reason to think that we should be more worried about the likelihood that RB (by itself)—or approaches that make RB *normative* for the tradition in question—will lead to these consequences than RMB.

Disingenuous? Sacrilegious? Addressing moral and theological concerns

It is difficult to disentangle the worries about RMB that appear to plague APR scholars. Worries about deceptiveness are tied to concerns about the purported non-seriousness of the religious make-believer, and both are tied to the view that RMB is somehow suboptimal or less preferable than RB. Still, it is perhaps worth addressing these concerns individually.

(When) is RMB deceptive?

We have seen above that it is make-believe's playful aspect—its immersiveness and autotelicity or non-fungibility—that generally rules out its being deceptive, since the pretense involved in deception is almost always predominantly instrumental. I maintain that this will be the case for RMB as well. Those who make-believe religiously in an *earnestly playful* sense are not trying to get others to come to believe something false about them or their doxastic status. If, as I have suggested, religiosity demands a kind of RMB, and if RMB of the kind described above is compatible with both committed RB and committed religious non-belief (hereafter "RNB"),[6] then committed religious believers and committed religious non-believers alike will *share* in the communal project of RMB. Each of them (individually and, presumably, collectively) will have to willingly adopt the relevant *as-if* stance and earnest lusory attitude to count as engaging religiously, and not just faithfully. They are no more trying to deceive each other (or anyone else for that matter) than those wearing rally caps at a baseball game, who may or may not believe in the efficacy of the superstition. Religion in this sense is *simulative*, not *dis*simulative.

Of course, deceptive *pretense* of a non-playful (and therefore non-make-believing) kind in the context of religious participation is certainly possible and may also involve the religious imagination. Take the example from Chapter 4 of the deconverted Muslim woman who temporarily (but inauthentically) commits herself to religious practice when visiting her parents. In such cases, we can imagine that she might attempt to conceal her deconversion, and she will likely have to pretend to care about religion, perhaps even adopt certain *as-if* stances, in order to be convincing to her parents (or to allow them to remain in the false belief) that she is still a faithful Muslim. Or consider someone employing religious imaginings while pretending to be authentically religiously committed in order to, e.g., receive a relative's inheritance, gain a political advantage (see: the US National Prayer Breakfast), or even to avoid spiritual abuse from their religious community. As Van Leeuwen puts it, "The religious faker [. . .] may imagine the stories and doctrines of their feigned religion, [but] they do not feel normative pressure to act in ways that express these imaginings *except insofar as they intend such actions to convince actual members of the sincerely faithful that they (the fakers) are also sincerely faithful*" (Van Leeuwen 2023: 174–5). However, these cases are a far cry from what I have characterized as RMB in this chapter. Not only do their actions lack the autotelicity and sincerity required of earnest play, they often have an ulterior motive (even if a sometimes morally permissible or even commendable one) that is itself not religiously motivated.[7]

In fact, the contexts in which the faithful religious non-believer is likely to be most motivated to deceptively *try* to conceal their actual doxastic state are precisely those in which belief is made *normative* or *ideal* for the tradition—especially those where those admitting a lack of doxastic conviction are shamed, disdained, or shunned, since their ability to remain a member of their religious community likely hinges on their ability to feign belief when not occurrently experiencing it. Therefore, some of the non-believing religious faithful might engage in deception in order to avoid being themselves harmed, but it is unclear how their deception harms the *believers* in the community.

Still, there are two related concerns in the vicinity of deception that are worth taking into consideration. First, one might worry that the non-believing religious make-believer unintentionally but recklessly *misleads* their believing counterparts into believing something false—namely that the former takes certain concepts to be real and propositions to be true which they actually do not believe. Yet similar to the above worry, it is difficult to see how, in the course of everyday religious practice, this really does harm to either party, nor to the tradition or community in question. Second, one might worry that non-doxastic RMB might lead to *self*-deception on the part of the non-believing make-believing subject. In the longstanding custom of "fake-it-till-you-make-it," one might worry that by engaging faithfully in religious practice involving RMB, the non-believer will become less sensitive to counterevidence and more likely to end up adopting beliefs that currently violate her own rational standards. This is a genuine concern, given religion's transformative propensities. However, one might also think that such practice can open an inquisitive subject up to *new* forms of evidence or ways of gathering and thinking about evidence that makes it more likely that they will acquire a *rational* confidence in the propositions of the tradition, and this result should, we might think, be welcomed by the believing faithful. In fact, a non-believing make-believer who is open enough to become or remain authentically committed to a religious tradition and to adopt an *as-if* stance with respect to that tradition might actually be *less* likely than their believing counterpart to become entrenched in the kind of dogmatism that leads to blind-spots or an inability to see genuine counterevidence as such, and *more* open to the possibility of revising their religious imaginings in light of relevant moral or metaphysical concerns. In this sense, although self-deception remains a constant concern for the religious make-believer, this concern applies to religious non-believers *and* believers alike, and the former might even have an epistemic "leg up" on the latter in terms of intellectual humility and imaginative openness.

Further, a religious community or tradition that makes belief a requirement for admission into or recognition by the community of the faithful—or that transforms a lack of full conviction into a sin, a vice, or some other moral or theological *failure*—seems more likely to encourage self-deception than one that does not explicitly or implicitly demand belief of its adherents. Where the alternative to normative conviction is either deception (concealing one's doubt from others) or deconversion (leaving the community altogether), it would not be surprising if we were to find those struggling with their belief doing everything they cognitively can—including engaging in self-deceptive strategies—to acquire, recover, maintain, or repair the requisite doxastic conviction, even in the face of what they take to be overwhelming evidence to the contrary.

Of course, I have maintained that RMB is not inherently or even commonly deceptive on the grounds that it is a form of *earnest play*. Therefore, it will help to, first, motivate the idea that RMB really is a form of *play*, before turning our attention to the second concern of those who find themselves philosophically or theologically allergic to the idea that the most authentic form of religiosity involves making-believe—namely, the worry that, *qua* playful make-believe, RMB lacks the appropriate attitudinal *seriousness* and/or theological *reverence*.

(When) is RMB playful? Can it really be earnest?

On the view I have defended here, the problem is not, *pace* Malcolm and Scott (2023), that the reasons of the faithful non-believer are non-epistemic. Rather, the worry for my view is that the primary reasons of such individuals for their religious participation might appear largely instrumental and prudential. If this is right, we might worry whether RMB can appropriately be characterized as a form of play, let alone earnest play, as I have maintained. This would again open up the door for the charge of deception—though, of course, the objector would still have to show that the instrumental reasons motivating the religious pretender result in deceptive intentions, or at least that their behavior is recklessly misleading. (As argued in the previous section, this is most likely to be the case in religious contexts with a strong normative belief-culture.) This fact notwithstanding, if RMB is supposed to be what it takes for the authentically committed religious practitioner to move *beyond* faith into genuine, living *religiosity*, it will be important to take the instrumentality and prudentiality concerns seriously, since many defenders of the religious life will likely balk at the idea that the truly religious individual is fundamentally calculating or self-centered in this way.

Importantly, however, this concern yet again applies to the faithful non-believer and faithful believer alike. Someone who believes that, say, God exists and the central propositions of their faith are true, but who commits herself religiously and adopts the *as-if* stance required for religiosity predominantly as a *means to some further end*—e.g., achieving some external reward or avoiding some harm (whether in this life or the next)—acts for equally instrumental and self-interested reasons. Like the professional athlete who has lost their love for the game (or perhaps never felt it in the first place) and engages in the sport solely to make money or achieve fame, they do not really *play*. For the athlete, the game is fungible and could just as well be any other game (or job, for that matter), so long as they are capable enough and the fiscal end result is the same. For the religiously committed—even, perhaps, those committed authentically in the sense that they "stand behind" or "reflectively endorse" their commitments in ways expressive of their core identity[8]—if their central reason(s) for pursuing the activity within the imaginative context dictated by a particular religious tradition are instrumental, then although they may religiously "pretend," perhaps even seriously, they do not *play*. They may thus display religious *faith* but not genuine *religiosity*. Someone pursuing religious participation solely to avoid damnation or pursue salvation may thus count as a person of faith, even perhaps authentic faith, but their faith can never (or only rarely) be transformed into religiosity. True, if the believing faithful think their faith is the only way to salvation—or if a particular faith is appropriately central to the identity of the non-believing faithful—the particular religious tradition or community will not, perhaps, be as easily fungible as the athlete's chosen sport. But if their reasons really are predominantly instrumental, they should be at least rationally prepared to convert should the exit costs be low enough and the prudential benefits of switching religions high enough.

Another way to think of the instrumentality issue in the case of religion is to consider Lebens' suggestion that the attitude central to holiness "is the antithesis of objectifying things" (Lebens 2020: 285). Lebens is here concerned with moral objectification in the context of Orthodox Judaism, but I think he is on to something regarding religiosity more generally. For the individual pursuing religion for instrumental reasons, religious participation and the activities it involves become *objectified*. They are a mere *tool* for pursuing some end independent of those activities that they care about. Still, it is important to see that the instrumental and the prudential can and do come apart. Even if they involve the objectification of religious practice and affirmation, not every case of instrumental religious participation need be centrally self-serving. The deconverted Muslim, for example, might commit herself predominantly out of filial piety. Another person might religiously commit for the sake of a spouse, a child, even an entire community.

At the same time, it would be strange—even for the authentically faithful—if genuinely religious subjects had *no* prudential reasons for religious participation or belonging whatsoever. This is significant because many defenders of religion also want to maintain that religion is or can be instrumentally "good" for people in various ways—both in this life and, within those religions whose imaginative contexts involve an afterlife, the next. And it would be unfair to insist that it is *always* religiously inappropriate to let those reasons (at least temporarily) take the driver's seat in a person's motivational and behavioral economy with respect to her faith. In other areas, to insist, say, that one's motivation for doing the right thing always be something like respect for the moral law or that one's drive to pursue philosophy be purely a matter of "love of wisdom" seems simply unreasonable.[9] Of course, this kind of "moral autonomy" or "intrinsic pursuit of wisdom for its own sake" can still stand as a kind of regulative ideal, provided one has the relevant psychological constitution and socioeconomic privilege of being able to take up and sustain the requisite attitudes for these stances and activities.

So it is, perhaps, with religious participation. We cannot always be moved by intrinsically religious reasons, so sometimes instrumental prudential reasons must be enough. But this is precisely part of what makes genuine religiosity so difficult. Taking up the particular *as-if* stance required by a particular imaginative religious context *and* simultaneously pursuing it, in some relevant sense, for the very sake of being able to enact that imagination itself is difficult—and it is one of the reasons many of us can experience the world under this aspect only fleetingly. For many of us, mundane reality breaks through too quickly, too easily, and we lose sight of the particular activity that partially constitutes the genuinely religious stance within that tradition. But this is where religious practice, especially religious *ritual*, can help. Even when operating under the guise of the instrumental and/or prudential, it can help us slowly but surely cultivate the relevant attitudes and capacities for taking up the make-believe stance that is part-and-parcel of religiosity.

Indeed, there is no contradiction in what we might call *practicing in order to play*. The athlete, the chess player, the pianist—to become any one of these kinds of players, one needs to learn *how* to play in the first place, acquire the skills to do so, and practice those skills (over and over) in order to become good enough to engage in the relevant kind of play activity. When one does this, one is often engaged in an instrumental project of *becoming a player* of a particular kind, and within this project, one might be motivated by all kinds of instrumental and prudential reasons (as well as further autotelic reasons). But these reasons can be channeled and directed by various forms of *ritual* and *transformed* into the kinds of attitudes, stances, and volitions necessary to play in the "right" kind of way.

I take this to be part of what is meant when Lebens talks about *striving to be holy*. While the play-activity itself might just *be* something like "enacting holiness," part of the striving is learning how to engage (within) the tradition, and this is bolstered by prescribed rituality. Howard Wettstein (2012) puts this well in his discussion of the cultivation of *yirat shamayim* in Judaism, or "the awe of heaven":

> We should remember, however, the magnitude and ambition of the project of facilitating *yirat shamayim*. While fixed prayer can and does degenerate into mechanical, unthinking, unfeeling performance, it offers great opportunities. [. . .] To engage regularly with [Biblical] literature—not merely to read the words but to declare them, to wrestle with them—is to occupy oneself with the project. Encounter with literature of such power, first thing in the morning for example, encourages the regularization of attitudes to which the literature so ably gives voice. Indeed, ritualization turns out to be a great virtue: we need not wait until the appropriate experiences present themselves.
>
> Wettstein 2012: 45

Here we see that engaging with holy words—reading, declaring, *wrestling* with them—can help individuals cultivate the right kinds of attitudes and stances, and to develop the right kinds of skills, to be able to engage skillfully and successfully (even if only temporarily), in the religious make-believe that enacts holiness.

So what kinds of play-activity can constitute religiosity, and what constitutes the lusory attitude religious "players" adopt? On my account, most generally, religious make-believers (whether of the RB or RNB variety) willfully and wittingly allow themselves to be guided and constrained by a cosmic narrative framework and its accompanying authorities, institutions, practices, norms, and propositions that collectively constitute the imaginative activity of existential meaning-making *just so the activity of existential meaning-making* can occur. That is, their particular form of RMB is a constitutive, non-fungible part of what it is to make existential meaning within a particular shared imaginative context.

This may take radically different forms, just as the things we classify as "sports" only loosely hang together in (at best) a cluster of family resemblances, though there may be specific aspects that make this kind of pursuit of existential hermeneutical understanding particularly religious, as opposed to other kinds of such meaning-making. Perhaps it is an enacting of holiness or the mutual recognition and creation of sacredness. Perhaps it is the fact that it institutes a cosmic narrative framework as opposed to some other sort of imaginative framework. My proposal is more mystical—that the meaning-making play-activity of RMB involves engaging in the kinds of imaginative make-believe that simultaneously turn one reflectively inward toward the self and actively outward toward the other (including the "Wholly Other")—where, if one achieves the lusory goal of such activity ("wins," perhaps, though I prefer alternative terms), the distinction between the inner and outer is ultimately *dissolved*. (I do not mean this as an annihilation of agency or absolution from responsibility. Rather, I mean something like the realization that one's self and interests are inseparable from the interests of others and that we are "bound" together in a shared divinity.) But I am not sure I even understand my own meaning here, and I suspect my own preferences for this kind of language are deeply informed by the shared imaginings one would expect from someone raised in the Christian tradition and currently immersed in late medieval mysticism. I therefore see the explication and delineation of the various forms that RMB (and alternative forms of existential meaning-making) can take as a comparative task for APR scholars from various religious and secular backgrounds to undertake together.

In any case, it is clear from what I have said that such activity can—indeed, must—be played with great earnestness. A "trifler" merely going through the motions is, to this extent, really only a "quasi"-player and does not exhibit the seriousness of the genuinely religious subject who is engaged in the kind of meaning-making that can only arise via RMB. They do not *care* about striving for holiness or cultivating a sense of the sacred or making existential meaning. (Of course, trifling can be a way of entering into the practices that can engender the kind of concern that might give rise to the lusory attitude.) Likewise, one must develop a sense for the "spirit" of the RMB in question and try to play accordingly. This has both an epistemic and an affective dimension. One must— by engaging with the tradition and the imaginative context woven within it— develop a careful *understanding* of both what one is doing and what is required of one to do it. But one must also cultivate a *respect* or *reverence* for such activity that motivationally underlies a commitment to playing in ways commensurate with that spirit. Finally, it should be clear from what I have said above that non-trifling religious play displays the kind of "existential earnestness" and all-encompassing "ultimate horizon" that "grips the whole of our being." It neither "objectifies," as Lebens puts it, nor does it relegate its objects to "the endless finiteness of [our] chains of means and ends," as Riezler warns against. RMB is, in this sense, truly religion at its highest and holiest.

Conclusion

In this chapter, I have tried to argue for the idea of RMB as the kind of playful pretense that can take a person beyond "mere" faith (which is difficult enough) to genuine religiosity. In so doing, I have motivated the claim that RMB is compatible with both RB and RNB. However, despite the fact that my doxastically permissive account of religious faith makes it significantly more inclusive and practice-oriented than the majority of approaches to faith in the APR literature, my account of RMB makes genuine religiosity more restrictive than might be expected, since—although it is open to people at all locations on the doxastic spectrum—the kind of earnest play set out above is, simply put, *hard*. It may be naturally easier for some individuals than others, but for most of us it takes significant training, practice, and dedication over time to be able to do regularly and well.

At the same time, there is also something simple and familiar about religiosity understood as a form of imaginative make-believe. As noted in Chapter 6, the term "make-believe" is often associated with the play of children. As we grow older, we often lose our sense of wonder and our ability for almost anything to be *seen as* something else, something *wholly other* than what it is. We are drawn into what Kurt Riezler called the "puny seriousness" of the everyday adult world of means and ends, in which all play becomes "mere" play. But religion can allow us to be "seriously gripped" by something *beyond* the mundane and to recover our child*like* (but by no means child*ish*) wonder at the world around us—to drop the "mere" and, as Plato suggests in the *Laws*, to "play the noblest games and be of another mind from what they are at present" (quoted in Huizinga 1949: 19).[10]

Notes

1   I am by no means the only philosopher who argues that sincere religious practice can and/or does involve make-believe. To take just a few recent examples, Robin Le

Poidivin (2020) speaks of "serious make-believe" as an option for the religiously motivated agnostic. In a similar vein, Carl-Johan Palmqvist (2023) has argued that the religious fictionalist participates in an "advanced form of participation-based fiction" in which they are "rationally required to role-play." Neil Van Leeuwen (2023) has recently published an entire book titled *Religion as Make-Believe* in which he argues that "one cognitive attitude that is both widespread and strikingly similar to make-believe imagining is religious credence, which is far different from factual belief" (97), though he ultimately thinks that religious credence is also theoretically distinct from make-believe imagining (172ff.). In the end, however, my account is most similar to that of Samuel Lebens (2020), whose account of religious make-believe I explicitly draw on here.

2   Although Lebens focuses largely on Howard-Snyder's account of propositional faith in his discussion of what he calls "sincere-frumkeit"—and although he characterizes faith as an *epistemic* attitude—he often speaks of "faith in" rather than "faith that" (see, e.g., p.279: "Sincere-frumkeit is what you have if you have faith in the tenets of your religion.") In fact, the way he talks about faith's role in sincere-frumkeit makes his view ultimately look much closer to my idea of authentic commitment than models centering mere hope or "right affect." Or perhaps my view of faith *just is* what Lebens is trying to get at with frumkeit. Whatever the case, his account is richer and more complex than I have room to spell out here.

3   On this point, see also Seligman (2010), who notes the importance of *ritual* as presenting us with an "opening to subjunctive worlds" enabling "a recognition of the ambiguous nature of empirical reality" and allowing for a kind of "play with different versions of reality" (23).

4   See Chapter 5 above.

5   Cited in Luhrmann (2020: 12).

6   For sake of ease, by RNB here I mean to refer to the cognitive orientation of anyone religiously committed in the sense for faith set out in Chapter 4 whose doxastic state does not meet the threshold for belief.

7   Note that whether we can *tell* the difference between authentically committed religious make-believers and deceptive religious pretenders is a different question than whether there *is* such a difference. In the context of everyday religious communities, we may not always be able to tell these individuals apart, and in many cases doing so would be both inappropriate and inefficient, especially given the cognitive heterogeneity of most communities at a time and most individuals over time, as discussed previously. In any case, I think we should be far more concerned about the "bad faith" of charlatan ministers preaching prosperity gospel to make gobs of money from their followers than about the non-believing (or even disbelieving) but authentically committed religious make-believers discussed here.

8 I am still unsure whether or not my authenticity criterion in Chapter 4 should preclude a faithful individual's committing themselves for instrumental reasons. If it does, then "authentic religious faith" will be much closer to "religiosity" than merely instrumental religious faith.

9 Compare the ways in which appeals to professional academics' "love of what they do" is often used by employers, journals, conferences, and funding bodies to exploitatively manipulate them into doing unpaid labor for the academy.

10 It is also, from within the Christian tradition, another way of interpreting Jesus's words in passages like Matthew 18:3: "Truly I tell you, unless you change and become like children, you will never enter the kingdom of heaven."

From Reform to Revolution

Playing the "Spoilsport"

On the one hand, when it comes to any particular religious tradition, many of the central concepts, objects, and propositions require the use of the imagination to be accessed and understood, regardless of where one's credence or level of doxastic confidence stands, and so make-believe is a natural bedfellow in the religious sphere. On the other hand, religion demands imaginings of the kind that push us to (and sometimes past) the limits of what we can successfully represent to ourselves in ways that can make regular and sustained make-believing of the religious sort a genuine challenge, even for the person of sincere, authentic, global faith as sketched out in Chapter 4. This is why we need useful models of the kind discussed in Chapters 2 and 3. Such models may not (always or even, in the case of God, ever) fully capture reality, but as we saw in the case of the enslaved Isabella's transformation into the civil rights activist Sojourner Truth in Chapter 5, the reasons for model preference will not, in most cases, be wholly epistemic, and sometimes models that theologians might characterize as inaccurate, syncretistic, heterodox, or even heretical can actually better contribute to religious understanding and human flourishing than those striving exclusively for "truth" or "orthodoxy."

In the case of Sojourner Truth, however, I do not think it unreasonable to maintain that *both* the ever-watchful, wholly sovereign, wrathful Master-God (who dominates over all creation and exacts vengeance on those who stray), as well as the compassionate, emancipatory, "far-near" Friend-God (who indwells in all of creation and is a divine witness to, compassionate companion in, and deliverer from suffering and injustice), are *consistent* with the purportedly omniscient, omnipotent, omnipresent, wholly just God of orthodox Christianity. That is, they both fall, for better or worse, within the historical "spirit" of the Christian meaning-making enterprise as it has been traditionally practiced. Yet the dominant model in Isabella's ante-bellum Southern-US context was God-as-master, and it was this model that needed to be resisted—from both an individual and a social standpoint.

It is for this reason, that religious communities must constantly be (re)negotiating the boundaries of the imaginative in their traditions and perhaps even the "spirit" of the play-framework itself. The good thing about make-believe is that, although it comes with rules and constraints, it is also eminently *flexible*. Indeed, problems tend to arise when players take their games, even their make-believe, *too* seriously. Although earnestness is important to certain forms of play to prevent it from falling into triviality and irreverence, such seriousness can also lead to a *deficiency* in playfulness, which can in turn give rise to a kind of "bad faith" amongst players, who are no longer willing or able to see that the game is socially constructed and agreed upon—and could be reimagined, reformed, or even transformed into something else entirely.

We can say something similar concerning the "earnestly playful" activity within particular RMB-frameworks. Although the content of a religious tradition is deeply informed by already-existing historical and contemporary social-imaginaries that play a central role in setting the confines of which imaginings and behaviors are considered appropriate or permissible (the "rules of play," as it were), religion is at the same time a *dynamic* and *living* social activity, one that is constantly being reiterated and renegotiated in the intersubjective ritualistic and discursive spaces in which it takes place. Religiously make-believing is, therefore, more than just standing imaginatively in some relevant relation to static and rigid "things-already-made." It is a matter of being actively engaged in a creative, interactive process of *things-in-the-making* (Ockman 2000). Or, to echo Hans Vaihinger's seminal work on "the philosophy of *as-if*," we might claim that the religious imagination is best associated, not with the Latin noun *fictio*, but rather with the verb *fingere*—with the activity "of constructing, forming, giving shape, elaborating, presenting, artistically fashioning" (Vaihinger 1935: 81).

In this vein, I suspect that religious traditions and communities that have become devoid of a certain kind of imaginative playfulness are more likely to fall into a kind of *bad faith* and to become rigid and dogmatic in ways that make participants prone to falling into intellectual vices and traps that could themselves have detrimental consequences. For example, C. Thi Nguyen (2022) argues that some belief systems persist, not because they are truth- or understanding-conducive but because they are "sticky" in ways that epistemically "trap" participants into preventing those within the system from seeing or acknowledging good counterevidence or viable alternative perspectives.

One potential antidote to epistemic traps, Nguyen suggests, is cultivating the virtue of what he calls *intellectual playfulness*. Intellectual playfulness gives us the freedom to "try out new perspectives for fun" (Nguyen 2022: 277) and to "explore ideas unconstrained by the need to optimize for truth every step along the way" (281), as opposed to merely entertaining alternatives under the constraints of our current epistemic and imaginative frameworks, which—to again channel Wittgenstein—often "take us captive" without our noticing. Its autotelic aspects—including the fact that such "random intellectual walks," as Nguyen calls them, are simply *enjoyable* for many rational inquirers—allow intellectual play to "directly motivate epistemic agents to explore the space of possibilities, sometimes leaving behind considerations of plausibility" (282), and this can make room for the exploration of perspectives "that their current background beliefs treat as beyond the pale" (281).

Given the potential of religiously committed communities to both create and fall into epistemic traps, those concerned with defending the epistemic respectability of religious commitment would do well to encourage the cultivation among such communities of a kind of "meta-playfulness" that allows for the adoption of intentionally playful attitudes regarding the very imaginings that constrain their discourse and activity. In some cases, this may involve "playing the gadfly" and intentionally introducing playful-yet-disruptive "epistemic frictions" or "resistant imaginings" like those discussed in previous chapters, which can function to challenge overly comfortable imaginings and their enactment within the relevant paracosm. In others, reflecting "just for the sake of it" on alternative religious perspectives, allowing them to "resonate" and creatively mix with one's own experience, can open up spaces for increased insight, understanding, and innovation even with respect to one's own preferred perspective. The cultivation of such intellectual playfulness by itself might not ward off all tendencies toward intellectual vice (and, as Nguyen points out, it brings with it some risks of its own), but adding it to one's repertoire of intellectual skills and habits can shore up one's resistance to epistemic traps and the kind of intellectual close-mindedness that sometimes accompanies the convictions (and committed imaginings) we care deeply about.[1]

At the same time, as we saw in Chapter 6, the mere fact that one's activity is playful does not a virtue make. The phrase "we were *just* playing/joking/messing around" most commonly functions to serve as an excuse, not seldomly for bad behavior. And in cases where genuine harm has been caused by the play in question, such excuses do not exculpate. (This is especially so if, as Riezler might put it, the activity is no *mere* play.) Thus, in cases where the imaginative framework itself, the concepts and discourse employed within its scope, or the way that those concepts are imaginatively enacted are *self-undermining*, *harmful*, or otherwise *detrimental* to those participating in and/or affected by the play, the very play-activity under discussion may require disruption.

This latter kind of disruption may require a different kind of Suitsian "quasi-player" than the "trifler" we encountered previously. The trifler, as we saw, abides by the constraints of the play-context but cares little about bringing about or accomplishing the activity made possible by such constraints. The *spoilsport*, on the other hand, rejects both rules and intra-lusory goals—that is, their activity centrally disrupts or undermines the very activity itself. I think there are (at least) two kinds of spoilsport: the kind who "spoils" the play by simply *failing to care* at all about the play-activity in question or its rules, and the kind whose behavior actively *calls into question* the value of the particular play-activity itself or the way it is conducted. The former is often just a nuisance.[2] The latter, however, is a threat to the very activity itself (and any institutions grounded in it). Yet such threats can be crucial to play-contexts—especially when, say, the way a play-activity has evolved comes to undermine the integrity of that activity, or when the very "spirit" of the activity itself needs to be interrogated.

In the religious realm, "theological spoilsports" may help aspiring and actual religious (make-)believers see the ways in which their tradition, its models, and its institutions are *not* just "fixed givens" and how they might indeed be fruitfully revised, reformed, or even rejected in favor of alternatives. (Even if it's true that God exists and is unchanging, this by no means entails that our ways of accessing and understanding the divine must remain static!) Historically, some theological spoilsports are remembered as much-needed "reformers," others as condemnable "heretics." Some were lionized, even canonized, others burned, exiled, or excommunicated. (And given the vagaries of history, not a few were burned first and celebrated later.)

Of course, spoilsports are not merely of consequence in how religion proceeds on the ground. They are also important in those disciplines that take religion as their subject matter. I think it especially incumbent upon those of us theologians and philosophers—whose job it is to explore, elucidate, interrogate, and even, perhaps, improve upon religious imaginings of religious traditions—not only to adopt an intentionally and earnestly playful attitude with respect to the relevant religious imaginings that are treated within the scope of the scholarly discourse, but sometimes to call into question the very spirit of that discourse altogether. Sometimes, even if an academic discourse can be characterized as "playful," it is not *appropriately* so, as when the kind of play in question is harmful to those it affects or when it undermines its own integrity and intra-lusory aim.

This kind of "spoilsportsmanship" is my aim in the final two chapters of this book, where I will raise concerns about the kind of "ivory-tower play" engaged in by APR scholars in their discussions of *theodicy*. While the tone of Chapter 8 will be significantly more serious than one might expect from someone who professes to be engaged in play, the seriousness will be necessary here in order to show how one favored form of approaching the problem of evil and theodicy is itself a kind of *merely* "playing around" with ideas—one that, like "locker-room talk" or other forms of dangerous play cannot be excused by mere appeal to its playful aspects, or to its separateness from ordinary life. Chapter 9, then, will return to a spirit of earnest playfulness by drawing creatively on medieval mystagogical literature to develop a different mode of discourse, one that promises to make the discipline of APR more inclusive, less harmful, and more responsive to those who genuinely *need* its deliverances.

Notes

1   We might even consider the possibility that intellectual playfulness can help ward off intellectually vicious forms of resilience in cases of propositional and objectual faith.
2   Of course, ceasing to care about the rules and goals of a play-activity may itself be a way of pointing out the absurdity or lack of value of that activity. (On this point, see the 1999 film *Office Space*.)

Part Three

Revolution

8

Beyond Theodicy

Faith-shaking Trauma and the "Purely Intellectual" Approach

Content warning: This chapter contains frank discussions of pregnancy and pregnancy loss a warning about what's coming.

The kind of scholarship that is not ultimately edifying is precisely thereby unchristian. Everything specifically Christian must resemble in its approach the doctor's bedside manner: even if only medical experts understand it, it should never be forgotten that it is occurring at the bedside of a sick person. [. . .] [It should be] qualitatively different from the kind of scholarship that is "indifferent," whose lofty "heroism" is so far from Christianly heroism that it [rather resembles] a kind of inhuman[e] curiosity.
Søren Kierkegaard, Preface to The Sickness Unto Death

"Oh me, what am I like? I am not like this earth, for the earth produces its fruit in season and blesses you, Lord."
Anna's lament, Protevangelium of James 3:8

Introduction

In this book, I have appealed to epistemic, practical, and social considerations to make a case for "looking beyond" in analytic philosophy of religion (APR). In this chapter, I want to bring some additional moral and pastoral dimensions to bear on the discourse in APR—though, as we shall see, these are themselves tied up closely with epistemic, practical, and social concerns in ways that should give pause to philosophers in APR (even those pursuing more "traditional" or "mainstream" approaches).

I should begin this chapter by granting that, despite the immense value of public-facing work, it is wholly unreasonable to demand that everything produced within the sphere of a discipline be accessible to laypersons or scholars outside the discipline. There is always a degree of distance between experts and non-experts, and it is usually appropriate for the experts to discuss matters at a shared level of understanding, especially within research contexts. At the same time, in addition to thinking about the benefits of our inquiries to us as theorizers or to the ongoing discourses within the discipline itself, as professional philosophers[1]—that is, as those kinds of academic experts who explore for a living the underlying features of reality, the contours of our lived experience in the world and in relation to others, and the possibility of living good and meaningful lives in the context of that experience—I think we also acquire special moral obligations vis-à-vis the public at large that might not apply to all members of the academy.[2] I therefore maintain that we also have a special responsibility to take into careful consideration:

- the *subjects* of the discourse (i.e., those whose experiences provide the impetus, input, or data for our philosophizing) and our respective *positionality* vis-à-vis those subjects;
- the *recipients* of the discourse (i.e., those to whom our ideas and ways of talking about them are addressed and/or communicated); and
- the *impact* of our discourse (i.e., the perlocutionary effects our discussions are likely to have on others).

In other words, we need to ask ourselves who and what we are philosophizing *about*, who our (intended and actual) *audiences* are, and who might plausibly end up being *affected* by our discourse, whether or not they are a direct recipient of it.

Importantly, this means thinking not only about the content of our discourse, but also about *how* we conduct it. If it should turn out that either of these aspects of our discourse is likely to cause more harm than good[3] for those concerned, then we should think very carefully about the wisdom of continuing to engage in it as we do. Therefore, in what follows, I will argue for a more "care-full" approach to doing philosophy in general and to doing philosophy of religion in particular—one that thinks as much about impact as it does truth, as much about concern as it does correctness, and as much about leaving the world better than we found as it does winning arguments or getting more publications, citations, clicks, or followers.

To illustrate my point, I will attempt to "play the spoilsport" regarding a common approach in APR to addressing the problem of evil and the accompanying discourse surrounding *theodicy*, as it is a topic regarding which our philosophizing not only takes the real-world experience of living creatures as its subject matter but also finds a significant audience and influence beyond the academy, whether we like it or not. In this chapter, drawing on insights from the discussion of objectivity set out in Chapter 1, I will explore the ways in which I take APR's current approach to theodicy to be epistemically and morally *dangerous*, both impeding important forms of existential, experiential, and religious understanding of the kind I discussed in Chapters 2 and 3 and preventing us from addressing and responding appropriately to real people in the real world whose experiences of real evil present them with a challenge to the kind of faith-constituting religious commitment I talked about in Chapter 4. Along the way, I will briefly discuss and respond to a few objections raised by APR scholars who wish to continue doing "business as usual" and, I will suggest, against APR's relatively defensive approach to theodicy (i.e., as yet another challenge for theism that the "rational theist" must counter), that we can find more compassionate philosophical approaches that are both theoretically and theologically viable, as well as morally and epistemically preferable to what we currently encounter in mainstream APR. With the support of some ideas from late medieval German mysticism, then, the final chapter of this book will draw on some of the insights from Chapters 5–7, in order to playfully but earnestly explore how such alternative approaches might be developed.

A note to the reader: In this chapter I will discuss my own experience of miscarriage as a way to help explain my ideas a bit better, since (a) I find concrete examples are always helpful to make somewhat nebulous ideas more accessible, and (b) some of my interlocutors seem to think my concerns involve a kind of moral self-righteousness, grandstanding, or straightforward "rudeness," when my concerns really live in a much darker space. For example, in a recent response to the single (very short) paper I have published on this topic (Griffioen 2018), Perry Hendricks writes: "My response to [Griffioen's arguments]? In short: Oh, please." He continues: "If you think my short response is rude (or whatever), I can't imagine how rude you must think it is for proponents of moral anti-theodicy to respond to theodicy by claiming it's immoral!" The footnote to this comment reads: "Isn't it a convenient position that those you disagree with are immoral?" (Hendricks 2023: 5).

I suppose this might be convenient (though sad) if that's what I was claiming.[4] I will admit that I can see how, despite their best intentions, the arguments of moral anti-theodicists can sometimes feel a bit "*ad hominem-y*" to those who prefer to stick with the *status quo* mode of theodicizing. I therefore want to emphasize at the outset that, in making theodicy-critical comments grounded in moral, social, and epistemic concerns, I am neither trying to shut down conversation nor to say anything about the characters of mainstream theodicy-"stans," and I do not I think I do so anywhere in the text Hendricks cites. Perhaps that article was too brief—or maybe the overall thrust was not clear enough to grasp—but my intention, both there and here, is neither to malign the character of any particular philosopher or group of philosophers, nor to reject the theodical enterprise altogether. Rather, my aim is to point to the ways in which I take certain modes of current theodical theorizing to be (actually, not just hypothetically) epistemically and morally *dangerous*, both to the well-being of those who suffer and to ourselves as philosophical theorists, such that we would do well to look for alternative approaches.

Thus—and this is apparently worth stating explicitly—even when I use examples from particular philosophers below to make my point, I by no means presume (nor intend to imply) that they and their ilk are bad people with bad intentions. Moreover, as I say below, I am not claiming that any or all theodical approaches are *false*, let alone that they are false *because* their proponents are immoral. I tend to believe, or hope anyway, that most philosophers of religion are pretty OK people and that we as a discipline could, if we made a concerted effort, do *better* theodicy. The problem I am raising in this chapter has to do with the fact that we—and here I mean all of us (myself included)—often fail to reflect on how our ways of speaking and philosophizing can both do harm to others and make us worse off as moral and epistemic agents, and it is these meta-philosophical worries that concern me here.

Additionally, as will become clear, I flat-out disagree with Hendricks that "theodicies in academia are typically carefully enough talked about that these worries aren't relevant" (7), and I hope that my reflections below on miscarriage can help show that my concerns are not a matter of unreasonable "pearl clutching," as he maintains (8). Rather, they point to something that negatively affects real people—both within and outside the profession—and which thus might be worth taking a bit more seriously. (I take up Hendricks' somewhat less flippant comments in my discussion of objections below.)

It is also important to be clear at the outset that, *pace* Hendricks, I do not take the mere attempt to reconcile theism and evil to be morally problematic, and unlike some anti-theodicists I do not reject all attempts at theodicizing. In fact, I am not sure that we *can* escape theodical reasoning altogether. We certainly cannot avoid wrestling with the problem of evil if we are to remain morally and theologically responsible philosophical theists. As Marilyn McCord Adams, never wholly without her pastoral hat on, rightly noted:

> Many [...] participants in horrors, sooner or later, not at every stage but eventually, over and over, raise questions of *meaning* [...]. They demand of *us*, their friends and counselors, not only that we sit *shiva* with them, but also that we help them try to *make sense* of their experience. [....] Delicate and perilous as this assignment is, participants in horrors themselves often thrust it upon us. Philosophical reflection on horrors *takes up the challenge.*
>
> McCord Adams 1999: 187–88, emphases mine

Importantly, though, genuinely taking up this challenge presumably involves searching for an approach that does not do *additional* moral or epistemic damage—both to those to whom we are responding and to ourselves as epistemic and moral agents—and this, as we shall see, is where I am less disposed than Hendricks to let the discipline off the hook. Still, while I will be largely critical of how APR tends to proceed with respect to theodicy in this chapter, I do intend for my approach here and in the next chapter to be remedial, not an outright rejection of philosophical theodicizing. In this sense, Hendricks and I agree that my worries "are objections to *careless* theodicy, not to *careful* theodicy" (7). However, I'm pretty sure moving to a more careful theodicy will take a bit more effort and consideration than (to take his somewhat sardonic example) adopting the "rule of thumb" (!) that we shouldn't hand out copies of Swinburne's *Providence and the Problem of Evil* at children's hospitals (8). In Chapter 9, therefore, I will discuss one way of thinking about how APR might go about taking its task of careful theodicy more seriously.

Theorizing about theodicy: the "theodical" terrain

I will assume for reasons of brevity that the reader is familiar with the problem of evil in its traditional (logical and evidential) formulations.[5] Quite obviously, there are various ways to spell out the problem, depending on the kind of evil one focuses on and how one divides up the moral terrain. For my purposes here, I want to focus specifically on the evil suffered by those human persons who have undergone some form of *faith-shaking trauma* (hereafter, FST).[6] An experience (or set of experiences) is traumatic to the extent that it, as Judith Herman (2015) puts it, "overwhelms the ordinary human adaptations to life"

(33), and it is faith-shaking when it presents enough of an existential disruption to cause an otherwise authentically committed religious subject to seriously consider abandoning their religious commitment as a result of or on the grounds of their suffering.[7] FST can involve experiences of the kinds of "horrendous," "appalling," or "radical" evils discussed in some of the APR literature, but it may also include the cumulative experience over time of less obvious stressors or structural injustices that ultimately end up overwhelming a person with respect to their faith—for example, the suffering undergone from a severe or chronic physical and/or mental illness/injury that prevent one from going on as before, the witnessing of/to the suffering of others (including such horrors as animal suffering, global pandemics, or ecological devastation) that simply becomes too much for someone, the accumulated experience of discrimination or microaggression in one's religious community, a sense developed over time that one is powerless in the face of the evil and injustices of the world, and so on. Although I think my argument would still hold if we restricted the class of persons concerned to those who have undergone horrendous suffering of the extreme kinds typically referenced by philosophers, I want to extend the scope of my concern to cases like the above in order to counter the common excuse given in these contexts that the affected group is relatively small.[8] That is, while I think the effect of traditional theodical discourse in APR on those who have undergone what most anyone would recognize as extreme traumatic suffering should already be enough to make us hesitate regarding the way we conduct such approaches, it will not do to respond that the class of those affected is so small as to not warrant genuine change on our part.

I do not have the space here to go through the dominant theodical approaches in any major detail but I tend to think about them in terms of five broad categories, which I have characterized thusly with respect to human suffering:[9]

- *"it's-our-fault" approaches*—explain some or all human suffering as either punishment for or the logical/metaphysical consequence of human sin or (abuse of) free will, either our own or others' (e.g., our ancestors')
- *"big-picture" approaches*—assume that God (necessarily or voluntarily) creates the best possible or most God-feasible world, and that world is *our* world, with all its suffering—or that there is otherwise some other larger "picture" or "plan" we cannot see that explains the existence of evil
- *"character-" or "soul-building" approaches*—view human adversity and suffering in general as important or necessary for the cultivation of certain higher-order goods or virtues (e.g., compassion, empathy, personal or

spiritual growth, etc.); relate suffering to the greater human good that can come from it

- *"relationship-building" approaches*— claim that experiences of suffering, while bad, can also be occasions for coming to experience divine intimacy, feeling God's presence, or otherwise drawing closer to God through hardship; relates human suffering to the opportunities for divine-human relationships that can arise from or be strengthened by it

- *"skeptical theist" approaches*— maintain that, given the limits of our finite human cognition, we should not expect to be able to identify or understand God's reasons for permitting evil (or even, perhaps, to comprehend the *nature* of divine reasons in the first place), but deny that our inability to justifiably locate a morally sufficient reason for evil is a compelling reason to reject theism.

Two things are noteworthy here. First, perhaps with the exception of skeptical theism, in each of these types of approaches, the evil in question is transformed into something no longer straightforwardly gratuitous. On such accounts, although the suffering that results from such evils may still be admitted to be subjectively bad, in theodicy it is generally transmuted into either an instrumental good or an unfortunate byproduct. Even in the case of skeptical theism, which does not itself provide an explanation that would constitute a morally sufficient reason for the divine to permit the intensity or magnitude of the human suffering we encounter in the world, the assumption seems to be that there *is* such a reason, and if we were in an epistemic position to occupy the God's-eye perspective, we would be in possession of that reason. In this sense, theodical approaches, even if not explicit about it, often focus their efforts on defending a form of classical perfect-being theism by concluding that human suffering is *not*, contrary to our experience, gratuitous (or that we are in no epistemic position to conclude that it is).

Second, and perhaps even more significantly, note the way the problem has come to be treated in these approaches. In contrast to Elie Wiesel's play, *The Trial of God*, in which—drawing on true events Wiesel claims to have experienced in Auschwitz[10]—three *Purimschpieler* put God on trial after arriving at a village recently destroyed in a *pogrom*, in APR it is no longer *God* who needs justifying to the religiously faithful. Instead, the discourse has, yet again, largely shifted to a justification of the *belief* of the (classical mono-)theist to the atheist. One might counter here that in practice this really amounts to the same thing. That is, the same arguments we can use to justify God against human accusations of maliciousness, complicity, apathy, or neglect can be used to defend human beings against the critical arrows of the atheist. This may well be correct—at least on some ways of framing things. But it does not change the fact that the issue has been transformed into a largely *theoretical* problem, while losing sight of the deeply *religious* struggle that motivates it. As Charles Kielkopf put it, the question becomes one of trying to figure out how someone could rationally "accept propositions to the effect that there is [such] evil in a world created by an all-good and all-powerful God," rather than the specifically religious problem "of bringing oneself to call God good while living amongst the pain and suffering of [God's] creation" (Kielkopf 1970: 34).

Of course, in many contemporary societies it is certainly the case that unbelief is a live option (or, in some places, even the norm). However, I would venture to say that, for the large majority of religious adherents who have undergone FST—even if they might sometimes wonder whether their theistic belief is warranted, or whether they should "adjust their credences" given their experiences—their central concern is not really about whether or not they are rational, let alone about whether the atheist challenger is being unfair or unreasonable. Their concern is not to combat militant atheism, and they likely won't be satisfied with a "for-all-we-know" kind of answer. Rather, the issue for them is deeply *practical*, even *existential*, and it comes with serious personal and theological consequences. For example, theologian Karen O'Donnell reports her own difficulties with worshiping in the aftermath of her repeated miscarriages (O'Donnell 2022: 95), and she observes the need of many women struggling with reproductive loss to seek out "a safer theological space of which to be part" (211–12) than those typically offered them by churches employing versions of the theodical approaches mentioned above (and the views of divine providence associated with them). Absent such spaces, such women are likely to cease worshipping altogether. Here, the problem is not merely a theoretical issue or a concern about rational (in-)consistency. It is a problem of *deconversion*—and this should give any APR scholar interested in defending and preserving theism (let alone "putting butts in the pews") a reason to pay attention.

Here I do not mean to imply that theistic philosophers interested primarily in the theoretical question do not also have a deeply vested existential interest in the answer, nor that the theoretical problem is irrelevant to the religious problem. It is theologically important, and philosophers have expertise that can be useful in answering it. But it is also important to note that those who investigate the theoretical question predominantly in order to "combat" the atheist—to "win" the "contest" over who is or is not (more) rational—seem to be engaged in a different activity with a different target audience than someone who is concerned with the question from a primarily religious standpoint.

Still, what's the problem? Why can't theistic philosophers interested in *that* project just remain in their isolated corners of academia as they do battle with the atheist or competing theistic views via dueling publications or by participating in yet another podcast or live debate between a prominent (usually white, male) theist and an equally prominent (also usually white, male) atheist?[11] To understand the force of the worry, we need to consider the ways in which APR's proceeding as usual has *real potential to do real harm to real people*. I will therefore proceed with a brief, partly autobiographical reflection on miscarriage to explain from a more personal perspective how traditional theodicies are often experienced as insufficient for addressing the person who has undergone a particular form of FST. I will then go on in Section 8.3 to claim that the discursive and addressive *mode* of much of APR's theodical theorizing—by means of which much of the content of such theodicies is derived and/or elucidated—runs a real risk of doing moral and epistemic damage that might outweigh the overall epistemic benefits potentially gained from such an approach.

A brief interruption: some reflections on miscarriage and theodicy

Spontaneous abortion, also known as miscarriage, is for many people with wombs the kind of bodily and psychological trauma that can shake someone's religious commitment to its very core. (It certainly shook—and still shakes—my own.) At the same time, it is also remarkably common. If you yourself have not experienced a miscarriage over the course of your sexually active lifetime, chances are very high that you have relatives, colleagues, and friends who have. Of those who know they are pregnant (and are thus in a position to potentially experience their loss as an occasion for grief), the rate of miscarriage is as high as 1 in 5.[12]

Despite its frequency, however, miscarriage is commonly associated with some *failure* on the part of the miscarrying person, not least in religious contexts. For example, in addition to imputations of acting unsuitably (e.g., failing to do the appropriate "pregnancy-promoting" things or to abstain from any and all of the myriad of *potentially* pregnancy-threatening activities), persons who have lost a pregnancy are often implicitly or explicitly charged with failures to *know correctly* (e.g., not recognizing they were pregnant earlier or failing to take a pregnancy test soon enough), to *feel appropriately* (e.g., feeling overly stressed or anxious, failing to be hopeful or optimistic) or *to will sufficiently* (e.g., not wanting it enough, not praying hard enough, or failing to have enough faith in God). Yet the large majority of miscarriages, especially those that occur early in a pregnancy, are due to genetic or medical causes over which the pregnant person has no control (Bardos et al. 2015; Melo et al. 2023). Thus, if one will excuse the pun, misconceptions about the causes of miscarriage abound.[13]

These misconceptions, and the culture of blame that surrounds them, often lead women and other persons capable of getting pregnant to construct harmful narratives of self-blame to explain their losses, even as they simultaneously experience a debilitating and demoralizing lack of control over their own cramping, bleeding, and tissue-passing bodies in relative isolation within a society that doesn't talk about pregnancy loss (Layne 2003). The collective silence concerning miscarriage also renders it largely invisible on the public and pastoral levels, not to mention in intellectual spaces. As one respondent in Millicent Feske's study of infertility and pregnancy loss noted, people often "don't understand the deep emotional scars, fears, and death of dreams" that accompany even early pregnancy loss (Feske 2012: 3.1). The phrase "death of dreams" here illustrates well the simultaneously backward- and forward-looking grief of miscarriage. One grieves not only the life that was lost, but also (or especially) the loss of an entire future—of an imagined person (the child), identity (mother/parent), and relationship (parent-child) that one had come to desire, hope for, or anticipate. As Alison Reiheld puts it, "the person who has miscarried is in the archetypal situation of 'no-longer' and 'not-yet,' for she will never parent the child who might have been" (Reiheld 2015: 11).

In religious contexts, a baby is often viewed as a blessing conceived with the help of the Divine. In the Hebrew and Christian Bibles, as well as in the Qur'an, for example, God is represented as being able to "open" and "close" wombs, and "barren" women pray to God for children.[14] In most of these narratives, their petitions are eventually answered (usually positively), and little mention is made of the repeated losses the women in question undoubtedly endured or the toll it may have taken on both their bodies and their minds, apart from the distress they express over being unable to bear their husbands a male heir. This deeply engrained idea of pregnancy as a sign of God's favor or a promise fulfilled—and infertility as an absence of divine blessing (Warner 2019)—means that even today there are very few social or religious scripts for dealing with pregnancy loss (O'Donnell 2022; Reiheld 2015).[15] It should come as no surprise, then, that women from these traditions who miscarry would turn to theodicies to help them make sense of their losses. However, as Feske notes from her interactions with her interviewees: "The classic answers of Christian theodicy are rarely experienced as satisfactory or helpful by those who are searching for answers to the conflict between traditional understandings of God and their personal experiences of loss and emptiness" (Feske 2012: 3.2).

Similarly, Nicole Johnson (2014), after interviewing several Christian laywomen who had undergone miscarriages, notes that her interviewees displayed a significant tension between, on the one hand, affirming the standard theodical approaches they encountered, and, on the other hand, feeling strong cognitive and emotional discomfort with the idea that God must will or have good reasons for allowing their miscarriages. In fact, when asked to elaborate, each of the interviewed women ultimately tried to revise the "standard" theodical position presented to them by their churches with respect to their own losses. Johnson emphasizes that the tension these individuals exhibited toward theodical approaches cannot just be chalked up to the stereotype of the grieving-woman-as-irrational. Rather, she claims, it is indicative of a larger confusion or inconsistency that "runs rampant through lay Christian perspectives on suffering." Yet these "lay perspectives" are not seldomly themselves inspired by the philosophical theodicies pushed by many APR scholars.

Feske's and Johnson's observations track my own experiences of pregnancy loss. As a philosopher who came up in the analytic tradition, I had long been able to take up the intellectual and imaginative stances demanded by APR-style theodicizing, and I could run the arguments. I could abstract away from my own experience and imagine wild "for-all-we-know" possible worlds that could wiggle me out of various formulations of the theoretical problem of evil. But, especially after my struggle with infertility and pregnancy loss, such approaches proved wholly inert in my cognitive and behavioral economy. Despite being familiar with the dominant philosophical theodicies in the APR literature and able to take up all the relevant intellectual stances, I still could not see how to reconcile *these* losses in *this* world with the God whom *I* was supposed to love and who was supposed to love *me*:

- "It's-our-fault" theodicies simply reinforced the implicit, neoliberal accusation implicit in much Anglo-American-European fertility culture that if *I* wasn't "producing," then *I* must somehow be to blame (e.g., miscarriage as the result of my lack of sufficient faith or a punishment for an earlier induced abortion). Lapsarian theodicies made me ask why *I* specifically had to bear the reproductive damage of someone *else's* mistake when others didn't. Free will defenses either collapsed into lapsarian theodicies or made me wonder why, if human free will was such a great good, it was a good closed off to *me* with respect to deciding what happens in my own womb, not to mention a good refused to the human being I wanted to bring into the world to enjoy such freedom.

- "Big-picture" theodicies initially made some sense of the gross inefficiency of human reproduction considered as a natural evil. Perhaps, even though it seems implausible, it couldn't nomologically have been otherwise in the best world that it was feasible for God to create. But it still didn't help me understand why *I* had to be one of the unlucky "super-inefficient" ones with a womb first opened, then closed.

- I didn't come to feel "closer" to God or more "intimate" with Jesus, nor did I think it was appropriate to try to use or view my miscarriage as an "opportunity" to do so.

- Neither could I see it as being in any way necessary for my "personal growth" or for "edifying my soul," and I resented the implication that if I *didn't* grow from it I was somehow psychologically or spiritually "deficient." Further, even if I *have* personally grown from what I have made out of my experience—and even if I *did* have my "rainbow baby" in the end—the suggestion that this should somehow "explain," "justify," "cancel out," "make good," or even "defeat" my pregnancy losses is repugnant to me.

- I will admit that considering my epistemic limitations helped a little at first. Maybe God's reasons are so radically beyond my ability to comprehend them that I should just "trust" that God had my "best interest" in mind or "had a plan for me." However, skeptical theism's suggestion that I doubt my own experience of pregnancy loss as a genuine (non-gratuitous) evil ended up feeling less like an invitation to intellectual humility and more like gaslighting. Moreover, if the nature and scope of God's reasons are so radically different from my own and so radically outstrip my ability to comprehend them, why should I assume God is the kind of being who has *reasons* like ours at all—let alone reasons for *my* miscarriage—or who *cares* (in a way continuous with or analogous to the way humans care) about my well-being? Reflecting on the divine's radical transcendence ultimately served mostly to amplify my sense of God's hiddenness—to alienate me from, not reconcile me with, the divine. If there was any comfort in this view, it was simply that perhaps God doesn't care about *anyone*.

These concerns persist in my mind today, and I still find it difficult to worship in a tradition that barely acknowledges my kind of pain. Moreover, in the time that has passed, as I came to realize just how common pregnancy loss actually is, it made me think about all the pregnant persons of faith (including Scriptural examples) who have grappled individually with similar problems *in the particular* as I have, and how they, too, lack(ed) the cultural and theological scripts to find their way back into society and back to faith. How many reproductive people struggle with faith like I do but don't talk about it, and for how many more struggling individuals do the theodicies they encounter from their communities (whether in person or online) only serve to add to their pain and *smother* their search for understanding? How many people find themselves, like me, unable to self-honestly accept or defend such theodicies—and for how many of them, does this inability *estrange* them from both their God and their religious community?

Miscarriage is one of a vast range of FSTs that make people's lives on this earth qualitatively worse in ways that alienate them from their faith and threaten to extinguish their commitment. I can only try here to convey how the content of many traditional theodicies can be insufficient to assist women and other persons with a uterus with just one of these religious problems or help them repair or recover their faith. For my part, I must admit that it is hard for me to see how, even if one or more of these theodical approaches should actually turn out to be *true*, that this would really make much of a practical difference to those of us struggling to maintain a relationship with the divine and a sense of religious commitment as they wrestle with broken bodies and minds in what *presents itself to us* as a broken world.

Of course, this reflection does not show that the kind of scholarship that will genuinely help religious strugglers like me with their faith really ought to be the concern of the theistic philosopher. I suggested above that many APR scholars putting forward theodical approaches in the largely theoretical mode seem to be engaged in a different project than those for whom the religious problem is immediate, pressing, and deeply existentially weighty. Certainly, these two projects can sometimes converge, but quite often they do not, with philosophical theodicists taking a page out of the "not-my-job" playbook and maintaining that their theodicies are simply not intended *for* the religious struggler at all. That is, they want to do *purely* intellectual philosophy—to theodicize in such a way that neither addresses nor takes particular sufferers into account, except insofar as the type or magnitude of their experiences of evil constitutes the data necessary to generate the problem in the first place. In the next section, I want to talk more about why I think the way theodicy is done in APR not only *fails to help* religious strugglers, it is actually epistemically and morally *dangerous* to all concerned. That is, there is a very real threat that such theodicizing will make both those who have undergone FST and those who theorize without addressing them *worse off* in the long run, regardless of "whom" such theodicies are intended for.

Doing damage? The dangers of the "purely intellectual" approach

I want to begin with an example from one prominent proponent of the approach I am critiquing here, who at least does his audience the favor of making explicit what many APR scholars merely assume.[16] In his heavily influential book on the problem of evil (developed from his public Gifford lectures), Peter van Inwagen (2006) claims that, although it would be "stupid and cruel" of him to give his kind of philosophical response to the problem of evil to a mother who has just lost a child, asking a philosopher to develop a more "suitable" approach for such audiences is simply too demanding:

> It is asking too much, it is asking the wrong thing entirely, of a philosopher's or theologian's response to the argument from evil, to ask that it be suitable reading for a mother who has lost a child. But if one cannot ask, one can at any rate hope, that it will be suitable reading for a pastor whose duty it is to minister to people in situations like hers. [. . .] I will not, in these lectures, try to say anything to bring that hope to fulfillment. It is not, in my view, advisable to try to do that sort of thing. [. . .] The task I propose for myself is a purely intellectual one.
>
> van Inwagen 2006: 11–2

Let us call van Inwagen's preferred philosophical approach to the problem of evil (and those approaches similar to it) the "purely intellectual" (or "PI") approach. To avoid any unnecessary confusion, allow me to first state my points of agreement with what I think van Inwagen is saying here and what *doesn't* follow from them.

First, I do not think the attempt to transform the discourse surrounding the problem of evil into a purely intellectual enterprise of the kind van Inwagen describes is a self-defeating project. That is, I don't think that van Inwagen and his like-minded theodical ilk are trying to do the impossible in taking up a PI approach, even if (as discussed in Chapter 1) they may sometimes overlook how the influence of socio-ethical-political concerns on their epistemologies might violate their own standards of intellectual "purity." However, even if taking up a

PI stance is *possible* with respect to theodicy, it is a further question as to whether it is morally or epistemically *advisable*.

Second, I agree with Van Inwagen's assumption that analytic philosophers of religion are not generally the best people to dispense advice to those who have suffered FST. They usually have little to no pastoral or therapeutic training, and it is good to be wary of overreaching where one has no expertise. However, this does not entail that the PI approach is the only way for philosophers to proverbially "stay in their lane." Although its professional demographics might tell a different story, philosophy is a remarkably diverse enterprise, and despite APR's preference for the PI mode of discourse, this does not mean we cannot locate alternative (potentially less dangerous) approaches from elsewhere in the discipline. Or, if we can't, nothing says we can't undertake the project of developing them ourselves.

Finally, I agree that it would be good if there were something in PI approaches that could be useful for those members of religious communities who do have the requisite pastoral training. However, we should ensure that this proviso is not just another way of excusing ourselves from our moral and epistemic responsibilities toward them. It is not enough to merely "hope," as van Inwagen does, that there might be something useful in one's intellectual work for the "appropriately-trained" pastor while simultaneously refusing to consider the mother who has lost her child—especially since, as Bethany Sollereder points out, "the usefulness of the book to the pastor is almost wholly determined by what *can* be said to the grieving mother" (Sollereder 2021: 384).

Moreover, especially in an increasingly connected world, it is not unlikely that the mother herself might stumble across such theodicies on her own, especially if those she leans on for spiritual guidance lack the theological scripts necessary to assist her. Even if the grieving mother is not intended (or, in this case, intended *not*) to be the audience for such arguments, collateral damage is still damage, and when it is done to those who have already undergone serious suffering, philosophers cannot excuse themselves by simply making of it a "potentially foreseen but unintended consequence"—nor can they distance themselves from it by simply failing to see it. In fact, if there is reason to think that APR theodicizing in the PI mode runs the risk of promoting intellectual vices that reduce theorizers' ability to see and take seriously such suffering, then just as we are responsible for combatting the other epistemic and moral vices that we fall prey to, we are responsible for genuine vigilance and self-work (not just lip service) in this respect too.

Indeed, it will not do to simply assert that theoretical theodicies are simply not *for* the religious struggler who has undergone FST or to reiterate that the PI theodicist is "merely" trying to counter objections to theism. Confining philosophical discussions to scholarly contexts does not shield suffering individuals from encountering these discussions. To begin with, FST touches many *within* the academy itself, so restricting one's discussion to scholarly contexts is not particularly likely to keep those affected by FST out, unless it is stipulated that those who are struggling religiously bracket their concerns in pursuit of the "purely intellectual" project. (I suspect not a few scholars find themselves in this position, and I address this gatekeeping problem below.[17]) In my own case, it happened more than once that, when I asked what a scholar's particular theodical approach would make of someone who had suffered pregnancy loss, the response went something like, "Oh, of *course* we wouldn't say this to someone who's just had a miscarriage"—when, of course, they just had.

As concerns erecting a sort of "barrier" between those inside and outside of the academy, it is worth noting that the metaphor of the "ivory tower" is (and always has been) a somewhat infelicitous fiction, especially with respect to the ways philosophical theology has consistently bled into the religious life and vice versa. Religious institutions and leaders, historically and today, have drawn deeply from the well of philosophical theodicies in their sermons and pastoral work, and the prevalence of theodical discourse in online podcasts, videos, discussion forums, and social media makes them easier than ever to find for someone who is looking for answers.[18] In the end, not only does the PI approach fail to remain in the ivory tower, that tower is (in some ways for better, in some for worse) in the process of being deconstructed. Therefore, even if philosophers like van Inwagen refuse to directly *address* religious strugglers who have suffered FST, it does not follow that such strugglers are unlikely to be downstream (or even direct) *recipients* of such theorizing.

To repeat, the mere fact that philosophers *can* take up a PI stance with respect to the problem of evil, does not mean they *should*. Yet in many circles and settings (including the typical Western philosophy of religion classroom), APR appears to simply assume that treating theodicizing as a purely intellectual activity in the service of purely intellectual ends is unproblematic and, presumably, *harmless*. What I want to show is that this assumption is by no means self-evident. Indeed, if there is reason to think that theodical approaches of this kind are epistemically or morally dangerous—that is, if they run the risk of doing real harm without countervailing benefits—then that might count more than a little against doing theodicy in the PI mode. Moreover, even if philosophers should end up concluding that this way of proceeding is epistemically and morally *permissible*, there remains the question of whether an alternative approach might not be *preferable*. If so, the traditional APR theodicist will have to seriously consider whether their preferred way of doing things is, in fact, theologically valuable enough to just continue on "as usual."

In the end, we may not have duties to directly minister to the mother who has lost a child with our philosophical theorizing, but it seems reasonable to think that we have at least indirect duties not to engage in theorizing that is likely to cause her (or us) further harm. And even if not morally demanded, if we do really care about the suffering of the mother and those like her, an approach that provides *some* beneficial hermeneutical resources for such individuals may be a morally preferable form of philosophical theorizing to that which would produce something "stupid and cruel" if uttered directly to them.

It is thus worth looking a bit more closely at the kinds of harms PI theodicizing risks causing. As stated above, I do not wish to impugn the moral character of anyone who engages in theodicizing in the PI mode. Instead, as noted, I want to talk about the *threat*, both epistemic and moral, that such theodicizing poses— not only to others but also to ourselves as philosophical theorizers. I maintain that the PI approach runs a serious risk of inflicting three significant categories of damage that call for a reevaluation of the approach, even perhaps by its own standards. First, such theorizing can cause epistemic and moral harms to those who have undergone traumatic suffering. Second, it may promote intellectual and moral vices in the theorists themselves. And third, it has the potential to undermine the integrity of the very project of theodicy itself by doing damage to the discipline. In what follows, I lay out each of these dangers in more detail.

Damage to those who suffer: epistemic injustice, gaslighting, and the erasure of morally significant evil

I maintain that the PI approach seriously risks committing *epistemic* and *moral harms* against those who have suffered FST in at least three ways:

Intellectual exclusion and testimonial silencing

First, there is the preferred methodology that is taken to largely constitute the PI mode of inquiry. We have already seen that theoretical theodicists often think it important to distance themselves from real, existent suffering, preferring abstract and impartial approaches to the problem and implicitly reinforcing the idea discussed in Chapter 1 that such cognitive distancing is necessary to achieve the "objectivity" demanded by the "rigorous" level of philosophical discourse. In such arenas, emotion and subjective experiential investment are often seen (perhaps rightly[19]) as having the potential to destabilize such discourse. However, the injunction of such an approach to regard the problem from a universal and impartial standpoint also threatens to *depersonalize* and *neutralize* the particular and personal testimony of those who have genuinely suffered FST. It does so by only granting a seat at the theoretical table to either those individuals who largely enjoy the "luxury of ignorance" (Medina 2013b: 31) regarding such forms of suffering and can thereby easily distance themselves from them, or those who are able and willing to "academically dissociate" from their own experiences of FST and to regard them from a cognitively abstract and affectively dispassionate standpoint.

This can serve to create an insular epistemological framework for theodical discourse in which the testimony of anyone from outside the theodical "bubble" who is unable or unwilling to sufficiently abstract away from their own experience is not taken seriously. Such a demand, as Ian J. Kidd has pointed out, "is apt to distract attention away from the empirical realities of suffering, not least the social identities of the sufferers, thereby occluding the testimonies and experiences of the sufferers" (Kidd 2017: 391). It thus threatens to perpetrate what are sometimes called *testimonial injustices* against those who have undergone FST, effectively "add[ing] silencing to the experience of suffering" (391). In addition, insofar as being silenced or not taken seriously can compound one's suffering by reinforcing feelings about not being "worthy" of having a seat at the discursive table, it can also lead to what Kristie Dotson calls *testimonial smothering*, or "the truncating of one's own testimony in order to insure that the testimony contains only content for which one's audience demonstrates testimonial competence" (Dotson 2011: 244).[20] And insofar as someone who might have the courage to challenge the dominant view gets shut down or excluded in such ways, it might feel like a form of intellectual belittlement bordering on outright *humiliation*.[21]

Hermeneutical lacunae and the erasure of evil

Second, the abstract transmutation and universalization of the concrete "bad things" experienced into "necessary evils" in the service of some "greater" (but largely unknown) good, "unfortunate byproducts" of a fallen world, or disguised "opportunities" for individual spiritual or moral growth, can function to epistemically *gaslight* those who have undergone FST by calling their encounters with evil into question and undermining their sense of innocence and unjust suffering in a way that ultimately alienates them from their own experience. Theodical approaches that make evil unrecognizable even to those who have experienced it first-hand threaten, therefore, to perpetrate additional *hermeneutical injustices* against those who struggle with FST by contributing to already-existing conceptual lacunae and gaps in understanding that prevent the latter from being able to adequately conceptualize and speak about their experiences—and this, in turn, can make their testimony continue to appear non-credible to theodical theorizers.[22]

Morally, many anti-theodicists have already noted the ways in which the perlocutionary effects of theodicizing in the PI mode listed above function either to essentially *erase* the badness of the morally significant evil suffered or to implicitly hold the individual *responsible*, if not for their suffering itself, then for failing to grow or to come closer to God by way of that suffering. Such approaches might make room for belief in the "omni-God" of traditional perfect-being theism, but they do so by failing either to condemn the source of suffering as genuinely evil or to preserve the innocence or non-culpability of the individual who undergoes it. Importantly, this is not just a matter of "disinterested" or "dispassionate" scholastic abstraction; it also involves an *unwillingness* to consider the negative impact and even re-traumatizing potential that such theorizing may have on those who actually suffer.[23] And this does significant disrespect to the fundamental dignity of those past and present individuals who have undergone FST (see, e.g., Betenson 2016; Trakakis 2008).

Addressive neglect and withholding of output

Third, the unwillingness of APR scholars to *address* those who have suffered FST (or to even consider them as proper recipients of their discourse) might perpetrate a further kind of harm to those who struggle with FST, namely that of "removing any sense that it is relevant or imperative to attend to them" (Kidd 2017: 391). In refusing to take up the entreaty discussed by McCord Adams above that we help those who have undergone FST make sense of their suffering, this kind of *addressive neglect* can do further moral damage by implying that those engaged in "intellectually rigorous" theodicizing simply don't care about them (except insofar as their suffering is abstractly utilized to get the problem of evil off the ground).

However, addressive neglect also has two significant epistemic implications. To begin with, it is an additional way of restricting who is allowed to contribute to the *production* of potential theodical knowledge—this time excluding religious strugglers, not in their capacity as straightforward testimonial givers of knowledge but rather as *fellow inquirers*, as agents capable of epistemic cooperation with the theodical project. Such exclusion is, ironically, often motivated by the idea that such individuals are incapable of the "right" kind of epistemic receptivity to the theodical approaches developed in the PI mode. That is, given their "special" experiential situation (as sufferers of FST), they are not in a position to be able to appreciate the "insights" of the theodical enterprise in the first place and therefore are in no position to contribute to it. And this is, as Ben Kotzee (2017: 329) has pointed out, a denial of a particular kind of epistemic credibility, namely that required for the successful *uptake* of knowledge. In this sense, insofar as it explicitly intends to create a barrier between those who theorize and those who might be negatively impacted, the proposed PI approach to theodicy might border on what Carla Camona describes as a "[withholding of] epistemic output as a result of wrongfully assessing a hearer-to-be's epistemic capacity" (Carmona 2021: 578).

Damage to those who theorize: intellectual and moral vice

Even if one is inclined to dismiss the concerns raised in the previous section, it is not only the wellbeing of those who have undergone FST that is at risk here. The methodological appeal to abstraction and neutrality in the service of the PI approach to theodicizing also threatens to promote intellectual and moral vice in theodical theorizers themselves. On the one hand, when scholars abstractly "filter out" the actual perspectives and social identities of those who suffer in the interest of developing solutions to the problem of evil, they run a significant risk that those remaining in the intellectual "room" will come to have distorted beliefs or narratives about what it means to suffer in that way. That is, in their pursuit of the mere *possibility* of theistic knowledge or rationality, they might distance themselves so far from *actual* suffering that they fail to grasp what is genuinely at stake when it comes to the problem of evil.

On the other hand, when the debate does admit the voices of those who suffer but implicitly expects of them a distanced neutrality with respect to their experience—or when it superimposes upon their suffering a universality that belies that experience—it yet again runs the risk of failing to take their expertise in the relevant domain seriously. Both ways of proceeding are apt to foster a kind of *epistemic arrogance* of the kind discussed in Chapter 1 by yet again reinforcing the confusion between the dominant and the default perspectives and continuing to propagate the idea that the loudest, most visible, or best funded voices in the discipline—or those with the highest educational credentials and scholarly "prestige" behind them—are, in fact, the most "objective," "impartial," and "universal" ones, and therefore the ones best-positioned to weigh in on the theodical debate.

Now there are clearly aspects in which their intellectual training in logic and argumentation make philosophers epistemic authorities of a very particular kind, but this expertise will not always (or perhaps even commonly) go hand in hand with authority on *the experience of traumatic human suffering*, and these two dimensions should not be confused. I am thus concerned that the presumption in the PI theodical enterprise concerning who will be doing the speaking about evil, who is being addressed, and who being asked *neither* to speak *nor* to consider themselves addressed might give rise to both a kind of "meta-insensitivity" to the theorizers' own epistemic weaknesses in this domain and perhaps even to a degree of *epistemic disdain* for those outside the philosophical community. Theodicizing in the PI mode can, as Katherine Dormandy puts it, lead to a lack of receptivity "to the idea that certain people outside [one's] own belief-forming community have anything to offer epistemically" and a failure "generally to take them seriously as interlocutors" (Dormandy 2022: 8). This, in turn, can lead to a paucity of diverse perspectives in the PI theodical literature, which can again reinforce the idea that the dominant perspective is the only relevant one and further entrench theorizers in forms of disciplinarily-sanctioned intellectual vice.

These manifestations of epistemic vice can also easily give rise over time to a more pernicious form of intellectual corruption, namely what Dormandy calls *epistemic cold-heartedness*, or "not caring about other people's epistemic aims, so that, to the extent that it is in your power to help them meet these aims (and not an unreasonable burden on yourself), you nonetheless decline to" (9). The explicit refusal of scholars theodicizing in the PI mode to address the existential need for understanding and the inability to find meaning that lies at the core of the problem of evil as confronted by the religious struggler can foster such cold-heartedness and further isolate them from real suffering in the real world—and thereby from the very *reality* of the "bad things" that cause such suffering.

This cluster of intellectual vices can easily bleed into one's moral character as well, especially insofar as it might lead one to demonstrate a lack of *concern* and *compassion* for those who have undergone traumatic suffering, assuming one can still see such suffering at all. Given what we saw above about the ways theodical approaches can harm such individuals, we have good reason to believe that continually reasoning about evil in this manner—i.e., taking a prescriptively abstract and disaffected approach to explain evil away in defense of a particular form of perfect-being theism—could morally *desensitize* individuals (and entire groups) to genuine evil and make them less inclined to *act* to counter it. Put a bit differently, insensitive, indifferent, or unsympathetic discourse can, over time, make us insensitive, indifferent, and unsympathetic people.

Returning to van Inwagen, he (to his credit, I suppose) recognizes that it would be "abysmally stupid and cruel" to follow his "first inclination" and say to the mother who has lost a child to leukemia:

> But you already knew that the children of lots of other mothers have died of leukemia. You were willing to say that [God] must have had some good reason in those cases. Surely you see that it's just irrational to have a different response when it's your own child who dies of leukemia?
>
> van Inwagen 2006: 10

If what I have said above is plausible, then perhaps the insight here should not be that we should restrict our discourse to exclude those whom such an answer might hurt but rather instead to question the very nature of the discourse that makes us "have to bite back an impulse" to respond with "abysmally stupid and cruel" things in the first place.

Overall, the theodical approach in the PI mode can be harmful to the character of theodicists themselves, insofar as it contributes to the vicious tendency many of us in positions of relative socio-economic privilege already have both to ignore suffering in ways that make us unable to see it and to engage in practices that further desensitize us to its badness—or what German theologian Dorothee Sölle (1973) labeled *Verdummung* and *Desensibilisierung*. And if a certain discursive practice is likely to make us less, not more, sensitive (epistemically and morally) to the suffering of others—especially when the reality of their suffering is what underlies and enables our discourse in the first place—then we must think very carefully about whether such a practice is worth it.

Damage to the discipline: intellectual theodicy and the threat of theoretical irrelevance

Finally, as suggested earlier, I worry that the PI approach places itself in an artificial epistemic bubble that excludes the kinds of diversity of perspectives and epistemic frictions necessary to make real progress on the problem of evil itself, even by the standards of those who endorse such an approach. There are a few ways in which epistemic insularity threatens the theodical enterprise that are worth mentioning here.

To begin with, the demand for impartiality and universality in APR can serve a disciplinary *gatekeeping* function that ends up (further) marginalizing relevant voices and interests. We have already seen the ways in which this can serve to exclude those individuals (among them scholars) who have actually undergone FST and are unable or unwilling to divorce their lived experience and interests from their thought about evil in the way demanded by the impartiality-culture of APR. Yet it would be a somewhat odd result if a debate that takes human suffering and pain as one of its key data points were to be framed in such a way that the voices or concerns of those who suffer did not really end up *mattering* much to that debate. Moreover, it seems to be closing the discipline off to important perspectives that could make it more, not less, epistemically perspicuous and thereby potentially lead to innovative theodical methodologies and approaches that are both more compassionate *and* theoretically satisfying. This, as Michelle Panchuk remarks, "distorts the results of our philosophical inquiry [such that our] theories end up incomplete at best, and false or positively harmful at worst" (Panchuk 2019: 56).

Moreover, in its attempt to remain in the realm of the "purely intellectual," theodical discourse in APR tends to largely eschew the more particular and perspectival contributions of other disciplines in the humanities, as well as the empirical deliverances of the social and natural sciences. It thus not only largely ignores many genres of literature, theater, film, and poetry which provide human beings with alternative modes of imaginatively articulating and reflecting on the problem of evil, it also inadequately engages with the valuable insights of scholars in religious studies, anthropology and sociology of religion, neuroscience, psychology, medicine, and related disciplines. Yet it could be immensely helpful to APR to engage with these disciplines on this subject. Likewise, and perhaps even more importantly, additional interaction with those engaged in explicitly pastoral work and spiritual care (e.g., ministers, chaplains, social workers, counselors, coaches, etc.) could forge new pathways for theodical inquiry going forward.[24] Finally, more *comparative* work between members of various religious traditions and global backgrounds would also be welcome in this vein, as philosophers search for important points of resonance and genuinely innovative approaches that go beyond merely making one more minute move in a game intended for only a few.

The objection from modal weakness and the demand for data

There is much more to be said here, but given the limited amount of space I have, it is perhaps worth looking at a few objections before I turn in the next chapter to the question of *how* APR might go about reorienting itself in less harmful directions.

As one proponent of objections I commonly hear in the discursive space of APR, I would like to again take up Perry Hendrick's summary dismissal of moral anti-theodicy, of which he (mistakenly) takes me to be a proponent. His main criticism rests on my use of words like "might" and "may" when making claims about the harms that certain forms of theodicizing *can* cause. Whereas my attempt was to refrain from making overly strong claims that are clearly indefensible (e.g., "every instance of theodicizing in this mode contributes to the cultivation of this vice" or "theodicies of this kind harm all individuals who have undergone FST"), Hendricks seems to transform my (perhaps overly cautious) rhetoric into a claim about *conceivability*. He claims in response that it's also *possible* by not practicing theodicy in the PI mode, some people *might* end up convinced by the atheist argument from evil, convert to atheism, (thereby?) become moral antirealists, and then (as such?) become insensitive to the suffering of others (Hendricks 2023: 6). Similarly, with respect to epistemic harms, he claims that "we might tend to become overly gullible, or [. . .] harm ourselves as epistemic agents by walling off any investigation into whether there are (or could be) reasons God has for permitting evil, or we might flout a general epistemic duty to pursue truth" (7). He then goes on to maintain that "these arguments *at best* merely show that we should be careful when talking about theodicy, not that we shouldn't do it at all" (7). However, his central worry regarding my use of modally weak language seems to be that it is an *empirical* question whether theodicy in the PI mode is actually harmful to those who suffer and that I have not produced sufficient evidence to show that the harm I point to is more likely than the just-so story about the dudes who become insensitive, anti realist jerks because philosophers didn't do theodicy. "[Critics of philosophical theodicy] give no data to back up their claims," he writes, "nor do they consider potential harms that come from not practicing theodicy, nor do they consider different methods of theodicy that would make it unlikely any harm would result" (7).

Let's take these concerns in order. First, the claim that my arguments merely show that we should be more careful about how we do theodicy, not give up the theodical project altogether, is not an objection; that's my view. However, I strongly suspect Hendricks and I differ in what careful and compassionate theodicy looks like and how easy it is to accomplish. He claims that "when practicing theodicy, we could remind ourselves about the very real suffering in the world and that we should work to alleviate it. *This isn't hard to do*." Likewise: "we can *just* change how we practice theodicy to reduce or eliminate any threat of moral insensitivity there may be" (6–7, my emphases). Perhaps, for Hendricks, real-world suffering is easily kept present to the mind while engaging in abstract philosophical reasoning. I, for my part, am not always so virtuous. From my relatively privileged perspective as a white, middle-class, cisgender, English-speaking, US-American expat scholar in Europe, it takes significant mental and emotional effort for me to both recognize and take seriously the reality and extent of creaturely suffering in the world, let alone to non-self-deceptively commit myself to combatting it in ways that can make an actual difference. If the arguments I have made in this chapter are at all plausible, and there is a real need for reform to our theodical discourse, I find it highly unlikely that APR will, with a snap of its collective fingers, "just" be able to change how it practices theodicy overnight. To hearken back to the interlude that preceded this unit, it will take a concerted effort of imagination, earnest playfulness, and philosophical innovation that, as I will suggest in the next chapter, we are unlikely to be able to accomplish on our own.

Second, I agree with Hendricks that whether or not theodicy in the PI mode is harmful to those who have undergone FST is, at least to a certain degree, an empirical matter. This provides yet another good reason for increased collaboration with researchers in the psychological and social sciences, as well as those involved in pastoral and palliative care, counseling, therapy, and social work to develop empirical studies surrounding theodicy and spiritual, psychological, and bodily well-being.[25] But this is all in addition to really trying to *listen* to the voices and testimony of those scholars and non-scholars who have struggled with their faith in light of trauma and to *hear* their complaints. *Even* if it should turn out, as Hendricks supposes, that "it's dubious to think they're credible sources when making claims about whether their suffering is all-things-considered permissible or unlikely given theism" (7), *and* it's true that they lack justification for claiming that there is "axiologically gratuitous evil" (see Chapter 9 of Hendricks 2023)—and *even* if we stipulate that the FSTs they suffered and the persistent struggles that follow them will actually be defeated in the "life to come"—such individuals will nevertheless likely be the some of the most credible sources we have on the way our theodical discourse affects their subjective well-being in *this* life, and it seems like that should count for something. In any case, it might be worth asking them, if one is not ready to go to the lengths of reading the extensive extant literature and autoethnographic research being done in fields like feminist, queer, and liberation theology, research on spiritual trauma, and the like.

At the same time, there will be serious limitations to what we can measure here. If relying solely on self-reporting questionnaires, we may run into a different problem of reliability than Hendricks anticipates, namely that religious strugglers belonging to particular traditions in which conviction is strongly normed might be hesitant to report anything that contradicts their tradition for fear of what it might mean for the state of their faith or salvation. Likewise, we will also have to distinguish between perceived or subjective senses of well-being and more objective accounts of human flourishing and figure out which kind of well-being we can and want to control for. A lot therefore depends on getting clear about what exactly we are trying to measure and how we go about measuring it. This is true both for critics like myself who are claiming PI theodicizing is harmful for many who undergo FST and for those appealing to data concerning the benefits of such theodicizing, as is becoming more common in the linking of soul- or relationship-building theodicies to the psychological research on post-traumatic growth.[26]

An additional concern is that it is often extremely difficult to detect testimonial and hermeneutical injustices, since they result in a *lack* or *gap* in testimonial sources of evidence and the conceptual resources needed for such testimony. As Dotson points out, "the burden of proving the practice of silencing can appear impossible to meet," especially in cases of testimonial smothering, "which may not admit of witnesses" as readily as other forms of silencing (Dotson 2011: 251). If there are such gaps, we might not expect them to show up in certain kinds of quantitative self-reporting studies, and we may need other methods (e.g., autoethnographies, behavioral studies, physiological measurements, qualitative studies conducted in safe pastoral settings, etc.) to detect them.

All this is to say that the "empirical" question(s) under discussion would need an entire interdisciplinary research program to even *begin* to tackle this issue properly. Until then, we are left with individual, often fragmented or incomplete pieces of testimony and our philosophical methods (which need not involve the abstraction and insular seclusion of the PI mode). The question, then, comes down to how great the potential is that theoretical theodicizing of the kind APR tends to engage in will do genuine damage—including further damage to already vulnerable individuals—as well as the extent of that potential damage, whether it is outweighed by the purported benefits of theodicizing in the purely intellectual mode, and whether there might not be a more consider-ate and care-full way of thinking about theodicy that is less likely to run the risk of such harm. I suspect that Hendricks and I have different intuitions about the likelihood and extent of potential harm; I hope that my personal and philosophical appeals here have made my perspective on the matter a bit more plausible. For my part, I would need to hear more on what the *upshot* of PI theodicy is, whom it is likely to benefit, and why it is more like the virtuous form of imaginative play that leads us *out* of epistemic and moral traps (Nguyen 2022), as opposed to the harmful play of activities like "locker-room talk" that preserves privilege and further marginalizes and hurts the vulnerable.

In any case, if we are really concerned to "change how we practice theodicy to reduce or eliminate any threat of moral [and, we may add, epistemic] insensitivity," this will have to involve an extended, collaborative effort on the part of APR scholars and a willingness to take the meta-disciplinary claims seriously. Merely "demanding the data" from theodicy-critical scholars like myself and refusing to consider genuine alternatives until one has conclusive data in hand would appear more like an attempt at sea-lioning—or even, perhaps, an implicit *noseeum* inference (i.e., concluding from APR's failure to *recognize* evidence for theodical harm that there probably is no such evidence)—than a good-faith attempt to consider what those like myself wrestling with FST are trying to say. It is thus my sincere hope that this is only the beginning of a meta-disciplinary conversation, not the end.

Conclusion

Ultimately, by failing to include, engage with, or address relevant voices and disciplines, APR's pursuit of the PI theodical project closes off avenues on all sides for important religious (and theodical) understanding. It thereby severely restricts the actual epistemic perspicuity of the intellectual theodical enterprise itself, limiting its ability to make plausible that its potential for epistemic benefit outweighs the risks of its causing additional epistemic and moral damage to the parties involved, let alone to track the truth. If the limited doxastic and alethic profits of the PI theodical strategy are outweighed or undermined by the likelihood of actual harms, both epistemic and moral, that it may cause, then we have good reason to reconsider such an approach—or at least to open it up to those it has traditionally excluded.

Notes

1 I am sensitive here to the fact that many professionally-trained philosophers find themselves without (full-time, stable) jobs in academia, and as someone currently preparing to leave the full-time academic grind, I wholly embrace the idea that one can be a "professional" philosopher without being occurrently employed *as* a philosopher in academia. As far as I am concerned, independent researchers, unemployed academics, philosophical counselors, and all those with the requisite training for whom doing philosophy constitutes (or would constitute, if employed in their field of choice) a significant part of their professional lives fall under the "professional philosopher" umbrella.

2 Personally, I think the first three points here apply to *all* academic disciplines, but whether or not one agrees with me on this, I think philosophers (and perhaps the humanities at large) need to be especially "care-full" and "consider-ate" in these regards.

3 My use of "likely to cause more harm than good" here is an unfortunate but expedient shorthand. I am hesitant to appeal to solely consequentialist considerations, first, because (at least amongst some philosophers) this often leads to being pulled into a series of abstruse Bayesian calculations and minute philosophy "moves" that rarely help us with decision procedures in the actual world. Second, I think some of the central harms we need to take into account involve, for example, whether certain central deontological considerations like respect for the dignity or integrity of persons are violated, whether the discourse is likely to hinder rather than promote the cultivation of moral, intellectual, or spiritual virtue, and so on. However, if someone in the meta-discourse insists on translating this into consequentialist "philosophy speak," I'd be inclined to appeal to a form of sophisticated value-adjusted possible-consequence utilitarianism here, combined with a form of value pluralism that allows for the incorporation of the relevant deontological and virtue-theoretic considerations.

4 It does, however, seem pretty convenient to simply dismiss one's opponents by performatively rolling one's eyes in print. (This is one reason I am hesitant to even discuss this passage here. But because it is so indicative of the kind of responses I receive from a certain faction of theist APR scholars when presenting on this issue, it seems prudent to address it.)

5 For an overview, see, e.g., Peterson (2017); Tooley (2019).

6 In what follows, I will generally use the present perfect tense "has/have suffered," but I here also mean to include the present progressive "is suffering," since the kind of suffering brought about by FST is a diachronic phenomenon and can continue even when mitigated to some extent by other factors.

7 If one is uncomfortable with expanding the term 'trauma' to cover the kinds of cases discussed in this chapter, one may simply substitute the term "experience" for

"trauma" where appropriate and think about FS*E*s, not FS*T*s. I prefer the word "trauma" because it tends to imply a significant caesura or break in one's self-narrative, even if that caesura ultimately ends up later being "closed" or otherwise incorporated into that narrative. (Note, however, that incorporation into a self-narrative is *not* necessarily the same as an evil's being defeated!)

8   In fact, I think many of the experiential aspects of the COVID-19 pandemic can serve as reminders of how various "smaller" evils can, in certain circumstances, "chip away" at one's faith or otherwise become so disruptive and overwhelming that they end up undermining someone's religious commitment.

9   This is obviously not the only way of parsing up the theoretical terrain. Bethany Sollereder, for example, divides what she calls "classical theodicists" into two camps—*instrumentalists* and *individualists*. The former argue "that evil in an individual's life can be redeemed by being part of some greater good," whereas the latter claim "that each individual who suffers must find their own redemption or compensation" (Sollereder 2021: 383).

10 "[The play's] genesis: inside the kingdom of night, I witnessed a strange trial. Three rabbis—all erudite and pious men—decided one winter evening to indict God for allowing his children to be massacred. I remember: I was there, and I felt like crying. But there nobody cried" (Wiesel 1995: 1). See also *Jewish Chronicle* 2008.

11 I write this with not a little irony, but the question of "keeping it in-house" is one I very frequently encounter in some form or another when I suggest that we ought perhaps to "slow our theodical roll" in APR. I moreover seldomly hear women or non-white voices in the more visible spaces where these intellectual debates between theists and atheists tend to happen. (It is also worth noting here that the very fact that these podcasts and public debates are intended to be maximally *visible* actually undermines the defense that philosophers should just "keep it in the academy" and show the ways in which they, too, ultimately want their work to be public—even, perhaps, "viral.")

12 A *modest* estimate of the rate of pregnancy loss between fertilization and birth ranges somewhere between 40 and 60% of all pregnancies (Jarvis 2016).

13 A 2013 survey reports that, of 1,084 valid respondents (male and female) in the United States, 22% of all participants (falsely) believed that that lifestyle choice was the single most common cause of miscarriage (a belief that men were 2.6 times more likely to hold than women). Moreover, of the 160 respondents who reported a history of miscarriage, 47% reported feeling guilty and 41% reported feeling they had done something wrong (Bardos et al. 2015).

14 Compare Jacob's angry response in Genesis 30:2 to Rebecca's desperate exhortation, "Give me children or I shall die!": "Can I take the place of God, who has denied you fruit of the womb?"

15 One exception is the relatively modern Japanese Buddhist ritual of *mizuko kuyō* commemorating lost fetuses, in which the *mizuko* [水子] ("water child") is thought to go from the water of the womb to a more "original" liquid state in the other world, preparing it for rebirth. In many cases, statues of the traditional protector deity of children, *Jizo*, are erected at Buddhist temples or at special parks and playgrounds dedicated to the *mizuko* (Garcia and Brind'Amour 2007).

16 For additional examples, see Sollereder (2021).

17 I also suspect that some philosophers of religion tackle the problem of evil precisely *because* they have undergone some form of FST or have witnessed such suffering. That philosophical engagement of this kind can be therapeutic, I do not contest. (In some senses, it is for me, too.) What I resist is the requirement, whether explicit or implicit, that one approach this in a "purely intellectual," impersonal, abstract, and impartial manner. (I am also skeptical that the philosophical puzzling involved in this mode will be genuinely helpful to someone struggling religiously, but I suppose that is an empirical matter, as I discuss below.)

18 ChatGPT, for example, answers the question of why a loving God would allow my miscarriage by simply listing various philosophical theodicies.

19 The question is whether such a destabilization would be a bad thing. As I suggested earlier, I think such "disruptions" can place important and beneficial checks on powerful discourses.

20 What kind of "audience failure" (see Ramler 2023) is involved in these cases and whether it corresponds to the kind of pernicious testimonial incompetence discussed by Dotson is worth further discussion. For a plausible argument that APR's preferred methodology does lead to testimonial smothering in Dotson's sense and harms those in the discipline who express emotion or vulnerability in their philosophical engagement, see Panchuk (2018), whose concerns largely parallel my own here.

21 While epistemic *humility* is to be encouraged on all sides of a discourse, as comedian and author Hannah Gadsby (2018) has rightly noted, when self-deprecation comes from "somebody who already exists in the margins [. . .] it's not humility; it's humiliation."

22 On hermeneutical injustice in the context of religious trauma and spiritual violence, see Panchuk (2020). See also the recent work Panchuk and Hereth have been doing on the connections between traditional theodicy and gaslighting.

23 Neither of these need be *logical* implications of the view. It suffices that the discourse or its message contribute to an already-existing culture of, say, blaming the victim, making it even more likely that individuals will draw such conclusions. Compare, for example, Panchuk's description of listening to APR defenses of penal substitution "with shaking hands, racing heart, and tears welling in my eyes" (Panchuk 2019: 69), a feeling I know all too well in theodical contexts that make me feel blamed for my pregnancy losses all over again.

24 Compare here the more pastoral theodical approaches developed most prominently by John Swinton (2018).

25 This is currently research I am currently trying to get off the ground with respect to pregnancy loss and theodicy. Wish me luck!

26 For a critique of Eleonore Stump's attempt to link theodicy and the post-traumatic growth literature, see Panchuk (2024). For a critical diagnosis of the contemporary research on post-traumatic growth and a corrective proposal for future research programs, see Brady and Jayawickreme (2023).

Beyond Closure?

"Re-mystifying" Analytic Philosophy of Religion

*The third path is called a path and yet is a [kind of] being-home. [. . .] How
wonderful it is to be standing within and without, to grasp and to be grasped,
to see and to be that which is seen, to hold and to be held: That is the end,
where the spirit remains at rest in the unity of loving eternity.*
Meister Eckhart, Sermon on Mary and Martha

It is bad to begin many things and to bring none to an end.
Henry Suso, from the *Life of the Servant*

Introduction

The goal of this final chapter is not to weigh in on the evidential status of theistic
belief in the God of perfect-being theism, nor to provide a new theodicy. Rather, it
is an attempt to provide one possible conceptual *framework* for how to begin
developing more compassionate philosophical responses to the problem of what I
have called "faith-shaking trauma" (or FST)—responses that look beyond concerns
of mere rationality to meet human beings in the midst of their struggle and to
collectively pursue the project of reconciling the life of religious faith with the very
real effects of suffering. Such a project will need to address more than the cognitive
lives of religious believers. It must, as Michelle Panchuk (2019) puts it, "make room
for the whole self" and attempt to situate it within the collective epistemic, ethical,
and spiritual concerns of a religious community, in order to develop answers to the
religious question that Gustavo Gutiérrez (1987) construes as Job's question,
namely: "How are human beings to find a language applicable to God in the midst
of innocent suffering?" Put in the language of this book, the project of theodicy is
transformed from the question of the possibility or probability of God's existence

given the existence of evil and suffering to the question of how the religious imagination can meaningfully construe the divine in ways that are both appropriate to what the divine is (or might reasonably be) and responsive to the concrete situations and lived experience of those who have suffered FST.

In this spirit, I propose we attempt to move forward by first looking back, reconstruing (at least part of) APR's task as developing what the fourteenth-century German scholar and contemplative Henry Suso (a.k.a. Heinrich Seuse, d. 1366) called a *philosophia spiritualis,* or the pursuit of the epistemic, moral, personal, and spiritual transformation that can occur when we place the *love of wisdom*—not the desire for recognition, clicks, or winning debates, nor the need for publications, citations, or tenure, nor even the attempt to demonstrate the rationality of one's position at all costs—at the center of our focus. I will thus use a passage from Suso's *Vita*—together with related ideas from Suso's teacher, Meister Eckhart—to elucidate one common way of conceiving of the spiritual journey of the individual toward God in late medieval Rhineland mysticism (a tradition within which both figures are situated).[1] I will then propose that we can helpfully appropriate and adapt this historical contemplative program[2] to develop a framework for the fruitful transformation of the discipline of APR, as we search for a more "com-passionate" approach to theodical discourse and a philosophy of religion prepared to "transgress" its traditional boundaries as it collectively pursues the love of wisdom, a commitment to solidarity, and the will to actively resist evil where it is encountered.

Deconstructing the self, imag(in)ing God, and being drawn beyond: a mystical program of spiritual transformation

In Chapter 49 of his *Vita,* Suso claims that "a person of releasement [*ein gelassener mensch*] needs to be unformed [*entbildet*] from creatures, [re-]formed [*gebildet*] with Christ, and transformed [*überbildet*] in the Godhead" (Seuse 1907: 168).[3]

This passage is notoriously difficult to translate and contains several creative plays on words in the Middle High German. For example, although the extolled "mystical virtue" of *gelâzenheit* exemplified by the *gelassener mensch* is sometimes translated as "serenity" or "equanimity," it is derived from the verb meaning to "let go," "leave," or "release" (*lâzen*) and is thus also sometimes translated as "detachment" or even "abandonment" (e.g., abandoning oneself to God). I prefer the term "releasement," as it can connote both activity (to release or let go *of* something) or passivity (to be released or let go *from* something *by* someone), a tension frequently played on by Suso, as well as by his teacher, Meister Eckhart (Griffioen and Zahedi 2018). In this sense, a *gelassener mensch* can be understood both as a person who has "been released" from some attachment or confinement and as someone who has "let go" of something. Importantly, however, since the participial adjective *gelassen* modifies *mensch* here, the term refers to something more like a character trait or virtue (i.e., *gelâzen*heit). It thus picks out someone who has internalized the practice of detachment and (absent backsliding) remains in the "state" of having-[been]-released.

Another fascinating ambiguity has to do with the root verb *bilden* in *entbildet*, *gebildet*, and *überbildet*, which can mean "to form," "to educate," or "to edify" but whose noun form *bild* refers most directly to an *image*. In this sense, one can also read this passage as claiming that the "released" person needs to become "de-imaged," "imaged," and "beyond-imaged." Although Suso borrows his use of *entbilden* from Eckhart to refer to detaching oneself from the false, illusory, or transient objects of our misdirected desires, he is even more friendly than his predecessor to the pragmatic use of concrete (even visual) imagery to promote understanding in pastoral contexts—so much so that the *Vita* concludes with Suso acquiescing to the request of his interlocutor (and possible "ghostwriter"), the nun and abbess Elsbeth Stagel, for an "illustrative representation" (*bildgebender glichnus*) of his mystical thought using "vivid speech" (*bildlicher rede*) so that she may better come to understand his meaning. And though he responds to her by asking rhetorically how one could possibly "shape without imagery [*bildlos gebilden*] and demonstrate without method [*wiselos bewisen*] that which lies beyond all sense and human reason," he nevertheless proposes to "exorcise the image by way of images" (*bild mit bilden us tribe*) and to "conclude a long speech with short words" (Seuse 1907: 191)—a proposal commensurate with my insistence in this book that religious models need not be strictly true to be epistemically valuable.[4]

Although Suso's approach is explicitly Christian, the tripartite structure of his "mystical path" follows a common depiction of the spiritual journey to the Divine in various contemplative traditions, especially those grounded in Neoplatonist thought. According to this framework, the individual must first be *purged* or *cleansed* of vicious attachment and falsehood (the so-called *via purgativa*) before they can become *illuminated* or *enlightened* by the light of wisdom (the *via illuminativa*). This clears the way intellectually for the genuine *contemplation* of higher things and ultimately for the complete *transformation* of the whole person by way of an epistemic and/or experiential union with the divine (the *via unitiva*). Before we turn to the application of this "mystical method" in APR, it will be instructive to look at these stages a bit more carefully.

The *via purgativa*

As mentioned above, the notion of *entbilden* in Eckhart and Suso implies that, to develop *gelâzenheit*, we must first "let go of" the misleading creaturely images to which we are both cognitively habituated and affectively attached. Importantly, however, it is not merely the images themselves and our mistaken ideas about their significance to which we become attached. We also become caught up in particular ways of expressing ("*form*-ulating") those ideas. We are trapped by our "forms" of discourse, which in turn "shape" how we experience the objects of that discourse.

The concern for the mystic, then, has both a cognitive-epistemic aspect (how to become able to recognize and take seriously the idea that one's attachments are illusory, insignificant, or injurious) and an affective-volitional dimension (how to successfully become disengaged from them). Importantly, for Suso (again following Eckhart), becoming appropriately *abgescheiden* ("detached" or "distanced") from idolatrous attachments involves developing a kind of *passive receptivity*, such that an Other (here: the Divine) can "break through" [*durchbrechen*] and "*en*-lighten" the individual concerning that which they are currently unable to see clearly. This act of "*in*-formation" is not something the spiritual wayfarer can accomplish wholly on their own. A fundamental act of divine *grace* is required to help us "turn away" (literally: to "convert" us)[5] from our misdirected cognitive and affective attachments and toward the "light" of divine illumination.

Still, the normative flavor of mystagogical texts like the *Vita* and the continual exhortations of spiritual directors like Eckhart and Suso that their readers develop the receptivity characteristic of detachment and releasement suggest that they think that we *can* in some sense be active participants in the pursuit of the kind of passivity needed to "be turned" in the appropriate ways. Indeed, the ascetic practices of renunciation they suggest for the mystical beginner represent a kind of *instruction in deconstruction*—a "learned un-learning," as it were (and yet another way of thinking about *entbilden*)—that can make a person more receptive to acts of divine grace. By asking the *anvahender mensch*, as Suso calls the spiritual "newbie," to refrain from certain habitual and pleasurable activities (by, e.g., fasting or practicing celibacy), to give up objects and lifestyles they enjoy (by, e.g., giving away possessions or taking vows of poverty), to make themself uncomfortable (by, e.g., wearing scratchy undergarments or living in small, bare cells), to meditate on and identify with the struggles and suffering of spiritual exemplars (in the Christian tradition, usually Christ, Mary, and the saints or martyrs), and so on, individuals can prepare themselves to be "unmade" from the secular world, "released" from idolatrous attachment and "turned" toward the illuminative activity of loving and pursuing wisdom, the *philosophia spiritualis.*

The *via illuminativa*

Despite its reliance on grace, the *via purgativa* is arguably the most difficult stage for spiritual wayfarers to traverse. It is, in essence, a sustained series of exercises in humility and self-control that must be continually cultivated and practiced in order to prevent backsliding. However, once one has been appropriately detached from illusions and idolatry with the help of divine grace, the primary spiritual task shifts from *de*construction and *un*formation to *re*construction and *re*formation of the self by way of *in*struction and *in*formation. Having unlearned old ways of thinking about ourselves, the world, and God, we need to be *remade* by the divine in order to be able to pursue genuine wisdom. Importantly, however, despite the emphasis on "de-imaging" in the *via purgativa*, walking the path of the *via illuminativa* does not necessarily mean being *imageless*—especially in traditions like Christianity that emphasize the human being as created *imaginem dei.* In fact, in the tradition within which Suso and his ilk operate, the medium of divine illumination is usually equated specifically with the divine Word or Wisdom, i.e., Christ the *logos*, whose "image" can be "poured into" (literally: *in-*form) the soul that has been "emptied" of (self-)deceptive attachments.

It is also notable that neither Eckhart nor Suso shies away here from using rich and complex imagery to convey their messages concerning this and subsequent stages. Their writings are intended to be instructive, not iconoclastic, and the question for these thinkers therefore becomes, not how to speak of God without imagery, but rather *which imaginings of the divine* can be useful in edifying or "building up" (*bilden*) their audience and bringing them to a deeper understanding of the medium by which the imageless divine is encountered. For example, Eckhart's imagery of the divine "in-flowing" (*învliezen*) characteristic of the *via illuminativa* is explicitly Marian and uterine. In several places in his vernacular works, he speaks of the soul emptied of idols and false attachments as a fertile "ground" that can be impregnated by and subsequently birth the "Word" (or *logos*) in its own depths. Here, the soul receptively *conceives* the image of the Divine and actively *labors* to bring it to productive *fruition*. Suso's imagery, for its part, lies more in the medieval courtly love and Boethian consolation traditions. In a series of dialogues, the love-sick "Servant" (Suso, as a stand-in for the searching soul) engages in intellectually sophisticated intercourse with his mistress and beloved, "Eternal Wisdom" (*Sophia*, the stand-in for the *logos*), who appears to her devoted "knight" in a "spiritual and ineffable form," instructing him in various theological and philosophical matters and ultimately leading him "through sweet and sour" to the "right path of divine truth" (Seuse 1907: 200).

Further, Eckhart and Suso both argue for the permissibility of using various context-sensitive metaphors, voices, and imagery in order to illuminate their readers who find themselves in different kinds of social and pastoral situations. For example, Eckhart writes in his *Commentary on John* that the reader should be able to "freely take now one [interpretation] and now the other as seems useful to him" (Eckhart 1981: 135), even where those interpretations might stand in conflict with one another if placed side by side. Suso likewise notes that, to be accessible to a wide range of readers, he does "as a teacher should do" and speaks in different voices: "now [. . .] as a sinful person, then as a perfected person; sometimes in the form of the love-sick soul, at other times as a servant with whom Eternal Wisdom converses" (Seuse 1907: 198). In this sense, both thinkers adopt a fundamentally *pragmatic* and *pluralistic* approach to their theoretical and mystagogical projects. This is no small point, since it reveals that, even where their projects are strongly epistemological, they are guided by a concern for accessibility and a sense of what their discourse is or could be used *for*.

The *via unitiva*

Of course, the "imaginative" edification in the mystagogical works of Eckhart and Suso is only meant as a stepping-stone to a greater *understanding*, which their models and modes of discourse can ultimately only gesture at. The attempt is thereby, as Wittgenstein might have put it, to "show" what they think cannot directly be "said." Like the ability of the soul to become emptied and detached, they maintain that genuine illumination must ultimately come from without— and only as the recipient of this latter kind of illumination is one in a position to adequately *contemplate* higher and more eternal truths and ultimately to achieve a kind of *union* between the knower and the thing known, the lover and the beloved, the seeker and the thing sought.

However, contrary to what we find in many contemporary interpretations of mystical texts, the *via unitiva* is not usually aimed at achieving some particular, remarkable, episodic religious experience. For many contemplative authors, an unexpected encounter with the divine (e.g., an experience of "presence," "togetherness," "oneness," or even "self-annihilation") is what *prompts* them to set out on their spiritual journey—and can only represent a fleeting "glimpse" or "foretaste" of true spiritual union with the divine. In fact, in some texts union with God is decidedly *anti-experiential*, at least insofar as experience is taken to have a subject-object structure that is purportedly dissolved when the soul truly "ascends" to God. Many of these more "annihilative" mystics—but also some of their more "affective" counterparts[6]—additionally tend to think that genuine, sustained union with the Divine is only possible *post mortem*.

Whatever the case, the goal of the spiritual journey in *this* life is to be able to grasp that which one before could only gesture at—to be *drawn beyond* a merely propositional theology to a deeper understanding of eternal truths—and to have one's will aligned with them, which is nothing more than being aligned with the very will of the divine itself. It is, to again crib Wittgenstein (who himself is cribbing the Rhineland mystics), a matter of "kicking away the ladder" one has used to climb to such heights (or, in Eckhart's case, depths). Put in Suso's terms, the image has been successfully *exorcised*, and one no longer has need of heuristic models to comprehend the divine. This, according to Suso, is the wisdom we should love and pursue in a *philosophia spiritualis*.

This climax of the mystical journey, therefore, results in a fundamental *trans-formation*—perhaps even a *loss*—of one's (sense of) self and attachments to ownership (e.g., of one's own actions) that occurs when one achieves full *con-formance* with the will of God and divine purposes.

The return to the world

It is perhaps already clear that the spiritual itinerary set out by figures like Eckhart and Suso, although diachronic and dynamic, is not simply a temporal matter of moving from one stage to the next. Given the limited kinds of creatures we are, backsliding is inevitable. As one pursues wisdom, one must therefore be diligent not to fall back into old habits and ways of thinking. Likewise, as with any virtue, conforming one's will to the Divine takes sustained *practice* and *habituation*. So long as we are embodied creatures with limited cognitive capacities and tendencies toward vice, internalizing the *gelâzenheit* necessary for any of the later stages is likely the most difficult project one can undertake as a human being—one that, at least in this life, will never fully be completed. As Suso writes of the person who has seemingly left his self and his worldly attachments behind, "in the next instant he comes back to his old, wicked self and is the same as he always was, and he has to let go of himself over and over again" (Seuse 1907: 161).

Even those few saintly exemplars who are able to habitualize such detachment and align their wills with the divine purpose remain finite, embodied creatures in the world, and as such they are not freed from the constraints of that world but rather continue to have moral and spiritual duties to creation and their fellow human beings. That is, they remain *in* the world even if no longer *of* the world. This is an important and often overlooked point in discussions of mysticism—namely, that there is ultimately no distinction between the *vita activa* and the *vita contemplativa*. "It is actually the same thing," Eckhart writes, "for we take [. . .] from the same ground of contemplation and make it fruitful in works, and thus the object of contemplation is achieved. [. . .] God's purpose in the union of contemplation is fruitfulness in works: for in contemplation you serve yourself alone, but in works of charity you serve the many" (Eckhart 2009: 48–9).

Indeed, one of the greatest lessons of contemplative thinkers like Eckhart and Suso—and one we see borne out in what we know of their lives—is that the intellectual, the spiritual, and the pastoral are not neatly, nor even ideally, divorceable. Not only do we deceive ourselves if we think our "purely intellectual" endeavors have nothing to do with those outside our intellectual circles, in trying to hermetically seal ourselves off from them, we fail to fulfil some of our most basic duties toward our fellow human beings (today encapsulated in terms like *recognition, treating with dignity, solidarity*, and the like). It is therefore worth thinking more closely about how we might use the evocative Rhineland language of imaging and formation as a springboard for an earnestly playful adaptation of the three stages of spiritual development discussed above—i.e., detachment/ unformation, illumination/reform[ation], and union/transformation—to the case of APR, so that it may better proceed with respect to developing care-full, consider-ate, and ultimately *com-passionate* theodicies that actively work to recognize, to reckon with, and ultimately to resist evil within a theistic framework.

Revolutionary formations: deconstructing the discipline, reforming the discourse, transforming ourselves

To begin, as I have already suggested in various places in this book, I think APR has become excessively *attached* (both intellectually and affectively[7]) to the epistemic value of rationality in the service of defending theism from the atheist challenge. As I argued in the last chapter, I think this narrow focus has led to APR scholars placing an overly high significance on the problem of evil construed as a fundamentally *theoretical* problem of defending theistic belief, one best approached in a "purely intellectual" ("PI") mode of discourse. This has led it to largely fail to address the problem as it presents itself to an overwhelming number of religious practitioners who have experienced what I have called "faith-shaking trauma" ("FST")—or traumatic experience of the kind that threatens their commitment to their religious community or tradition and thereby transforms the possibility of *deconversion* into a live option for them.

APR's disciplinary overattachment to the theoretical problem, I suggested, runs a high risk of leading to troubling consequences, including a systemic failure (perhaps even bordering on an inability) to *see* the perspectives of those who have undergone FST, to *hear* their testimony regarding the badness of their suffering, and to *take seriously* challenges and methodological alternatives to the APR *status quo* that would better support them in their struggle with the theodical problem construed as an essentially religious problem. This is epistemically worrisome insofar as it creates intellectually significant "blind spots" within the discipline and its scholars while simultaneously perpetrating epistemic injustices against those whose suffering constitutes part of the "dataset" for the problem of evil in the first place. It is morally troublesome, insofar as it can lead to a kind of insensitivity to genuine suffering and even an inability to recognize and resist evil where it occurs.

Shaking APR out of its contentedness with the unambitious project of defending the possibility that theistic belief could constitute knowledge and turning it away from its insistence on the PI approach to theodicy (even if only for a time) may thus require, as Eckhart might have put it, a "breaking through" of perspectives from the periphery of the discipline (or from outside it altogether). Here, it may be helpful to recall the discussion of *epistemic frictions* from Chapter 2. There, I noted the epistemic value of disruption, including how the subversion of cherished models and modes of discourse can help combat uncritical dogmatism and contribute to achieving a more comprehensive understanding of a subject matter. To put it in more "mystical terms," epistemic frictions can provide a crucial impetus for a discipline to "let go" or "detach" itself from the models it holds sacrosanct—and to open itself up to a reconsideration of how the field proceeds. In the context of theodicy, these epistemic frictions can be provided by the testimony of those who have undergone FST—who, I suggest, are in a unique epistemological position to provide such testimony.

True, there is often a fundamental *lack* of understanding at the core of much trauma (e.g., the radical "break" in one's self-narrative or the inability to integrate one's experience into one's previous view of one's self, the world, and God). And it is this lack of understanding that often underlies a large part of the religious problem of theodicy. However, this does not mean that those who have undergone FST are in an intellectually less advantageous position than those treating the problem of evil in the PI mode. In a certain respect, the former's experiences force them into a vantage point that is more perspicuous than the latter, since they have, to some extent, already been detached from the problem of evil as purely theoretical and compelled to see how things look from *outside* the dominant models favored by APR. Their testimony, then, may be useful in upsetting the comfortable "equilibrium" of scholars who desire to simply remain in the PI mode involved in defending traditional perfect-being theism, and in some cases it might even be able to help turn them away from some of the more harmful theodical approaches performed in that mode.

Of course, we[8] as scholars must also become open to being turned in this way and receptive to taking such disruptions seriously, and this often takes a concerted effort. Although traditionally marginalized voices might, on occasion, simply "break through" a scholarly discourse so forcefully that a discipline is more-or-less compelled to reckon with them, such cases are relatively rare. Sometimes the introduction of smaller, subtler disruptions through a concerted, often collective effort—and sustained through a series of iterative performances, or what José Medina (2013b) calls "chained action"—are likewise able to upset or erode a discourse over time. In many cases, however, some activity on the part of allies and those in positions of privilege in the discipline will be necessary for epistemic frictions to gain the traction required for them to perform their disruptive function. In this sense, APR as a discipline need not (and *should* not) be wholly passive with respect to "frictional input," especially given its epistemic potential to turn us toward what we cannot (yet) see. As with the ascetic cultivation of the "mystical" virtues of *gelâzenheit* and *abgescheidenheit*, we can therefore work to undertake certain practices as scholars in the service of actively *seeking out* possible epistemic frictions[9]—not only to our favored theoretical theodical approaches but also to the preferred modes of discourse that accompany them.

For some of us, of course, this might be easier said than done. We might need to start small: for example, by simply making an effort to *refrain* from certain habitual microaggressions in academic settings—a roll of the eyes, a dismissive smirk, a snarky comment—when we encounter perspectives or approaches that radically diverge from our own preferred way of doing things. Indeed, when we force ourselves to *act* like we're taking someone seriously, we might find ourselves *actually* taking them more seriously and thereby come to encounter reasonable perspectives we hadn't considered before. More proactively, we might, for example, make a concerted effort to *read* texts from outside APR's traditional borders (and even outside philosophy itself), including those composed by persons situated radically differently from us. We can attempt to *diversify* who we invite to speak at a conference or who we include on our syllabi. And, as suggested in the previous chapter, we can begin to reflect more carefully on the *aim* and *impact* of our discourse—not only its intended illocutionary function but also its actual or likely perlocutionary effects on those who might be direct, peripheral, or downstream recipients of it. By engaging in a kind of "academic asceticism" (or "disciplinary discipline") of scholarly self-restraint and collective self-reflection, and by actively seeking out epistemic frictions, we may find our own thought moved in illuminating directions that surprise us.

We also need to seek out voices—scholarly and otherwise—of those who have undergone FST, both within the discipline and (especially, I think) from outside it.[10] However, becoming receptive to such voices in ways that can counter the harmful epistemic and moral dangers of theodicizing in the PI mode will involve the cultivation of a special kind of passivity—one that can open us up to a kind of testimonial "grace." In particular, we need to learn how to *refrain from speaking*, a task of extreme difficulty for many philosophers—myself included. We have a tendency to want to contribute our thoughts to a discussion (and, usually, to raise objections) at the first opportunity. Yet if part of our duty as philosophers of religion is, as Marilyn McCord Adams (1999) claimed, to work with those who have suffered to help them (and us) make sense of their experience, we must *unlearn* our propensity to speak and first practice being *still*—to sit passively in silence and let others speak. Only in this way can someone's gracious testimonial act about their suffering allow us to truly witness to it.

Put a bit differently, in order to be genuinely responsive to the demands of those who suffer and to actively begin developing philosophical and theological models that can adequately address that suffering, we first need to *listen* to those voices trying to escape the isolating silence typified by our social scripts surrounding traumatic suffering. As Dorothee Sölle put it: "The first step towards overcoming suffering is [...] to find a language that leads out of the uncomprehended suffering that makes one mute, a language of lament, of crying, of pain, a language that at least says what the situation is" (Sölle 1975: 70). We therefore need to let the attempts of those voices to locate a language that can "at least say what the situation is" *break through* the walls of our preferred modes of intellectual discourse. Only then can we take their suffering seriously and work together to develop a philosophy capable of appropriately resisting it.

We also must not forget that testimonial articulations of this kind are, in fact, acts of undeserved *grace*—especially given the ways that extreme suffering both isolates and makes communication difficult, together with the exacerbation of such isolating silence by the unease and insensitivity of those who either prefer to look away in discomfort or fail to register it altogether. Indeed, just as members of oppressed groups do not have a civic or moral duty to educate members of relevantly privileged circles, let alone provide them with already-worked-out plans for the annihilation or amelioration of the oppression in question, those who have suffered FST and are both capable and courageous enough to give voice to their complaints are under no obligation to share their testimony or use it in the service of "illuminating" APR scholars, even if we can hope that they will. In this sense, an individual's testimony concerning the badness of their FST (as well as regarding the (in)ability of any particular theodicy to reconcile that experience with their faith) is wholly *supererogatory*. If anything, it is our duty as philosophers to *welcome* that difficult testimony when it is offered—and to do our best to really hear and acknowledge it, rather than simply offloading any response to ministers, counselors, or social workers.

As the voices of those who have suffered FST and those who stand on the margins of the discipline (groups which may have significant overlap) begin to penetrate the discourse of APR, we may find ourselves intellectually "informed" and "illuminated" in ways we did not expect. Likewise, rather than merely desiring to protect ourselves from intellectual vulnerability, we may find ourselves "graced" with a more other-directed desire for a compassionate theodical approach that turns us *outward* and makes the discipline more public-facing. As we move beyond the PI mode, then, we will likely need to alter our ways of thinking and speaking and to begin to explore which imaginings of the divine can be both epistemically *instructive* and practically *constructive*, theologically satisfying and pastorally useful. In line with Eckhart's pregnancy metaphors, it will become necessary to "gestate" more *therapeutic* theodical models and to work collectively to bring them to "fruition" (Griffioen 2018).[11] Ideally, such models will be therapeutic in two senses: They will be philosophically remedial for the discipline, helping us diagnose its shortcomings and counteract its harms, and they will be genuinely helpful to those struggling with FST.

Developing such models will mean looking "beyond belief" and experimenting playfully-yet-earnestly with ways of thinking about God that may not, strictly speaking, be true or rational to believe but which can be "illuminative" in other ways that promote religious understanding and the ability to make existential meaning in the face of the reality of evil. In so doing, the hope is that we will find new alternatives to old ways of thinking that *reshape* and ultimately *transform* the discipline for the better. When we do this, we may find ourselves "turned toward" each other—brought together in a kind of affective and volitional alignment—in ways that can be genuinely *transformative* for us as philosophers and individuals, for the discipline of APR, and, most importantly, for those who struggle with faith in the face of evil and suffering. We can return to the world of academic philosophy *changed*, finding new ways of addressing our "old" philosophy of religion with an altered, more outward-looking, *political* consciousness and new cognitive habits—and we can finally take up the challenge diagnosed by McCord Adams of tackling the problem of theodicy in solidarity, rather than in solitude.

What will be the defining characteristics of such theodicies? Will they be recognizable *as* theodicies? Do they need to be? I cannot—yet—say what a sustained, collective effort at theodical transformation will look like. It may turn out that there can only be theodicies in the particular and plural, not some overarching, one-size-fits-all theodical approach. Perhaps they will be irreducibly theological and tradition-specific (though perhaps this will amount merely to making what is already implicit, explicit). Or perhaps they will adopt what Sölle might have called a "mysticism of resistance," flipping theodicy on its head by centering Job instead of God, making our imaginative models of the Divine adequate to the badness of the evil suffered rather than the other way around, and emphasizing the sufficiency of human individuals to stand together in solidarity to both say "NO" to the world as it is and "YES" to bringing about the (perhaps impossible) kingdom of God.

Conclusion: going in for revelation

In this chapter, as in the entirety of this book, I have asked APR to look beyond its traditional horizons—and to reorient, reform, perhaps even revolutionize its approach to traditional problems and debates. I have suggested it "let go" of some of its more obsessive attachments and find more "edifying" discourses that can "trans-form" it for the better. This is the challenge for an APR of the future: not just to spin its wheels or run around in circles, nor to assume that the limits of the discipline need to be where they have traditionally been placed. But rather to pivot in different directions and see where it takes us.

Some who read this will be disappointed or dissatisfied that the book ends here—open-ended, without closure. I remind them, however, that we who remain in the grips of faith-shaking trauma—we, too, lack closure. The problem when one proposes to undertake a journey of transformation, whether individual or collective, is that one never really knows where one will end up—or how the preferences and predilections of those being transformed will be changed. As L.A. Paul suggests at the close of *Transformative Experience*, we may sometimes need to simply go in for "valuing experience for its own sake, that is, for the revelation it brings" (Paul 2014: 178). Instead of "choosing the status quo," she writes, we can "choose to create and discover new preferences, that is, to experience the way our preferences will evolve, and often, in the process, to create and discover a new self"—or, the case of APR, a new (or *renewed*) discipline. To undertake this project, Paul suggests, is to engage in "one of the most important games of life," namely "the game of Revelation, a game played for the sake of play itself" (178). It is my hope for the discipline that, by playing this game in earnest, it may create the conditions for a genuine *philosophia spiritualis*—or at least for a pursuit of wisdom and understanding that is both revelatory and, we may hope, relevant.

Notes

1   Whether Suso was ever directly taught by Meister Eckhart is unclear. He spent time in both Strasbourg and Cologne, where he certainly came under the influence of Eckhartian thought, and he was likely removed from his lectorship in Konstanz for defending Eckhartian ideas. But the only "documented" encounter we know of between Suso and Eckhart comes from Suso's own *Vita*, where he claims the already-deceased Meister appeared to him in a dream to instruct him about "true detachment." For comprehensive discussions of Eckhart, Suso, and other late medieval Rhineland mystics, see McGinn (2005).

2   My project should not be confused with Suso's own mystagogical project. As I have argued elsewhere (Griffioen 2023a), in addition to understanding the task of the history of philosophy as purely exegetical, evaluative, or comparative we can also engage in what I call *recognizable appropriation*, in which we recover and adapt

historical texts and ideas for contemporary philosophical or public-facing purposes in ways that need not correspond to the author's intent—but which does not distort their thought so much as to make it wholly unrecognizable.

3 The entire sentence reads: *Ein gelassener mensch műss entbildet werden von der creatur, gebildet werden mit Cristo, und überbildet in der gotheit.* All translations of Suso's Middle High German in this section are mine. I have taken the Eckhart translations from the most commonly cited translations of his work.

4 Suso also likely oversaw the illustration of an early edition of the *Vita*, which contains several images of the scenes and ideas contained in the book.

5 The MHG verb *kêren* is used as a translation of the Latin *conversio* and the Greek μετανοέω in these texts and points at another central metaphor trading on the ambiguity between active and passive—namely that of *turning* and *being turned*. See, e.g., Kaffanke (2015).

6 On the annihilative/affective distinction, see Van Dyke (2022). On my concerns regarding the sharpness of the distinction, see Griffioen (2023c).

7 That the attachment is also affective can be seen by the disproportionately angry defensiveness some philosophers show when the *status quo* way of proceeding is challenged—an interesting phenomenon given an epistemological framework that equates anger and partiality with irrationality.

8 I use the first-person plural here to indicate, first, that I, too, have a long way to go in the respects I discuss here and, second, that these movements are best achieved collectively, rather than individually.

9 Helen De Cruz (2020) recommends something like this this with respect to the introduction of non-Western voices and religious traditions into APR discourse.

10 It is especially here that APR needs to interact more with its empirical disciplinary neighbors, as well as with community and pastoral figures.

11 At the same time, we may also struggle with the analogues of infertility and miscarriage here. Some of our imaginings may, for various reasons need to be aborted. (Perhaps we discover they are not workable or are likewise harmful. Perhaps the vicissitudes of the academic life prevent us from taking them further. Etc.) Indeed, just as in pregnancy, even if we are fortunate enough to have the security and space to nourish these ideas, it is still likely to be a genuine intellectual and moral struggle as we do so.

Works Cited

Abel, Darrel. 1978. "Robert Frost's 'True Make-Believe.'" *Texas Studies in Literature and Language* 20 (4): 552–78. https://www.jstor.org/stable/40754553.

Adams, Robert M. 1997. "Symbolic Value." *Midwest Studies in Philosophy* 21 (1): 1–15. https://doi.org/10.1111/j.1475-4975.1997.tb00513.x.

Alcoff, Linda, and Elizabeth Potter, eds. 1993. *Feminist Epistemologies*. New York: Routledge.

Alston, William P. 1993. *Perceiving God: The Epistemology of Religious Experience*. Ithaca: Cornell University Press.

Alston, William P. 1996. "Belief, Acceptance, and Religious Faith." In *Faith, Freedom and Rationality: Essays in the Philosophy of Religion*, edited by Jeff Jordan and Daniel Howard-Snyder, 3–27. Lanham, MD: Rowman & Littlefield.

Ammerman, Nancy T. 2020. "Rethinking Religion: Toward a Practice Approach." *American Journal of Sociology* 126 (1): 6–51. https://doi.org/10.1086/709779.

Andersen, Elizabeth. 2000. *The Voices of Mechthild of Magdeburg*. Wien: Lang.

Anderson, Elizabeth. 2006. "The Epistemology of Democracy." *Episteme* 3 (1): 8–22. https://dx.doi.org/10.1353/epi.0.0000.

Arcadi, James M. 2017. "Analytic Theology as Declarative Theology." *TheoLogica* 1 (1): 37–52. https://doi.org/10.14428/thl.v1i1.73.

Arnal, William E., and Russell T. McCutcheon. 2013. *The Sacred Is the Profane: The Political Nature of "Religion"*. New York: Oxford University Press.

Audi, Robert. 2011. "Faith, Faithfulness, and Virtue." *Faith and Philosophy* 28 (3): 294–309. https://doi.org/10.5840/faithphil201128328.

Audi, Robert. 2013. *Rationality and Religious Commitment*. Oxford: Clarendon Press.

Austin, J. L. 1962. *How to Do Things with Words*. Oxford: Oxford University Press.

Avigad, Jeremy. 2018. "Principia: Is It Possible That, in the New Millennium, the Mathematical Method Is No Longer Fundamental to Philosophy?" *Aeon*. https://aeon.co/essays/does-philosophy-still-need-mathematics-and-vice-versa. Accessed 21 December, 2024.

Bagger, Matthew C. 2007. *The Uses of Paradox: Religion, Self-Transformation, and the Absurd*. New York: Columbia University Press.

Barbour, Ian G. 1974. *Myths, Models and Paradigms: A Comparative Study in Science & Religion*. San Francisco: HarperOne.

Bardos, Jonah, Daniel Hercz, Jenna Friedenthal, Stacey A. Missmer, and Zev Williams. 2015. "A National Survey on Public Perceptions of Miscarriage." *Obstetrics and Gynecology* 125 (6): 1313–20. https://doi.org/10.1097/AOG.0000000000000859.

Barr, Beth Allison. 2021. *The Making of Biblical Womanhood: How the Subjugation of Women Became Gospel Truth*. Grand Rapids, MI: Brazos Press.

Baumberger, Christoph, and Georg Brun. 2016. "Dimensions of Objectual Understanding." In Grimm, Baumberger, and Ammon 2016, 165–89.

Baumberger, Christoph, and Georg Brun. 2021. "Reflective Equilibrium and Understanding." *Synthese* 198: 7923–47. https://doi.org/10.1007/s11229-020-02556-9.

Betenson, Toby. 2016. "Anti-Theodicy." *Philosophy Compass* 11 (1): 56–65. https://doi.org/10.1111/phc3.12289.

Bishop, John. 2002. "Faith as Doxastic Venture." *Religious Studies* 38 (4): 471–87. https://doi.org/10.1017/S0034412502006121.

Bishop, John. 2007. *Believing by Faith: An Essay in the Epistemology and Ethics of Religious Belief*. Oxford: Clarendon Press.

Blackmon, Michael. 2017. "This Woman Reimagined Michelangelo's "The Creation of Adam" with Black Women and It's Beautiful." Accessed 21 December, 2024. https://www.buzzfeed.com/michaelblackmon/god-is-a-black-woman.

Boon, Mieke. 2012. "Understanding Scientific Practices: The Role of Robustness Notions." In *Characterizing the Robustness of Science*, edited by Léna Soler, Emiliano Trizio, Thomas Nickles, and William Wimsatt, 289–315. Dordrecht: Springer Netherlands. https://doi.org/10.1007/978-94-007-2759-5_12

Boscaljon, Daniel. 2013. *Vigilant Faith: Passionate Agnosticism in a Secular World*. Charlottesville: University of Virginia Press.

Bostic, Joy R. 2013. *African American Female Mysticism: Nineteenth-Century Religious Activism*. New York: Palgrave Macmillan.

Brady, Michael, and Eranda Jayawickreme. 2023. "A Philosophical Approach to Improving Empirical Research on Posttraumatic Growth." *Philosophical Psychology*, 38 (2): 796–819. https://doi.org/10.1080/09515089.2023.2213251.

Brown, David. 2007. *Discipleship and Imagination: Christian Tradition and Truth*. Oxford: Oxford University Press.

Brown, David. 2008. *Tradition and Imagination: Revelation and Change*. Oxford: Oxford University Press.

Bruner, Jason. 2021. *Imagining Persecution: Why American Christians Believe There Is a Global War Against Their Faith*. New Brunswick, NJ: Rutgers University Press.

Buchak, Lara. 2012. "Can It Be Rational to Have Faith?" In *Probability in the Philosophy of Religion*, edited by Jake Chandler and Victoria S. Harrison, 225–47. Oxford: Oxford University Press.

Buchak, Lara. 2017a. "Faith and Steadfastness in the Face of Counter-Evidence." *International Journal for Philosophy of Religion* 81 (1–2): 113–33. https://doi.org/10.1007/s11153-016-9609-7.

Buchak, Lara. 2017b. "Reason and Faith." In *The Oxford Handbook of the Epistemology of Theology*, edited by William J. Abraham and Frederick D. Aquino, 46–63. Oxford: Oxford University Press.

Buchak, Lara. 2022. "Faith and Traditions." *Noûs* 57 (3): 740–59. https://doi.org/10.1111/nous.12427.

Burley, Mikel. 2020. *A Radical Pluralist Philosophy of Religion: Cross-Cultural, Multireligious, Interdisciplinary*. London: Bloomsbury.

Burley, Mikel. 2022. "The Nature and Significance of the Hindu Divine Mother in Embodied Thealogical Perspective." *Religious Studies* 58 (S1): S4–S16. https://doi.org/10.1017/S0034412521000263.

Bynum, Caroline Walker. 1988. *Holy Feast and Holy Fast: The Religious Significance of Food to Medieval Women*. Berkeley, CA: University of California Press.

Caputo, John D. 2013. *The Insistence of God: A Theology of Perhaps*. Bloomington, IN: Indiana University Press.

Carmona, Carla. 2021. "Silencing by Not Telling: Testimonial Void as a New Kind of Testimonial Injustice." *Social Epistemology* 35 (6): 577–92. https://doi.org/10.1080/02691728.2021.1887395.

Chandrasekhar, Subrahmanyan. 1989. "The Perception of Beauty and the Pursuit of Science." *Bulletin of the American Academy of Arts and Sciences* 43 (3): 14–29. https://doi.org/10.2307/3824649.

Chandrasekhar, Subrahanyan. 2010. "Beauty and the Quest for Beauty in Science." *Physics Today* 63 (12): 57–62. https://doi.org/10.1063/1.3529003.

Chang, Ruth. 2013. "Commitment, Reasons, and the Will." In *Oxford Studies in Metaethics, Volume 8*, edited by Russ Shafer-Landau, 74–113: Oxford: Oxford University Press.

Clarke-Doane, Justin. 2020. *Morality and Mathematics*. Oxford: Oxford University Press.

Cohen, L. Jonathan. 1992. *An Essay on Belief and Acceptance*. Oxford: Clarendon Press.

Coomaraswamy, Ananda K. 1942. "Play and Seriousness." *Journal of Philosophy* 39 (20): 550–52. https://doi.org/10.2307/2018774.

Cottingham, John. 2005. *The Spiritual Dimension: Religion, Philosophy, and Human Value*. Cambridge: Cambridge University Press.

Coyne, Jerry. 2014. "The Best Argument for God? Really?" Accessed 21 December, 2024. https://whyevolutionistrue.wordpress.com/2014/06/27/the-best-argument-for-god-really/.

Csikszentmihalyi, Mihaly. 1975. *Beyond Boredom and Anxiety*. London: Jossey-Bass.

Csikszentmihalyi, Mihaly. 2013. *Flow: The Psychology of Optimal Experience*. New York: HarperCollins.

Cuneo, Terence. 2016. *Ritualized Faith: Essays on the Philosophy of Liturgy*. Oxford: Oxford University Press.

Currie, Gregory, and Ian Ravenscroft. 2002. *Recreative Minds: Imagination in Philosophy and Psychology*. Oxford: Oxford University Press.

Dancy, Jonathan. 2004. *Ethics Without Principles*. Oxford: Clarendon Press.

D'Arms, Justin, and Daniel Jacobson. 2000. "The Moralistic Fallacy: On the 'Appropriateness' of Emotions." *Philosophy and Phenomenological Research* 61 (1): 65–90. https://doi.org/10.2307/2653403.

Debus, Dorothea. 2016. "Imagination and Memory." In *The Routledge Handbook of Philosophy of Imagination*, edited by Amy Kind, 135–48. London: Routledge.

De Cruz, Helen. 2020. "Seeking Out Epistemic Friction in the Philosophy of Religion." In *Voices from the Edge: Centring Marginalized Perspectives in Analytic Theology*, edited by Michelle Panchuk and Michael C. Rea, 23–46. Oxford: Oxford University Press.

De Cruz, Helen (2024). *Wonderstruck: How Wonder and Awe Shape the Way We Think*. Princeton: Princeton University Press.

Deng, Natalja. 2015. "Religion for Naturalists." *International Journal for Philosophy of Religion* 78 (2): 195–214. https://doi.org/10.1007/s11153-015-9529-y.

Deonna, Julien A., and Fabrice Teroni. 2012. *The Emotions: A Philosophical Introduction*. London: Routledge.

De Regt, Henk W. 2015. "Scientific Understanding: Truth or Dare?" *Synthese* 192 (12): 3781–97. https://doi.org/10.1007/s11229-014-0538-7.

De Regt, Henk W., and Victor Gijsbers. 2016. "How False Theories Can Yield Genuine Understanding." In Grimm, Baumberger, and Ammon 2016, 50–75.

Dormandy, Katherine. 2022. "Epistemic Phariseeism." *Religious Studies* 59 (3): 515–32. https://doi.org/10.1017/S003441252200035X.

Dotson, Kristie. 2011. "Tracking Epistemic Violence, Tracking Practices of Silencing." *Hypatia* 26 (2): 236–57. https://doi.org/10.1111/j.1527-2001.2011.01177.x.

Du Mez, Kristin Kobes. 2020. *Jesus and John Wayne: How White Evangelicals Corrupted a Faith and Fractured a Nation*. New York: Liveright Publishing.

Eckhart of Hochheim (Meister Eckhart). 1981. *Meister Eckhart: The Essential Sermons, Commentaries, Treatises, and Defense*. New York: Paulist Press. Translated by E. Colledge and B. McGinn.

Eckhart of Hochheim (Meister Eckhart). 2009. New York: Crossroad Publishing. Translated by M. O'C Walshe.

Elgin, Catherine Z. 1996. *Considered Judgment*. Princeton, NJ: Princeton University Press.

Elgin, Catherine Z. 2006. "From Knowledge to Understanding." In *Epistemology Futures*, edited by Stephen C. Hetherington, 199–215. Oxford: Oxford University Press.

Elgin, Catherine Z. 2007. "Understanding and the Facts." *Philosophical Studies* 132 (1): 33–42. https://doi.org/10.1007/s11098-006-9054-z.

Elgin, Catherine Z. 2011. "Making Manifest: The Role of Exemplification in the Sciences and the Arts." *Principia* 15 (3): 399–413. https://doi.org/10.5007/1808-1711.2011v15n3p399.

Elgin, Catherine Z. 2017. *True Enough*. Cambridge, MA: MIT Press.

Elgin, Catherine Z. 2022. "Models as Felicitous Falsehoods." *Principia* 26 (1): 7–23. https://doi.org/10.5007/1808-1711.2022.e84576.

Eshleman, Andrew. 2016. "The Afterlife: Beyond Belief." *International Journal for Philosophy of Religion* 80 (2): 163–83. https://doi.org/10.1007/s11153-016-9565-2.

Feske, Millicent C. 2012. "Rachel's Lament: The Impact of Infertility and Pregnancy Loss Upon the Religious Faith of Ordinary Christians." *Journal of Pastoral Theology* 22 (1): 3.1–3.17. https://doi.org/10.1179/jpt.2012.22.1.003.

Forberg, Friedrich Karl. 1799. *Friedrich Carl Forbergs [...] Apologie Seines Angeblichen Atheismus*. Gotha: J. Perthes.

Frankfurt, Harry G. 1971. "Freedom of the Will and the Concept of a Person." *Journal of Philosophy* 68 (1): 5. https://doi.org/10.2307/2024717.

Fricker, Miranda. 2007. *Epistemic Injustice: Power and the Ethics of Knowing*. Oxford: Oxford University Press.

Gadsby, Hannah. *Nanette*. Netflix, 2018. Accessed August 15, 2023.

Gaesser, Brendan. 2013. "Constructing Memory, Imagination, and Empathy: A Cognitive Neuroscience Perspective." *Frontiers in Psychology* 3 (#576). https://doi.org/10.3389/fpsyg.2012.00576.

Gallagher, Shaun. 2005. *How the Body Shapes the Mind*. Oxford: Oxford University Press.

Garcia, Benjamin, and Katherine Brind'Amour. 2007. "Mizuko Kuyo." *Embryo Project Encyclopedia*. https://hdl.handle.net/10776/1716.

Gendler, Tamar Szabo. 2000. "The Puzzle of Imaginative Resistance." *Journal of Philosophy* 97 (2): 55–81. https://doi.org/10.2307/2678446.

Gendler, Tamar Szabó, and John Hawthorne, eds. 2002. *Conceivability and Possibility*. Oxford: Clarendon Press.

Gendler, Tamar Szabó, and Karson Kovakovich. 2006. "Genuine Rational Fictional Emotions." In *Contemporary Debates in Aesthetics and the Philosophy of Art*, edited by Matthew Kieran, 241–53. Oxford: Blackwell.

Goodman, Nelson, and Catherine Z. Elgin. 1988. *Reconceptions in Philosophy and Other Arts and Sciences*. Indianapolis, IN: Hackett.

Green, Garrett. 1989. *Imagining God: Theology and the Religious Imagination*. San Francisco: Harper & Row.

Griffioen, Amber L. 2010. *The Irrational Project: Toward a Different Understanding of Self-Deception:* Iowa Research Online. https://doi.org/10.17077/etd.95kp27df.

Griffioen, Amber L. 2015. "Why Jim Joyce Wasn't Wrong: Baseball and the Euthyphro Dilemma." *Journal of the Philosophy of Sport* 42 (3): 327–48. https://doi.org/10.1080/00948705.2015.1036874.

Griffioen, Amber L. 2016. "Prolegomena zu einer jeden künftigen ‚(Nicht-)Metaphysik' der Religion: (Anti-)Realismus, (Non-)Kognitivismus und die religiose Imagination." In *Gott ohne Theismus? Neue Positionen zu einer zeitlosen Frage*, edited by Rico Gutschmidt and Thomas Rentsch, 127–47. Münster: Mentis.

Griffioen, Amber L. 2018. "Therapeutic Theodicy? Suffering, Struggle, and the Shift from the God's-Eye View." *Religions* 9 (4): 99. https://doi.org/10.3390/rel9040099.

Griffioen, Amber L. 2021a. "Nowhere Men and Divine I's: Feminist Epistemology, Perfect Being Theism, and the God's-Eye View." *Journal of Analytic Theology* 9: 1–25. https://doi.org/10.12978/jat.2021-9.001217061713.

Griffioen, Amber L. 2021b. *Religious Experience*. Cambridge Elements in the Philosophy of Religion. Cambridge: Cambridge University Press. https://doi.org/10.1017/9781108699952.

Griffioen, Amber L. 2022. "Are You There, God? It's Me, the Theist: On the Viability and Virtuosity of Non-Doxastic Prayer." In *Reaching for God: New Theological Essays on Prayer*, edited by Oliver Crisp, James M. Arcadi, and Jordan Wessling, 38–58. Oxford: Oxford University Press.

Griffioen, Amber L. 2023a. "Forever Full, Eternally Empty: Using Meister Eckhart's Philosophical God to "Break Through" Bad Theology." Paper presented at the Conference on the History of Philosophy of Pregnancy, at the University of Dayton (6–8 October, 2023).

Griffioen, Amber L. 2023b. "Meister Eckhart." In *The Stanford Encyclopedia of Philosophy*, edited by Edward N. Zalta and Uri Nodelman. Stanford: Stanford University Metaphysics Research Lab. https://plato.stanford.edu/archives/sum2023/entries/meister-eckhart/.

Griffioen, Amber L. 2023c. "REVIEW: Christina Van Dyke, A Hidden Wisdom: Medieval Contemplatives on Self-Knowledge, Reason, Love, Persons, and Immortality." *Faith and Philosophy* (40) 3: 456–61.

Griffioen, Amber L. 2023d. "Toward a Philosophical Theology of Pregnancy Loss." In *Meanings of Mourning: Perspective on Death, Loss, and Grief*, edited by Mikołaj Sławkowski-Rode, 57–75. Lanham, MD: Lexington Books.

Griffioen, Amber L., and Mohammad Sadegh Zahedi. 2018. "Medieval Christian and Islamic Mysticism and the Problem of a 'Mystical Ethics'." In *The Cambridge Companion to Medieval Ethics*, edited by Thomas Williams, 280–305. Cambridge: Cambridge University Press.

Grimm, Stephen R. 2006. "Is Understanding a Species of Knowledge?" *The British Journal for the Philosophy of Science* 57 (3): 515–35. https://doi.org/10.1093/bjps/axl015.

Grimm, Stephen R., Christoph Baumberger, and Sabine Ammon, eds. 2016. *Explaining Understanding: New Perspectives from Epistemology and Philosophy of Science*. New York: Routledge.

Gutiérrez, Gustavo. 1987. *On Job: God-talk and the Suffering of the Innocent*. Maryknoll, NY: Orbis Books.

Gutiérrez, Gustavo. 1990. *The Truth Shall Make You Free: Confrontations*. Maryknoll, NY: Orbis Books. Translated by M.J. O'Connell.

Harding, Sandra. 1993. "Rethinking Standpoint Epistemology: What Is 'Strong Objectivity'?" In Alcoff and Potter 1993, 49–82.

Harris, Harriet A. 2005. "Does Analytical Philosophy Clip Our Wings? Reformed Epistemology as a Test Case." In *Faith and Philosophical Analysis: The Impact of Analytical Philosophy on the Philosophy of Religion* ed. Harriet A. Harris and Christopher J. Insole, 100–118. Burlington, VT: Ashgate.

Harrison, Victoria S. 2020. "Global Philosophy of Religion(s)." *Religious Studies* 56 (1): 20–31. https://doi.org/10.1017/S0034412519000647.

Hasker, William. 2005. "Analytic Philosophy of Religion." In *The Oxford Handbook of Philosophy of Religion*, edited by William J. Wainwright, 421–46. Oxford: Oxford University Press.

Heidegger, Martin. 1969. *Identity and Difference*. New York: Harper & Row. Translated by J. Stambaugh.

Hendricks, Perry. 2023. *Skeptical Theism*. Palgrave Frontiers in Philosophy of Religion. Cham: Palgrave Macmillan.

Herman, Judith Lewis. 2015. *Trauma and Recovery*. 3rd ed. New York: Basic Books.

Heschel, Abraham Joshua. 1955. *God in Search of Man: A Philosophy of Judaism*. New York: Farrar, Straus, & Cudahay.

Hieronymi, Pamela. 2008. "The Reasons of Trust." *Australasian Journal of Philosophy* 86 (2): 213–36. https://doi.org/10.1080/00048400801886496.

Hockett, Charles F. 1967. *Language, Mathematics, and Linguistics*. The Hague: Mouton.

Hossenfelder, Sabine. 2018. *Lost in Math: How Beauty Leads Physics Astray*. New York: Basic Books.

Howard-Snyder, Daniel. 2013. "Propositional Faith: What It Is and What It Is Not." *American Philosophical Quarterly* 50 (4): 357–72. https://www.jstor.org/stable/24475353.

Howard-Snyder, Daniel. 2016. "Does Faith Entail Belief?" *Faith and Philosophy* 33 (2): 142–62. https://doi.org/10.5840/faithphil201633059.

Howard-Snyder, Daniel. 2019a. "Can Fictionalists Have Faith? It All Depends." *Religious Studies* 55 (4): 447–68. https://doi.org/10.1017/S0034412518000161.

Howard-Snyder, Daniel. 2019b. "Three Arguments to Think That Faith Does Not Entail Belief." *Pacific Philosophical Quarterly* 100 (1): 114–28. https://doi.org/10.1111/papq.12237.

Howard-Snyder, Daniel, and Daniel J. McKaughan. 2022. "Theorizing About Faith with Lara Buchak." *Religious Studies* 58 (2): 297–326. https://doi.org/10.1017/S0034412520000359.

Huizinga, Johan. 1949. *Homo Ludens: A Study of the Play-Element in Culture*. London: Routledge & Kegan Paul.

Incurvati, Luca, and Julian J. Schlöder. 2019. "Weak Assertion." *Philosophical Quarterly* 69 (277): 741–70. https://doi.org/10.1093/pq/pqz016.

Insole, Christopher J. 2006. *The Realist Hope: A Critique of Anti-Realist Approaches in Contemporary Philosophical Theology*. Burlington, VT: Ashgate.

Jackson, Elizabeth. 2023. "Faithfully Taking Pascal's Wager." *Monist* 106 (1): 35–45. https://doi.org/10.1093/monist/onac021.

Jaeger, Gregg. 2016. "Grounding the Randomness of Quantum Measurement." *Philosophical Transactions of the Royal Society A: Mathematical, Physical and Engineering Sciences* 374. https://doi.org/10.1098/rsta.2015.0238.

James, William. 1907. *Pragmatism: A New Name for Some Old Ways of Thinking*. New York: Longmans, Green, and Co.

Jantzen, Grace. 1996. "Sources of Religious Knowledge." *Literature and Theology* 10 (2): 91–111. https://doi.org/10.1093/litthe/10.2.91.

Jantzen, Grace. 1999. *Becoming Divine: Toward a Feminist Philosophy of Religion*. Bloomington, IN: Indiana University Press.

Jarvis, Gavin E. 2016. "Early Embryo Mortality in Natural Human Reproduction: What the Data Say." *F1000Research* 5:2765. https://doi.org/10.12688/f1000research.8937.2.

Jay, Christopher. 2011. "Realistic Fictionalism." PhD thesis, University College London.

Jay, Christopher. 2014. "The Kantian Moral Hazard Argument for Religious Fictionalism." *International Journal for Philosophy of Religion* 75 (3): 207–32. https://doi.org/10.1007/s11153-013-9435-0.

Jeffrey, Anne. 2017. "Does Hope Morally Vindicate Faith?" *International Journal for Philosophy of Religion* 81 (1–2): 193–211. https://doi.org/10.1007/s11153-016-9603-0.

Jewish Chronicle. 2008. "Wiesel: Yes, We Really Did Put God on Trial." *The Jewish Chronicle*, September 19. https://www.thejc.com/news/uk-news/wiesel-yes-we-really-did-put-god-on-trial-1.5056.

Johnson, Nicole L. 2014. "Invisible Grief? Theological Reflections on Miscarriage." *The Other Journal: An Intersection of Theology & Culture* (23). https://theotherjournal.com/2014/03/17/invisible-grief-theological-reflections-on-miscarriage/.

Jonas, Silvia. 2016. "On Mathematical and Religious Belief, and on Epistemic Snobbery." *Philosophy* 91 (1): 69–92. https://doi.org/10.1017/S0031819115000431.

Jones, L. Serene. 2001. "Hope Deferred: Theological Reflections on Reproductive Loss (Infertility, Stillbirth, Miscarriage)." *Modern Theology* 17 (2): 227–45. https://doi.org/10.1111/1468-0025.00158.

Kaffanke, Jakobus. 2015. "Heinrich Seuses ‚geswinde kehr' als Ekstatische Konfession: Heinrich Seuse bei Martin Buber." In *Heinrich Seuse - Bruder Amandus*, edited by Jakobus Kaffanke, 111–26. Heinrich-Seuse-Forum Bd. 2. Münster: LIT.

Kane, Robert H. 1976. "Nature, Plenitude and Sufficient Reason." *American Philosophical Quarterly* 13 (1): 23–31. https://www.jstor.org/stable/20009600.

Kearney, Richard. 2011. *Anatheism: Returning to God After God.* New York: Columbia University Press.

Keltner, Dacher, and Jonathan Haidt. 2003. "Approaching Awe, a Moral, Spiritual, and Aesthetic Emotion." *Cognition & Emotion* 17 (2): 297–314. https://doi.org/10.1080/02699930302297.

Kermani, Navid. 2018. *Wonder Beyond Belief: On Christianity.* Cambridge: Polity Press. Translated by T. Crawford.

Kidd, Ian J. 2017. "Epistemic Injustice and Religion." In Kidd, Medina, and Pohlhaus 2017: 386–96.

Kidd, Ian James, José Medina, and Gaile M. Pohlhaus, eds. 2017. *The Routledge Handbook of Epistemic Injustice.* London: Routledge.

Kielkopf, Charles. 1970. "Emotivism as the Solution to the Problem of Evil." *Sophia* 9 (2): 34–8. https://doi.org/10.1007/BF02804175.

Kierkegaard, Søren. 1865. *Sygdommen til Døden : En christelig psychologisk Udvikling til Opbyggelse og Opvækkelse.* C.A. Reizel.

Kind, Amy, ed. 2016. *The Routledge Handbook of Philosophy of Imagination.* London: Routledge.

Kind, Amy. 2020. "Philosophical Perspectives on Imagination in the Western Tradition." In *The Cambridge Handbook of the Imagination*, edited by Anna Abraham, 64–79. Cambridge: Cambridge University Press.

Kind, Amy. 2023. "Why We Need Imagination." In *Contemporary Debates in Philosophy of Mind*, edited by Brian McLaughlin and L. J. Cohen. 2nd ed., 570–87. Malden, MA: Wiley-Blackwell.

Kind, Amy, and Peter Kung, eds. 2016. *Knowledge Through Imagination*. Oxford United Kingdom: Oxford University Press.

Klemm, David E., and William Schweiker. 2008. *Religion and the Human Future: An Essay on Theological Humanism*. Malden, MA: Blackwell.

Kotzee, Ben. 2017. "Education and Epistemic Injustice." In Kidd, Medina, and Pohlhaus 2017: 324–35.

Krieger, Martin H. 2004. "Some of What Mathematicians Do." *Notices of the American Mathematical Society* 51 (10): 1226–30.

Kvanvig, Jonathan L. 2003. *The Value of Knowledge and the Pursuit of Understanding*. Cambridge: Cambridge University Press.

Kvanvig, Jonathan L. 2013. "Affective Theism and People of Faith." *Midwest Studies in Philosophy* 37 (1): 109–28. https://doi.org/10.1111/misp.12003.

Kvanvig, Jonathan L. 2018. *Faith and Humility*. Oxford: Oxford University Press.

Langland-Hassan, Peter. 2020. *Explaining Imagination*. New York: Oxford University Press.

Layne, Linda L. 2003. *Motherhood Lost: A Feminist Account of Pregnancy Loss in America*. New York: Routledge.

Lebens, Samuel. 2020. *The Principles of Judaism*. Oxford: Oxford University Press.

Lebens, Samuel. 2021. "Will I Get a Job? Contextualism, Belief, and Faith." *Synthese* 199 (3–4): 5769–90. https://doi.org/10.1007/s11229-021-03045-3.

Legenhausen, Muhammad. 2013. "Responding to the Religious Reasons of Others: Resonance and Nonreductive Religious Pluralism." *European Journal for Philosophy of Religion* 5 (2): 23–46. https://doi.org/10.24204/ejpr.v5i2.232.

Le Poidevin, Robin. 1996. *Arguing for Atheism: An Introduction to the Philosophy of Religion*. London: Routledge.

Le Poidevin, Robin. 2019. *Religious Fictionalism*. Cambridge Elements in the Philosophy of Religion. Cambridge: Cambridge University Press.

Le Poidevin, Robin. 2020. "Fiction and the Agnostic." *European Journal for Philosophy of Religion* 12 (3): 163–81. https://doi.org/10.24204/ejpr.v12i3.3415.

Levin, Janet. 2011. "Imaginability, Possibility, and the Puzzle of Imaginative Resistance." *Canadian Journal of Philosophy* 41 (3): 391–422. https://doi.org/10.1353/cjp.2011.0027.

Levy, Neil. 2017. "Religious Beliefs Are Factual Beliefs: Content Does Not Correlate with Context Sensitivity." *Cognition* 161: 109–16. https://doi.org/10.1016/j.cognition.2017.01.012.

Lewis, David K. 1973. *Counterfactuals*. Oxford: Blackwell.

Liao, Shen-yi, and Tamar Gendler. 2020. "Imagination." In *The Stanford Encyclopedia of Philosophy*, edited by Edward N. Zalta. Stanford: Stanford University Metaphysics Research Lab. https://plato.stanford.edu/archives/sum2020/entries/imagination/.

Lillard, Angeline. 2002. "Just Through the Looking Glass: Children's Understanding of Pretense." In *Pretending and Imagination in Animals and Children*, edited by Robert W. Mitchell, 102–14. Cambridge: Cambridge University Press.

Lindemann, Hilde. 2014. *Holding and Letting Go: The Social Practice of Personal Identities*. New York: Oxford University Press.

Longino, Helen. 1993. "Subjects, Power and Knowledge: Description and Prescription in Feminist Philosophies of Science." In Alcoff and Potter 1993, 101–20.

Longino, Helen E. 1990. *Science as Social Knowledge: Values and Objectivity in Scientific Inquiry*. Princeton, NJ: Princeton University Press.

Luhrmann, T. M. 2020. *How God Becomes Real: Kindling the Presence of Invisible Others*. Princeton, NJ: Princeton University Press.

MacDonald, George. 1893. *A Dish of Orts*. London: Sampson Low, Marston & Co.

MacDonald, George. (1895). *A Dish of Orts*. London: S. Low, Marston, & Co.

Malcolm, Finlay. 2018. "Can Fictionalists Have Faith?" *Religious Studies* 54 (2): 215–32. https://doi.org/10.1017/S0034412517000063.

Malcolm, Finlay, and Michael Scott. 2023. *A Philosophy of Faith: Belief, Truth and Varieties of Commitment*. Routledge Studies in the Philosophy of Religion. New York: Routledge.

Marion, Jean-Luc. 1991. *God Without Being*. 2nd ed. Chicago: University of Chicago Press. Translated by T.A. Carlson.

McCord Adams, Marilyn . 1999. *Horrendous Evils and the Goodness of God*. Ithaca, NY: Cornell University Press.

McCord Adams, Marilyn. 2014. "What's Wrong with the Ontotheological Error?" *Journal of Analytic Theology* 2: 1–12. https://doi.org/10.12978/jat.2014-1.120013000318a.

McCrary, Charles A. 2022. *Sincerely Held: American Secularism and Its Believers*. Chicago: University of Chicago Press.

McFague, Sallie. 1987. *Models of God: Theology for an Ecological Nuclear Age*. London: SCM Press. Translated by T.A. Carlson.

McGinn, Bernard. 2005. *The Harvest of Mysticism in Medieval Germany*. The Presence of God: A History of Western Christian Mysticism 4. New York: Crossroad Publications.

McKaughan, Daniel J. 2013. "Authentic Faith and Acknowledged Risk: Dissolving the Problem of Faith and Reason." *Religious Studies* 49 (1): 101–24. https://doi.org/10.1017/S0034412512000200.

McKaughan, Daniel J. 2016. "Action-Centered Faith, Doubt, and Rationality." *Journal of Philosophical Research* 41 (9999): 71–90. https://doi.org/10.5840/jpr20165364.

McKaughan, Daniel J. 2018. "Faith Through the Dark of Night." *Faith and Philosophy* 35 (2): 195–218. https://doi.org/10.5840/faithphil2018327101.

McKaughan, Daniel J., and Daniel Howard-Snyder. 2023. "Faith and Faithfulness." *Faith and Philosophy* 39 (1): 1–25. https://doi.org/10.37977/faithphil.2022.39.1.1.

Medina, José. 2013a. "An Enactivist Approach to the Imagination: Embodied Enactments and 'Fictional Emotions.'" *American Philosophical Quarterly* 50 (3): 317–35. https://www.jstor.org/stable/24475354.

Medina, José. 2013b. *The Epistemology of Resistance: Gender and Racial Oppression, Epistemic Injustice, and Resistant Imaginations*. Oxford: Oxford University Press.

Melo, Pedro, Rima Dhillon-Smith, Md Asiful Islam, Adam Devall, and Arri Coomarasamy. 2023. "Genetic Causes of Sporadic and Recurrent Miscarriage." *Fertility and Sterility* 120 (5): 940–44. https://doi.org/10.1016/j.fertnstert.2023.08.952.

Mitchell, Basil. 2005. "Staking a Claim for Metaphysics." In Harris and Insole 2005, 21–32.

Mitchell, Robert W. 2007. "Pretense in Animals: The Continuing Relevance of Children's Pretense." In *Play and Development: Evolutionary, Sociocultural, and Functional Perspectives*, edited by Artin Göncü and Suzanne Gaskins, 51–75. Mahwah, NJ: Lawrence Erlbaum Associates.

Moran, Richard. 1994. "The Expression of Feeling in Imagination." *Philosophical Review* 103 (1): 75–106. https://doi.org/10.2307/2185873.

Moskowitz, Clara. 2014. "Equations Are Art Inside a Mathematician's Brain." *Nature*. https://doi.org/10.1038/nature.2014.14825.

Mugg, Joshua. 2022. "Faith Entails Belief: Three Avenues of Defense Against the Argument from Doubt." *Pacific Philosophical Quarterly* 103 (4): 816–36. https://doi.org/10.1111/papq.12374.

Müller, Olaf L. 2019. *Zu Schön, Um Falsch Zu Sein: Über Die Ästhetik in Der Naturwissenschaft*. Frankfurt a. M. S. Fischer.

Muyskens, James L. 1979. *The Sufficiency of Hope: The Conceptual Foundations of Religion*. Philadelphia: Temple University Press.

Myers, Joshua. 2024. "Imaginative Beliefs." *Inquiry* [online first]: 1–28. https://doi.org/10.1080/0020174X.2024.2312218.

Nguyen, C. Thi. 2020. *Games: Agency as Art*. New York: Oxford University Press.

Nguyen, C. Thi. 2022. "Playfulness Versus Epistemic Traps." In *Social Virtue Epistemology*, edited by Mark Alfano, Colin Klein, and Jeroen d. Ridder, 269–90. New York: Routledge.

Nichols, Shaun, ed. 2006. *The Architecture of the Imagination: New Essays on Pretence, Possibility, and Fiction*. New York: Oxford University Press.

Ockman, Joan. 2000. *The Pragmatist Imagination: Thinking About "Things in the Making"*. New York: Princeton Architectural Press.

O'Donnell, Karen. 2022. *The Dark Womb: Re-Conceiving Theology Through Reproductive Loss*. London: SCM Press.

Okshevsky, Walter C. 1992. "Epistemological and Hermeneutic Conceptions of the Nature of Understanding: The Cases of Paul H. Hirst and Martin Heidegger." *Educational Theory* 42 (1): 5–23. https://doi.org/10.1111/j.1741-5446.1992.00005.x.

Olyan, Saul M., and Martha C. Nussbaum, eds. 1998. *Sexual Orientation & Human Rights in American Religious Discourse*. New York: Oxford University Press.

Otto, Rudolf. 1958. *The Idea of the Holy*. New York: Oxford University Press. Translated by J.W. Harvey.

Palmqvist, Carl-Johan. 2021. "Forms of Belief-Less Religion: Why Non-Doxasticism Makes Fictionalism Redundant for the Pro-Religious Agnostic." *Religious Studies* 57 (1): 49–65. https://doi.org/10.1017/S0034412519000027.

Palmqvist, Carl-Johan. 2023. "Pretending to Be a Believer: On Understanding Religious Fictionalism as a Role-Playing Game." *Religious Studies* 59 (2): 276–90. https://doi.org/10.1017/S0034412522000312.

Panchuk, Michelle. 2018. "The Shattered Spiritual Self: A Philosophical Exploration of Religious Trauma." *Res Philosophica* 95 (3): 505–30. https://doi.org/10.11612/resphil.1684.

Panchuk, Michelle. 2019. "That We May Be Whole: Doing Philosophy of Religion with the Whole Self." In *The Lost Sheep in Philosophy of Religion: New Perspectives on Disability, Gender, Race, and Animals*, edited by Blake Hereth and Kevin Timpe, 55–76. Abdington-on-Thames: Routledge.

Panchuk, Michelle. 2020. "Distorting Concepts, Obscured Experiences: Hermeneutical Injustice in Religious Trauma and Spiritual Violence." *Hypatia* 35 (4): 607–25. https://doi.org/10.1017/hyp.2020.32.

Panchuk, Michelle. 2024. "What Doesn't Kill Me Makes Me Stronger? Post-Traumatic Growth and the Problem of Suffering." *Religious Studies* 60 (3): 428–44. https://doi.org/10.1017/S0034412523000999.

Paul, L.A. 2014. *Transformative Experience*. Oxford: Oxford University Press.

Pearson, Kathleen M. 1973. "Deception, Sportsmanship, and Ethics." *Quest* 19 (1): 115–18. https://doi.org/10.1080/00336297.1973.10519761.

Peterson, Michael L., ed. 2017. *The Problem of Evil: Selected Readings*. Second Edition. Notre Dame, IN: University of Notre Dame Press.

Pigliucci, Massimo. 2019. "Richard Feynman Was Wrong About Beauty and Truth in Science." Accessed February 15, 2024. https://aeon.co/ideas/richard-feynman-was-wrong-about-beauty-and-truth-in-science.

Pinn, Anthony B. 2015. *Humanism: Essays on Race, Religion and Popular Culture*. London: Bloomsbury Academic.

Plantinga, Alvin. 1983. "Reason and Belief in God." In *Faith and Rationality: Reason and Belief in God*, edited by Alvin Plantinga and Nicholas Wolstertorff, 16–93. Notre Dame, IN: University of Notre Dame Press.

Plantinga, Alvin. 2000. *Warranted Christian Belief*. New York: Oxford University Press.

Pojman, Louis P. 1991. "Faith, Doubt and Hope." In *Contemporary Classics in Philosophy of Religion*, edited by Ann Loades and Loyal D. Rue, 183–207. La Salle, IL: Open Court.

Potter, Kelli. 2013. "Religious Disagreement: Internal and External." *International Journal for Philosophy of Religion* 74 (1): 21–31. https://doi.org/10.1007/s11153-012-9393-y.

Potter, Kelli. Forthcoming. "The Significance of Heterodoxy." In *Radical Pluralism: Essays on Ethics, Diversity, and Religious Experience*, edited by Brian Birch and Patrick Horn. Tübingen: Mohr Siebeck.

Priest, Graham. 2016. "Thinking the Impossible." *Philosophical Studies* 173 (10): 2649–62. https://doi.org/10.1007/s11098-016-0668-5.

Pritchard, Duncan. 2010. "Understanding." In *The Nature and Value of Knowledge: Three Investigations*, edited by Duncan Pritchard, Alan Millar, and Adrian Haddock, 66–88. Oxford: Oxford University Press.

Rambo, Lewis R. 1993. *Understanding Religious Conversion*. New Haven, CT: Yale University.

Ramler, Mari E. 2023. "When God Hurts: The Rhetoric of Religious Trauma as Epistemic Pain." *Rhetoric Society Quarterly* 53 (2): 202–16. https://doi.org/10.1080/02773945.2022.2129755.

Rea, Michael C. 2009. "Introduction." In *Analytic Theology: New Essays in the Philosophy of Theology*, edited by Oliver Crisp and Michael C. Rea, 1–30. Oxford: Oxford University Press.

Reiheld, Alison. 2015. "'The Event That Was Nothing': Miscarriage as a Liminal Event." *Journal of Social Philosophy* 46 (1): 9–26. https://doi.org/10.1111/josp.12084.

Ricœur, Paul. 1995. *Figuring the Sacred: Religion, Narrative, and Imagination*. Minneapolis, MN: Fortress Press. Translated by D. Pellauer.

Riezler, Kurt. 1941. "Play and Seriousness." *Journal of Philosophy* 38 (19): 505–17. https://doi.org/10.2307/2017298.

Rucińska, Zuzanna, and Shaun Gallagher. 2021. "Making Imagination Even More Embodied: Imagination, Constraint and Epistemic Relevance." *Synthese* 199 (3–4): 8143–70. https://doi.org/10.1007/s11229-021-03156-x.

Russell, J. S. 1999. "Are Rules All an Umpire Has to Work with?" *Journal of the Philosophy of Sport* 26 (1): 27–49. https://doi.org/10.1080/00948705.1999.9714577.

Sartre, Jean-Paul. [1940] 2004. *The Imaginary: A Phenomenological Psychology of the Imagination*. London: Routledge. Translated by J. Webber.

Schilbrack, Kevin. 2014. *Philosophy and the Study of Religions: A Manifesto*. Malden, MA: Wiley-Blackwell.

Schmid, Stephen E. 2009. "Reconsidering Autotelic Play." *Journal of the Philosophy of Sport* 36 (2): 238–57. https://doi.org/10.1080/00948705.2009.9714759.

Seligman, Adam B. 2010. "Ritual and Sincerity: Certitude and the Other." *Philosophy & Social Criticism* 36 (1): 9–39. https://doi.org/10.1177/0191453709348416.

Seligman, Adam B., Robert P. Weller, Michael J. Puett, and Bennett Simon. 2008. *Ritual and Its Consequences: An Essay on the Limits of Sincerity*. Oxford: Oxford University Press.

Seuse, Heinrich (Henry Suso). 1907. *Heinrich Seuse: Deutsche Schriften*, ed. by K. Bihlmeyer. Stuttgart: W. Kohlhammer.

Seuse, Heinrich (Henry Suso). 1861. *Henrici Susonis seu fratris Amandi, Horologium sapientiae*. Cologne: J.M. Hebberle (H. Lempertz).

Sölle, Dorothee. 1973. *Leiden*. Kreuz Verlag.

Sölle, Dorothee. 1975. *Suffering*. Philadelphia: Fortress Press.

Sollereder, Bethany N. 2021. "Compassionate Theodicy: A Suggested Truce Between Intellectual and Practical Theodicy." *Modern Theology* 37 (2): 382–95. https://doi.org/10.1111/moth.12688.

Soskice, Janet. 1987. "Theological Realism." In *The Rationality of Religious Belief: Essays in Honour of Basil Mitchell*, edited by William J. Abraham and Steven W. Hotzer, 105–19. Oxford: Clarendon Press.

Stenmark, Mikael. 2015. "Competing Conceptions of God: The Personal God Versus the God Beyond Being." *Religious Studies* 51 (2): 205–20. https://doi.org/10.1017/S0034412514000304.

Strenski, Ivan. 2012. "Philosophy of (Lived) Religion." *Studies in Religion/Sciences Religieuses* 41 (1): 5–11. https://doi.org/10.1177/0008429811430052.

Strevens, Michael. 2016. "How Idealizations Provide Understanding." In Grimm, Baumberger, and Ammon 2016, 37–49.

Stringer, Martin D. 1996. "Towards a Situational Theory of Belief." *Journal of the Anthropological Society of Oxford* 27 (3): 217–34.

Stump, Eleonore. 2010. *Wandering in Darkness: Narrative and the Problem of Suffering*. Oxford: Oxford University Press.

Suits, Bernard. 1977. "Words on Play." *Journal of the Philosophy of Sport* 4 (1): 117–31. https://doi.org/10.1080/00948705.1977.10654132.

Suits, Bernard. 1978. *The Grasshopper: Games, Life, and Utopia*. Toronto: University of Toronto Press.

Swinburne, Richard. 2007. *Faith and Reason*. 2nd ed. Oxford: Clarendon Press.

Swinton, John. 2018. *Raging with Compassion: Pastoral Responses to the Problem of Evil*. London: SCM Press.

Taliaferro, Charles. 2005. *Evidence and Faith: Philosophy and Religion Since the Seventeenth Century*. Cambridge: Cambridge University Press.

Tillich, Paul. 1973. *Systematic Theology: Volume One*. Chicago: University of Chicago Press.

Timpe, Kevin. 2015. "On Analytic Theology." *Scientia et Fides* 3 (2): 9–22. https://doi.org/10.12775/SetF.2015.013.

Tooley, Michael. 2019. *The Problem of Evil*. Cambridge Elements in the Philosophy of Religion. Cambridge: Cambridge University Press.

Trakakis, Nick. 2008. *The End of Philosophy of Religion*. New York: Continuum.

Vaihinger, Hans. 1935. *The Philosophy of 'as If': A System of the Theoretical, Practical and Religious Fictions of Mankind*. 2nd ed. Translated by C. K. Ogden.

Van Dyke, Christina. 2022. *A Hidden Wisdom: Medieval Contemplatives on Self-Knowledge, Reason, Love, Persons, and Immortality*. Oxford: Oxford University Press.

Van Inwagen, Peter. 2006. *The Problem of Evil*. Oxford: Clarendon Press.

Van Leeuwen, Neil. 2011. "Imagination Is Where the Action Is." *Journal of Philosophy* 108 (2): 55–77. https://doi.org/10.5840/jphil201110823.

Van Leeuwen, Neil. 2014. "Religious Credence Is Not Factual Belief." *Cognition* 133 (3): 698–715. https://doi.org/10.1016/j.cognition.2014.08.015.

Van Leeuwen, Neil. 2017. "Two Paradigms for Religious Representation: The Physicist and the Playground (A Reply to Levy)." *Cognition* 164: 206–11. https://doi.org/10.1016/j.cognition.2017.03.021.

Van Leeuwen, Neil. 2023. *Religion as Make-Believe: A Theory of Belief, Imagination, and Group Identity*. Cambridge, MA: Harvard University Press.

Verbin, N. K. 2002. "Uncertainty and Religious Belief." *International Journal for Philosophy of Religion* 51 (1): 1–37. https://doi.org/10.1023/A:1012658403848.

von Stosch, Klaus. 2009. "Komparative Theologie Als Hauptaufgabe Der Theologie Der Zukunft." In *Komparative Theologie: Interreligiöse Vergleiche Als Weg Der Religionstheologie*, edited by Reinhold Bernhardt and Klaus von Stosch, 15–33. Zürich: Theologischer Verlag Zürich.

von Stosch, Klaus. 2012. "Comparative Theology as Challenge for the Theology of the 21st Century." *Religious Inquiries* 1 (2): 5–26. https://ri.urd.ac.ir/article_6271.html.

Wagner, Rachel. 2014. "The Importance of Playing in Earnest." In *Playing with Religion in Digital Games*, edited by Heidi A. Campbell and Gregory P. Grieve, 192–213. Bloomington, IN: Indiana University Press.

Wallace, R. Jay. 2001. "Normativity, Commitment, and Instrumental Reason." *Philosophers' Imprint* 1 (4): 1–26. https://hdl.handle.net/2027/spo.3521354.0001.004.

Walton, Kendall L. 1990. *Mimesis as Make Believe: On the Foundations of the Representational Arts*. Cambridge, MA: Harvard University Press.

Walton, Kendall L. 2006. "On the (So-Called) Puzzle of Imaginative Resistance." In *The Architecture of the Imagination: New Essays on Pretence, Possibility, and Fiction*, edited by Shaun Nichols, 137–48. New York: Oxford University Press.

Warner, Meg. 2019. "'Sing, O Barren One Who Did Not Bear': Childlessness, Blessing and Vocation in the Old Testament." *Modern Believing* 60 (2): 111–21. https://doi.org/10.3828/mb.2019.10.

Westphal, Merold. 2001. *Overcoming Onto-Theology: Toward a Postmodern Christian Faith*. New York: Fordham University Press.

Westphal, Merold. 2007. "The Importance of Overcoming Metaphysics of the Life of Faith." *Modern Theology* 23 (2): 253–78. https://doi.org/10.1111/j.1468-0025.2007.00372.x.

Wettstein, Howard K. 1997. "Awe and the Religious Life: A Naturalistic Perspective." *Midwest Studies in Philosophy* 21 (1): 257–80. https://doi.org/10.1111/j.1475-4975.1997.tb00527.x.

Wettstein, Howard K. 2012. *The Significance of Religious Experience*. New York: Oxford University Press.

Wiesel, Elie. 1995. *The Trial of God (As It Was Held on February 25, 1649, in Shamgorod): A Play*. New York: Schocken Books. Translated by M. Wiesel.

Williams, Bernard. 1981. "Persons, Character and Morality." In *Moral Luck: Philosophical Papers, 1973–1980*, edited by Bernard Williams, 1–19. Cambridge: Cambridge University Press.

Wittgenstein, Ludwig. 1953. *Philosophical Investigations: (Philosophische Untersuchungen)*. Oxford: Blackwell. Translated by G.E.M. Anscombe.

Wolterstorff, Nicholas. 1976. *Reason Within the Bounds of Religion*. Grand Rapids, MI: Eerdmans.

Wong, David B. 2020. "Soup, Harmony, and Disagreement." *Journal of the American Philosophical Association* 6 (2): 139–55. https://doi.org/10.1017/apa.2018.46.

Wood, William. 2021. *Analytic Theology and the Academic Study of Religion.* Oxford: Oxford University Press.

Yadav, Sameer. 2016. "Mystical Experience and the Apophatic Attitude." *Journal of Analytic Theology* 4: 17–43. https://doi.org/10.12978/jat.2016-4.180017240021a.

Young, Iris Marion. 2006. "Responsibility and Global Justice: A Social Connection Model." *Social Philosophy and Policy* 23 (1): 102–30. https://doi.org/10.1017/S0265052506060043.

Young, Iris Marion. 2011. *Justice and the Politics of Difference.* Princeton, NJ: Princeton University Press.

Zeki, Semir, John Paul Romaya, Dionigi M. T. Benincasa, and Michael F. Atiyah. 2014. "The Experience of Mathematical Beauty and Its Neural Correlates." *Frontiers in Human Neuroscience* 8 (68): 1–12. https://doi.org/10.3389/fnhum.2014.00068.

Index

abandonment (to God), *see* detachment

abgescheidenheit, abgescheiden, 210, 216;
    see also detachment; mysticism

abortion; 183, 186, 221n11; *see also*
    pregnancy loss

abstraction, 2, 17, 63, 185, 188, 191–2,
    194, 201n17

academia, ix, xi, 1, 6, 22n2, 132, 165n9,
    183, 188, 190, 201n1

acceptance
    and belief, 30, 41n7, 47, 61n8, 66, 77, 83,
        108, 116, 120–1, 125n20
    definition of, 30
    in faith contexts, 77, 82, 83, 85, 90,
        101n11
    imaginative, 58, 60n8, 108, 116, 119,
        120–1, 124n14, 125n20, 127,
        132–3, 147
    in play, 132–3, 134, 147
    religious, 45, 125n20, 127, 147, 151
    and resonance, 34–5
    of rules, 132, 137, 143n12
    in science and mathematics, 30

action
    chained, 119, 126n21, 216
    collective/communal/joint, 51, 73, 94,
        96, 149n1
    and conversion, 122n22
    and faith, 75, 83, 87, 95–6
    and imagination, 109, 113
    and motivation, *see* motivation
    symbolic, 51

Adams, Marilyn McCord, *see* McCord
    Adams, Marilyn

Adams, Robert M., 51

adequacy, 21, 30, 50, 54, 64, 115, 193, 219;
    see also appropriateness;
    fittingness

affective (attitudes, orientations, dimensions)
    in APR, 15, 214, 221n7
    as divorced from the epistemic in APR,
        15, 18, 154, 192

    in epistemology, 39
    and exemplification, 51
    in mysticism, 210, 213, 219, 221n6
    and play, 162
    in religion/religious faith, 15, 47, 73, 83,
        90–1, 95, 97, 99, 121, 127, 160
    resonances and dissonances, *see*
        resonance
    in science and mathematics, 34
    and the social imagination, 113, 117
    transformation, 127
    and understanding, 35, 39, 46, 58, 65

affirmation, 71, 77, 84, 91, 94, 102n19, 159

agency, 41n6, 88–9, 95, 96, 104n32, 109,
    112, 195, 213

agnosticism, agnostic, 27, 41n6, 65, 108,
    121, 148, 164n1; *see also* belief,
    suspension of; doubt; non-belief

agreement, consensus, 21, 30–1, 36, 38, 65,
    96; *see also* disagreement

alienation, 117, 186–7, 193

Alston, William P., 123n1, 124n12

Ammerman, Nancy T., 59n2, 72–3

Anderson, Elizabeth, 24n18

analytic philosophy, 2, 6, 7, 14, 41n10, 45,
    73, 87, 124n9, 183

analytic philosophy of religion (APR)
    adversarial nature of, xiii, 16
    vs. analytic theology, 6, 63–4
    constricted horizons of, 4–7
    critiques of, ix, 1–3, 15–19, 39, 57, 61n9,
        62n19, 188–97 (*see also*: this
        entire monograph)
    onto(theo)logical objections to,
        11–20, 22n3–4, 23n10–11,
        24n14, 53, 65–6, 72, 102n18,
        103n29, 107
    defensive stance of, 2, 14, 16, 20, 129,
        177, 221n7
    demographics of, 5–7, 183, 203n11
    end of, x
    future of, 63–7, 167–71, 219–20

gatekeeping in, 190, 197
insularity/isolation of, 2, 7, 20, 63, 183,
    192, 195, 197, 200
intellectualist, xi, 16–7, 72–3, 98–9 (*see
    also* theodicy, "purely
    intellectual" approach to)
irrelevance of, xii, 7, 13, 20, 57, 196–7,
    220
methodology of, 2, 7, 20, 191–2, 198,
    200, 204n20, 215
non-Christian perspectives in, 5–6,
    7n2, 116, 197
analytic theology (AT), *see* theology,
    analytic
Anselm of Canterbury
    fides quaerens intellectum, 14, 63,
        97–8
    Jesus as mother hen, 125n18
antirealism, antirealist, 13–14, 21, 23n10,
    30, 57, 65, 87, 97, 142n2, 198;
    see also fictionalism; realism,
    realist
anti-theodicy, 178, 193, 198; *see also*
    theodicy, moral and epistemic
    dangers of
apophaticism, *see* theology, apophatic
appropriateness, 42n13, 48–9, 55, 56, 119,
    134, 168, 171; *see also* fittingness
APR, *see* analytic philosophy of religion
Arcadi, James M., 6, 63–4
Arnal, William E., 22n6, 100n1
as-if stance, 132–3, 134, 135, 147, 152, 154,
    156–7, 159–60, 168
asceticism, 210, 216–7
AT, *see* analytic theology
atheism, atheist(s), viii, 2, 14–5, 22n7,
    23n10, 42n12, 60n6, 61n15 65,
    129, 181–3, 198, 203n11, 215
new" atheism, 11, 13 16, 21n1, 129
attachment (in mysticism), 209–15; *see
    also* detachment
Audi, Robert, 75, 93, 100n4, 100n6,
    105n45
Austin, J.L., 102n15
authenticity, 60n8, 85, 90–9, 103n29,
    103n37, 108, 121, 143n8, 147,
    151, 156–60, 164n2, 164n7,
    165n8, 180; *see also*
    commitment; faith

autotelicity, autotelic, 41n10, 132–4, 136,
    140, 142, 144n13, 152, 156, 161,
    169
awe, *see* wonder

Bacon, Francis, 35
bad faith, 91, 97, 164n7, 168; *see also*
    self-deception
Barbour, Ian G., 50, 60n3
beauty (in science and mathematics),
    34–5, 40n5, 41n12; *see also*
    values, aesthetic
belief, believer(s); *see also* certainty,
    subjective; disbelief,
    disbeliever(s); doubt; make-
    believe(rs); religious belief,
    believer(s)
    and acceptance, *see* acceptance, and
        belief
    and faith, 72, 75–83, 99, 108 (*see also*
        faith, doxastic models of)
    degrees of, 15, 72, 78–9, 108, 124n13,
        130
    imaginative, 124n13
    justified true, *see* knowledge
    rationality of, 26, 46; *see also*, religious
        belief/believer(s), rationality of
    religious, *see* religious belief/believer(s)
    suspension of, 47, 99, 109, 122n1
    taxonomy of (into belief, non-belief,
        disbelief), 122n1, 149
    theistic, *see* religious belief, theistic
Berkhof, Louis, 64
beyondness, x, 142
bild, bilden (*entbildet, gebildet, überbildet*),
    208–9, 211, 221n3; *see also*
    mysticism
birth, rebirth, 115, 125n17, 203n12,
    204n15, 211
Bishop, John, 76–7
blame, blameworthiness, xiii, 14, 103n26,
    183–4, 185, 204n23
bodies, *see* embodiment
Bostic, Joy R., 117–18
boundaries (borders, limits)
    disciplinary, x–xi, 4, 13, 16, 208, 217,
        220
    in imaginative play, 132, 134
    in religion, 44, 168,

breaking through (*durchbrechen*), 210,
215, 216, 218
Brown, David, 112, 124n14–15
Buchak, Lara, 76, 95, 98, 105n42
bullshit, ix,102n19
Burley, Mikel, 7n2, 45, 116

Cambridge Platonists, 4
cataphaticism, *see* theology, cataphatic
certainty, subjective (confidence,
credence), 15, 27–8, 36, 60n8,
72, 78–9, 86, 99, 108, 120–1,
122n1, 125n20, 129–30,
141n1,149, 153, 157, 163n1,167;
see also belief; doubt; religious
belief
CF model, *see* faith, commitment model of
Chandrasekhar, Subrahmanyan, 34–5
Chang, Ruth, 88–90, 97, 103n27, 104n32
Christ, *see* Jesus of Nazareth (Christ)
Christianity, Christians,xiv, 5–7, 14, 31,
50, 55, 61n18, 64, 67n6, 94,
103n24–25, 113–15, 118–19,
124n22, 125n18, 130, 162,
165n10, 167, 175, 184, 185, 209,
211; *see also* analytic theology,
Christian; theology, Christian
Clarke-Doane, Justin, 27
close-mindedness, 18, 169
cognition, cognitive
and affect, 35, 47, 58, 73, 85, 95, 113,
118
attunement, *see* resonance, cognitive
and authenticity, 93
centered in APR, 3, 14, 72–3, 75, 94,
98–9, 116–17
and faith, 3, 72–3, 85, 87, 95, 99, 108,
120–1
and imagination, 3, 99, 108, 111–12,
117, 120
in religion, 87, 93, 148–50, 163n1,
164n7
cognitivism, non-cognitivism, 13, 23n10,
116
Cohen, L. Jonathan, 30, 120, 122n1
commitment(s)
and acceptance, 28–9, 39, 41n7, 60n8,
108, 120–1, 127
analysis/nature of, 88–89, 103n27

and authenticity, 60n8, 90–3, 95, 97,
99, 104n37, 121, 156, 158, 159,
164n2, 164n7, 165n8
cognitive, 28, 41n7, 89, 90, 109, 113,
149
doxastic, 15, 54, 108, 117
and faith and, 90–9; *see also* faith,
commitment model of
and identity/identification, 89–91, 93,
97, 112, 121
moral, 45, 52, 88, 89103n26, 160
networks/systems of, 28, 46
practical/social, 45, 55, 85–6, 89–90, 91,
97
propositional, 26, 120
rationality/reasonability of, 28, 88–89,
92, 95, 97, 103n25, 103n29
as reason-giving, 88–9, 103n26, 103n29
religious, 6, 46, 64, 85–99, 105n40,
105n45, 108, 112, 127, 147–151,
160, 169, 180, 183, 187, 203n8
and transformation, 36, 52–3, 127
wielded to further epistemic ends, 28,
29, 46
and the will, *see* volition(al),
volitionality
community, communities
epistemic, 31, 195, 81
and faith, 74, 86–7, 92, 94, 98, 157–8
intellectual, scientific, 27, 37, 195
religious, 31, 55, 74, 79, 82, 84–7, 92, 94,
98, 111, 117–18, 143n9, 148–9,
156–8, 164n7, 168–9, 176, 180,
182, 187, 189, 207, 215
social, cultural, familial, 118–19, 133,
160, 221n10
comparative theology, *see* theology,
comparative
compassion, compassionate, 3, 118, 167,
177, 180, 195, 197, 199, 207, 218
confidence, *see* certainty (subjective); *see*
also belief; doubt; religious
belief
Confucius (Kŏngzĭ), 25, 36
consensus, *see* agreement; *see also*
disagreement
contemplation, 46, 154, 209, 212, 214
contemplative traditions, contemplatives,
see mysticism, mystics

context-dependence, -sensitivity, 54, 57,
    61n18, 64, 80, 122, 122n1,
    125n20, 134, 212
conversion, xii, 85, 86, 97, 102n22, 159,
    182, 198, 210; *see also*
    deconversion
Coomaraswamy, Ananda K., 138–9
correspondence (to reality), 27, 32, 49, 50,
    53, 111, 113
    see also factivity; tethering; truth
cosplay, 133, 140; *see also* role-playing
Cottingham, John, 46, 72, 84–5, 150
Coyne, Jerry, 1, 2
credence(s), *see* certainty, subjective; *see*
    also belief; doubt; religious belief
Csikszentmihalyi, Mihaly, 138, 141
Cuneo, Terence, 5, 51, 105n43, 127–8,
    142n1

Dancy, Jonathan, 24n16
deception, 82, 102n19, 129, 132, 135–7,
    149, 156–8
    definition of, 136
    in games, 132, 136, 143n11
    and make-believe/pretense, 129–32,
        135–7, 144n19, 156–8, 164n7
    self-, 79, 91, 102n16–18, 103n28, 130,
        149, 153, 157–8, 199, 211, 214
deconstruction (unformation, *entbilden*)
    academic, disciplinary, 190, 214–19
    instruction in, 210
    of the self in mysticism, 208–11
declarative theology, *see* theology,
    declarative
deconversion, 91, 92, 103n25, 156, 158,
    160, 182, 215
De Cruz, Helen, 6, 59, 221n9
Deng, Natalja, 102n20, 128
De Regt, Henk, 26, 29–30
detachment
    of analytic epistemology from socio-
        political considerations, 45
    of APR from lived religion, 5, 15, 17, 73
    as epistemic value (disinterestedness),
        16–17, 193
    in mystical contexts (*abgescheidenheit,*
        gelâzenheit), 208–10, 214,
        215–16, 220n1
    in play, 138

dignity, 33, 193, 202n3, 214
direction of fit, 47, 51, 55
disagreement
    as crucial for objectivity, 21, 37–8
    peer, 36, 65
    religious, 65, 105n44
    scientific, 30
disbelief, disbelievers, 22n7, 80, 82–83, 87,
    96–7, 99, 102n21, 108, 109, 121,
    123n1, 141n1, 153; *see also*
    belief; faith; non-belief
disembodiment, 17, 47, 117; *see also*
    embodiment
disinterestedness, *see* detachment
disruption, dissonance, xi, 35–9, 41n12,
    54, 169, 204n19; *see also*
    epistemic frictions; reflective
    equilibrium; resonance
    aesthetic/affective, 36, 39, 58
    in APR/AT, 45, 56, 58, 64–5, 96, 215–17
    cognitive/intellectual, 36, 50, 58, 169
    existential (in trauma), 180, 203n8
    imaginative, *see* imagination, resistant
    and "playing the spoilsport," 169–171
    of religious models, 54
    and social dynamics of understanding,
        35–7,
    and weirdness, 35
diversity, diversification
    lack of/need for in APR, 4–7, 21, 48,
        196–7, 214–19
    of perspectives, importance of, 21,
        37–8, 197
    of religious life and attitudes/
        commitments, 15, 43
Divine Mother
    in Hinduism (Kālī), 116
    Jesus as, 125n18
dogmatism, 157, 168, 215
Dormandy, Katherine, 195
Dotson, Kristie, 192, 200, 204n20
doubt (uncertainty), 76–81, 95–6, 101n10,
    149, 158, 186; *see also* faith;
    non-belief
doxasticism, *see* faith, models of, doxastic
durchbrechen, see breaking through
duties, obligations
    civic, legal, 89, 218
    epistemic, 65, 121, 198

moral, 89, 176, 191, 214, 218
    scholarly/vocational, 57, 176, 188, 191,
        217

earnestness (in play), 3, 99, 108, 122,
        129–30, 137, 138, 141–2, 147, 156,
        158–63, 168, 170–1; *see also*
        seriousness; sincerity
Eckhart of Hochheim (Meister Eckhart),
        61n10, 125n17, 207, 208–14, 215,
        218, 220n1
edification, v, 175, 186, 209, 211–12, 219;
        see also bild, bilden; forming,
        formation
elegance (in science and mathematics), *see*
        beauty
Elgin, Catherine Z., 26–33, 37–9, 41n8–9,
        47, 49–51, 58
embodiment; *see also* disembodiment
    human beings as, 45, 51
    and imagination, *see* imaginings,
        embodied
    and miscarriage, 183
    and mysticism, 213–14
    and religious practice/ritual, 15, 46,
        51–2, 56, 75, 84–5, 96, 98, 101n7,
        122, 154
emotion, *see* affective (the)
empathy, 153, 180
Endō, Shūsaku, 104n38
enlightenment, *see* illumination
Enlightenment, the (historical
        movement), 1, 21n1, 72
epistemic arrogance, 18, 38, 194–5
epistemic cold-heartedness, 195
epistemic friction(s), 36–9, 45, 64–5, 66n1,
        127, 196
    in APR/AT, 56, 64–5, 115, 196, 215–7,
        221n9
    and epistemology of resistance, 58–9,
        62n20
    and intellectual vice/virtue, 38, 50,
        169
    in religious contexts, 54
epistemic injustice, 15n24, 191–4, 200,
        215; *see also* gaslighting
    and addressive neglect, 193–4
    hermeneutical injustice, 192–3, 200
    testimonial injustice, 18, 191–2, 200

    testimonial silencing, 191–2
    testimonial smothering, 187, 192,
        200, 204n20
epistemic traps, 168–9
epistemic value (of a domain)
    of religion, xii, 3, 25, 39–40, 43–5,
        47–50, 53, 60n3, 71
    of science and mathematics, 25–8,
        29–30
    understanding and, 31–3,
epistemology
    feminist, ix, 45
    knowledge- vs. understanding-
        centered, 25–62, 63, 107–8,
        116
    religious, 2, 4, 39, 43–68
    of resistance, *see* resistance
    social, ix, 26, 35–9, 43, 53–9
    values in, *see* values, epistemic
error-theory, 13, 97
ethics, ethical concerns, 4, 44, 45, 47,
        51, 105n43, 127, 128, 188,
        207
evidentialism, 14, 23n11
evil; *see also* suffering; theodicy
    erasure of, 193
    gratuitousness of, 181, 186
    horrendous, 18, 180, 187
    moral, 114
    natural, 186
    problem of, 3, 12, 171, 175–201,
        204n17
    theoretical vs. religious, 182, 187,
        215–16
exemplars (moral, spiritual), 25, 51, 76, 79,
        120, 155, 211, 214
exemplification, 31–2, 50–2
existential
    challenges, 59n1, 182, 187, 195
    disruption, 180
    earnestness, 141–2, 163
    meaning-making (orientation), 43–6,
        47, 50, 60n3, 60n8, 71–2, 98,
        120, 122, 147, 161–2, 177, 219;
        see also understanding,
        hermeneutical
    narratives, 97, 105n45
eye-rolling, performative, 177, 202n4,
        216

factivity, 3, 29–30, 40n4, 41n9, 57; *see also* truth
faith
  and authenticity, 90–9, 159
  bad, *see* bad faith; *see also* self-deception
  and belief, *see* faith, doxastic vs. non-doxastic models of
  commitment model of (CF), 90–9, 108–9, 112, 121, 143n8
  devotional, 75, 80, 82, 86–7, 90, 93–4, 97–8, 104n37 151
  and doubt, 76–81, 87, 95–96
  doxastic vs. non-doxastic models of, 76–84, 99
  as doxastically permissive, 3, 99, 107–22, 129, 148, 163
  global, 75, 80, 82, 91, 92, 98, 99, 100n4, 100n6, 104n37, 167
  and hope, 77, 79, 87, 90, 96, 101n11, 113, 121, 164n2
  and identity, 91, 93, 97, 99
  and imagination, 107–22, 121
  (in)compatibility with disbelief, 80, 82–3, 87, 96–7, 99, 102n21 108, 121, 153
  institutional (creedal), 75, 100n6, 101n7
  locutions, in English, 74
  and make-believe, 147–63
  objectual (attitudinal), 75, 76–7, 80, 81, 82, 83 86, 87, 90, 95, 97, 100n4–6, 102n23, 108, 171n1
  propositional, 72, 75–83, 86, 94, 98, 100n5, 102n23, 105n42, 108, 116, 120–22, 129, 164n2
  rationality of, 72–3, 78, 79, 81, 92, 95, 97, 102n18, 103n29
  resilience of, 79, 82, 83, 87, 95, 105n41, 171n1
  and risk/venture, 76–8, 87, 96
  and trust, 77, 84, 90, 96, 101n12
  volitionality of, *see* volition(al), volitionality
faith-shaking trauma (FST), 179–80, 187, 190–1, 193, 195, 200, 207, 215; *see also* suffering; trauma
felicitous falsehoods, 26–7, 32, 49
Feske, Millicent C., 184–5
Feynman, Richard, 34
fiction(s), 15, 27, 60n5, 109, 111, 133, 148–9, 163n1, 190

fictionalism, fictionalist(s), 83, 87, 97, 102n20, 125n19, 128–9, 142n2, 153, 163n2
fittingness, 33, 37, 42n13, 49, 53–4; *see also* adequacy; appropriateness
flow, flowing, 125n17, 138, 141, 211
flourishing, xii, 43, 45, 51–2, 57, 60n3, 65, 112, 167, 200
Forberg, Friedrich Carl, v
forming, formation, 53, 209–11, 214; *see also* bild, *bilden*; reform/reformation; transformation
Frankfurt, Harry, 104n33
Fricker, Miranda, 41n7, 60n7, 113
frictions, epistemic, *see* epistemic frictions
frivolity (and play/make-believe), 135, 137–42, 147, 158
Frost, Robert, 150
frumkeit, 151, 164n2
Fry, Hayden, xiv
FST, *see* faith-shaking trauma

gadfly, Socratic, xiv, 96, 169
games, ix, 40n6, 41n10, 129, 131–2, 136, 138–40, 143n11–12, 144n15, 145n23, 145n25, 154, 163, 168; *see also* make-believe, play, sport(s)
gaslighting, 186, 191–2, 204n22
gelâzenheit, gelassen ("releasement"), 208–10, 213, 216, 221n3; *see also* abgescheidenheit; detachment; mysticism; virtue(s)/vice(s)
gender, 7, 19, 114–15
God
  attributes of, 4, 11, 20, 84, 115, 119, 167, 193, 211
  of classical theism, 4, 6, 7n1, 12, 17, 115, 181
  and evil, *see* evil, problem of; theodicy
  existence of, 4, 6, 7, 11, 13
  God's-eye view, *see* objectivity
  hiddenness of, 101n10, 186
  human being as image of, 56, 61n16, 114, 211
  as Master/King, 113–14, 117, 167
  as Mother, 115–16, 125n18
  racialization of, 114, 117–18, 167
Goodman, Nelson, 31, 37, 53

grace
    divine, 210
    testimonial, 217–18
Green, Garrett, 110–11
Gutiérrez, Gustavo, 85, 207

Harding, Sandra, 24n16
harmony, 25, 26, 36, 42n14; *see also*
        resonance; dissonance
Hayy ibn Yaqzan, 103n24
Heidegger, Martin, 12
Hendricks, Perry, 177–9, 198–201, 202n4
hermeneutical understanding, *see*
        understanding, hermeneutical
hermeneutical injustice, *see* epistemic
        injustice, hermeneutical
Herman, Judith Lewis, 179
Heschel, Abraham Joshua, 71, 84
heterodoxy/heteropraxis, 15, 23n12,
        101n7, 105n40 148–51, 167
Hinduism, 55, 116
Hockett, Charles F., 27
holiness, 130, 147, 151–3, 159, 161–3
hope, *see* faith, and hope
horizons, x–xi, 4–7, 139, 141, 163, 219
Hossenfelder, Sabine, 41n12
Howard-Snyder, Daniel, 76, 83, 95, 100n4,
        102n21, 164n2
Huizinga, Johan, 138, 147
humanism, 15, 22n7, 65, 67n7
humility, xiii, 50, 51, 105n43, 158, 186,
        204n21, 210, 217–18

idealizations
    in science, 26, 29, 32, 49
    in APR, 4, 20, 23n12
identity, identification; *see also*
        commitment; faith
    core, 90, 99, 97 159, 183
    disciplinary, ix–xi
    group/social, 112, 192
    and imagination, 112–13, 117
    individual, sense of self, 90–3, 112, 213
    loss of, xi, 141, 184, 213
    narrative, 90, 97
    religious, xii, 19, 74, 93, 94, 112, 150,
        159
    with spiritual exemplars, 211
    with target roles, 142n1

idolatry, 15, 50, 66, 210, 211
illumination, 125n17, 209–12, 214,
        217–19; *see also* mysticism,
        threefold path in
imagination, imaginings, 208, 211–12
    and acceptance, *see* acceptance,
        imaginative
    vs. belief, 109–10
    and commitment, 108
    and the doxastic permissiveness of
        faith, 107–22, 121
    embodied, 109, 115, 118, 122, 123n6, 154
    as faculty, 107, 123n2
    inaccessibility of objects of, 110–11
    and make-believe, 131–5, 140, 147–63
    religious, 3, 44, 58, 63–4, 66, 99, 107–22,
        127, 147–63, 208, 211–12,
        218–19, 221n11
    resistant, 64, 115, 169 (*see also*
        epistemic friction(s); disruption,
        dissonance)
    social, 94, 112–17, 123n2
    and understanding, 107–8, 111–12, 120
impartiality (as epistemic ideal/norm), 17,
        63, 191–2, 195, 197, 204n17; *see*
        also neutrality
indicative (mood), vs. subjunctive, *see*
        subjunctive
(in)fertility, 184, 185, 203n12, 211,
        221n11; *see also* pregnancy loss
(in)justice
    divine, 119–20, 167
    epistemic (hermeneutical, testimonial),
        see epistemic injustice
    social, xiii, 33, 55, 58, 120, 167
    structural, 180
insincerity, *see* sincerity
Insole, Christopher J., 23n10
insensitivity, *see* sensitivity
instrumentalism, theological, *see*
        fictionalism
intelligibility, *see* understanding
interdisciplinarity, interdisciplinary
        research, 59n2, 73, 94, 197, 200,
        201
interfaith/interreligious dialogue, 61, 65,
        94
intuition(s), philosophical, 20, 35, 76,
        78–9, 87, 103n24, 128, 201

irrationality, irrational, 12, 18, 23n12, 48,
  79, 83, 91, 95, 97, 102n18, 155
irreverence, *see* reverance
Isabella (Baumfree), *see* Truth, Sojourner
Islam, Muslim(s), ix, 7n3, 67n4, 74, 91,
  156, 160, 209
ivory tower, 2, 55, 171, 190

Jaeger, Gregg, 24n17
James, William, 11
Jantzen, Grace, ix, 15, 18, 20, 56–8, 62n19,
  112
Jesus of Nazareth (Christ); *see also* God;
  Trinity (the)
  Church as body of (Christ), 94
  as Divine Word/Wisdom (*logos*),
    125n18, 211–12
  (in)formation/impregnation of the
    soul by, 211
  on faith, 165n10
  as friend and companion, 118–20, 186
  as mother (hen), 125n18
  as spiritual exemplar, 211
  symbolism in Christian art, 31
Job (biblical narrative), 50, 207, 219
John of the Cross, 101n10
Johnson, Nicole L., 185
Jonas, Silvia, 40n2
Jones, L. Serene, 115
Judaism, Jewish, 7n3, 50, 67n3, 151–3,
  159, 161
Julian of Norwich, 125n18
justice, *see* (in)justice

Kālī, *see* Divine Mother
Kane, Robert H., 24n17
Kant, Immanuel, 12
Kermani, Navid, 67n6
Kidd, Ian J., 192–3
Kielkopf, Charles, 182
Kierkegaard, Søren, v, 175
kingdom of God, v, 219
knowledge
  as discovered, received, 47
  as justified true belief, 14, 16–17, 28,
    39, 128
  propositional, 3, 16, 26, 28–9, 39, 46,
    63, 65
  religious, 14, 19, 77, 98, 107

ritual, 127–8
  vs. understanding, 3, 25–40, 57–9,
    60n6, 63–5, 73, 77, 98, 107–8,
    128
Kotzee, Ben, 194
Kvanvig, Jonathan L., 28, 40n4, 40n6, 79,
  87, 105n43

lament, 104n37, 175, 217
language
  breakdown of, 115
  captivity to, 127, 142
  about faith, 73–4, 100n1, 100n3
  about God, 14, 49, 207
    masculine, 114–15
  in Rhineland mysticism, 208–9
  ordinary, 74, 100n3
  religious semantics, 125n19
  and theodicy, 207, 217–18
  usefulness in philosophy, 49, 100n3
LARPing, *see* role-playing
Layne, Linda L., 184
Lebens, Samuel, 7n3, 122n1, 151–4, 159,
  161, 163n1–,
Legenhausen, Muhammad, 34–6, 65
Le Poidevin, Robin, 22n8, 102n20,
  163n1
Lewis, David K., 24n17
liberation, xii, 103n24, 113, 118–19, 153
liberation theology, *see* theology,
  liberation
Lillard, Angeline, 144n16
Lincoln, Abraham, 21, 24n19
Lindemann, Hilde, 92
liturgy, *see* religious practice/praxis
"locker-room" talk, 137, 171, 201; *see also*
  play, harmful
logos, *see* Jesus of Nazareth (Christ)
Longino, Helen, 24n18, 37, 42n15
Luhrmann, Tanya, 134, 142, 147, 149–50,
  154
lusory attitude, 132, 143n12, 147, 161,
  162, 170

make-believe, make-believing
  and deception, 135–7, 156–8
  definition and features of, 134–5
  and play, ix, 3, 129, 131–42, 152, 156,
    159

and pretense, 128–32, 135–7
religious (RMB), 3, 99, 108, 122,
        128–30, 147–63
and seriousness/frivolity, 3, 129–30,
        137–42, 158
Malcolm, Finlay, 78, 80–1, 83, 101n14,
        101n8, 102n19, 104n37, 105n46,
        128–9, 143n4, 158
MaRTeR, *see* realism, metaphysically
        robust theistic
mathematics
    and beauty, 34–5, 41n12
    and realism, 27, 30, 32
    and understanding, 27–30, 32
McCord Adams, Marilyn, 22n5, 179, 193,
        217, 219
McCutcheon, Russell T., 22n6, 100n1
McFague, Sally, 57, 61n18, 114
McKaughan, Daniel J., 76, 77, 83, 95,
        101n10
Medina, José, 18–19, 24n18, 36, 38, 58,
        62n20, 112–13, 155, 117, 126n21,
        192, 216
meaning, meaning-making, *see also*
        understanding, hermeneutical
    direction of fit/fittingness of, 47–55
    existential, 43–6, 50, 52, 71, 98, 142,
        147, 161–2, 219
    in religion, xii, 12, 44, 52, 85, 98, 152,
        219
metaphor, x, xi, 31, 35, 36, 49, 114, 123n3,
        211, 218
metaphysics; *see also* realism; anti-realism
    and APR, 2, 12, 16, 47
    critiques of, 12, 22n3
metaphysically robust theistic realism
        (MaRTeR), *see* realism,
        metaphysically robust
microaggressions, 132, 180, 216
miscarriage, *see* pregnancy loss
Mitchell, Basil, 16
Mitchell, Robert W., 144n16
mizuko (*kuyō*), in Buddhism, 204n15
models
    change in, 53–5, 57
    cognitive, 72
    as felicitous falsehoods, 26–7, 32, 49
    fittingness of, 33, 37, 53–4
    of God, ix, 17–18, 55, 57, 113–20, 167

religious, 44, 47, 49–59, 108, 111, 167,
        209
    scientific, 26, 30–3, 49–50
monotheism; *see* theism
Mother Teresa, 76, 78–81
motivation
    and belief, 83, 105n41
    and faith, 82–3, 87, 94–5
    and playfulness, 169
    and prudential reasons, 160–1
    and reverence, 162
    and social imaginings, 113, 119
    and understanding, 33
    and wonder/awe, 34
Muslim, *see* Islam
Muyskens, James L., 101n11
mysterium tremendum et fascinans, 35
mysticism, mystagogy; *see also* Eckhart of
        Hochheim; Suso, Henry; Truth,
        Sojourner
    19th-c. African American female,
        117–20
    annihilative vs. affective, 213, 221n6
    Christian, ix, 103n24, 208–14
    Islamic, ix, 103n24, 209
    of resistance, 219
    Rhineland, 208–14, 215n7
    and theodicy, 177, 208–14
    threefold path in, 209–14
        via purgativa, 209–11
        via illuminativa, 209–12, 214
        via unitiva, 210, 212–13
    virtues in, 208–10, 216
myths, mythology, 31, 41n9, 57

narrative(s)
    and identity, 90, 97, 127
    frameworks, cosmic, 43–5, 50, 66, 72,
        84, 93, 111, 147, 161, 162
    frameworks, imaginative, xii, 44, 132,
        147, 161, 168
    historical, 130
    and religious understanding, 43–5, 85,
        98, 111, 119
natural theology, *see* theology, natural
neglect, addressive, 193–4
neoliberalism, neoliberal, 138, 142, 185
Neoplatonism, 209
neuroscience, 109, 124n10, 197

neutrality (as epistemic value/ideal), 17–19,
　　21, 55, 37, 113, 194; *see also*
　　detachment; impartiality
"new" atheism, *see* atheism
Nguyen, C. Thi, 145n25, 168–9, 201
Nietzsche, Friedrich, 53
non-belief, 80, 87, 99, 108, 122n1, 149,
　　156–9; *see also* agnosticism;
　　belief, suspension of; doubt;
　　faith
non-doxasticism, *see* faith, doxastic vs.
　　non-doxastic models of
normativity, normative, *see also* values
　　of belief in religious contexts, ix,
　　　102n19, 129, 149, 155, 157–8,
　　　200
　　and commitment, 89–91, 95, 103n26
　　of doxastic models of faith, 80–1,
　　　101n14, 102n19
　　in mysticism, 210–11

objectification, 12, 159–60, 163
objectivity
　　absolute/utter, 38–9, 57, 64, 113
　　normative frameworks of, 16–17, 26, 37,
　　　63, 177, 192
　　　social/polyphonic, 21, 25–6, 37–9, 58
　　　view from nowhere/God's-eye view,
　　　　2, 17–21, 38–9, 63–4, 113
　　values/ideals of, 16–21, 37, 54, 195 (*see
　　　also* value(s), epistemic)
obligations, *see* duties, obligations
Ockham's razor, 24n17
O'Donnell, Karen, 182, 105
"omni"-properties, divine, *see* God,
　　attributes of
ontological/ontotheological critiques (of
　　APR), *see* analytic philosophy of
　　religion, critiques of
ontotheology, 12, 22n4–5, 23n10
open-mindedness, openness, 18, 53, 58,
　　158
orientation, re-orientation
　　and disciplinary change, xi, 3, 59, 63–6,
　　　71–3, 93, 98, 107, 219
　　as epistemic, 52–3
　　existential, v, 3, 43, 46, 51, 90, 98, 99
　　religious, xii, 15, 44, 46, 52, 55, 73, 90, 96,
　　　98, 102n22, 111

orthodoxy, 6, 16, 54, 167
Otto, Rudolf, 35

Palmqvist, Carl-Johan, 121, 164n1
Panchuk, Michelle, 103n25, 197, 204n20,
　　204n22–23, 205n26, 207
paracosms, 134, 142, 147, 152, 169
paradigms, 36, 38, 52, 54, 61n15, 76; *see
　　also* models
partiality, 21, 24n16, 221n7; *see also*
　　impartiality
passivity, 53, 59, 96, 114, 122, 209, 210,
　　216–17
patriarchy, 113–15
Paul, L.A., 220
Pearson, Kathleen M., 143n11
perfect-being theology, *see* theism,
　　perfect-being
perlocutionary effects, 56, 79, 102n15, 176,
　　193, 217
Persephone, 31
perspectivity, perspectival, 17, 20, 27, 38–9,
　　54, 63–4; *see also* positionality
phenomenology, 35, 110, 122n1
philosophia spiritualis, 208, 211, 213, 220;
　　see also Suso, Henry
PI approach, *see* "purely intellectual"
　　approach (in APR)
Pigliucci, Massimo, 42n12
Pinn, Anthony B., 22n7, 44, 59n2, 67n7
Plantinga, Alvin, 23n11, 84
Plato, 147, 163
play
　　autotelicity of, 132–4, 136, 152, 156, 159
　　and earnestness/seriousness, 3, 129–30,
　　　137–42, 147
　　as "existential balm," 142, 145n25
　　harmful, 137, 169–71, 201
　　intellectual, 169
　　make-believe as, *see* make-believe
plenitude, principle of, 24n7
pluralism
　　in APR, ix, 64
　　epistemic, 41n11
　　religious, 65, 202n18
Pojman, Louis P., 101n11
Porete, Marguerite, 126n22
positionality, 19, 39, 151, 176
postcolonialism, 5, 16

postmodernism, xiv, 12, 16, 66

posttraumatic growth, 186, 200, 205n26

power, 57, 132

Potter, Kelli, 15, 101n7

practice/praxis, religious, *see* religious
        practice/praxis (participation)

pragmatism, 11, 33, 41n8, 61n10, 97, 209,
        212

prayer, 51, 118, 150, 154

pregnancy loss; *see also* abortion
    as faith-shaking trauma, 183–7
    and theodicy, 177, 183–7, 190, 196,
        202n11, 204n23, 205n25
    in Scripture, 184

pretense
    instrumental vs. autotelic, 132–4, 137,
        156, 158–61
    and make-believe, 3, 81, 102n19,
        128–32, 135–7
    and play, 128–32, 135–7
    and religion, 3, 81, 128–31, 147–63

Pritchard, Duncan, 41n9

privilege, 155, 160, 196, 199, 201, 216

projection, 13, 56, 112, 115, 122, 124n10, 134

Pseudo-Dionysius, 12

quasi-player, *see* spoilsport; trifler

Rambo, Lewis R., 102n22

rationality, reasonableness, *see also*
        (religious) belief; commitment;
        reasons, reasoning
    centrality in APR, 3–5, 11–12, 14, 15, 25,
        47–8, 63, 71–3, 81, 107, 111–12,
        120, 215
    as epistemic value, 17–18, 63 (*see also*
        objectivity; value(s), epistemic)

Rea, Michael C., 6, 64

realism, realist(s), 2, 13, 15, 27, 30, 32, 49;
        see also anti-realism
    definition of, 13
    metaphysically robust theistic
        (MaRTeR), 14–21, 25, 39, 47, 53,
        57, 63, 65, 72, 87

reasons, reasoning
    aesthetic, 34–5, 41n12, 121 (*see also*
        values, aesthetic)
    epistemic, 48, 72, 89 (*see also* values,
        epistemic)

intrinsic vs. instrumental, 41n10, 83, 87,
        97, 132–42, 142n2, 144n13–15,
        152, 156–61, 165n8 (*see also*
        autotelicity, autotelic)

moral, 62n19, 91, 103n26

philosophical, 209

practical/prudential/strategic, 15, 33,
        42n13, 45–7, 55, 85, 89–91, 97,
        103n29, 121, 158–61, 175, 182

social, political, 33, 45, 55, 85, 97, 175

theodical, 178, 181, 180–3, 188–91

receptivity, 52, 194–5, 210–11, 216–17; *see
        also* open-mindedness, openness

reflective equilibrium, 28, 29, 36, 39, 40n3,
        59, 65

reform, reformation, xi, 3, 4, 52, 63, 167,
        170, 209, 211, 214

Reiheld, Alison, 184

releasement, *see gelâzenheit, gelassen*

religion(s)
    affective and volitional aspects of, 15,
        73, 85
    benefits and harms of, xii, 15, 52, 86–7,
        114, 156
    cognitive aspects of, 3, 14, 72–3, 85
    epistemic value of, 3, 25, 39, 43–59
    factivity/truth of, 3, 13, 21, 57
    heterodoxy of, *see* heterodoxy/
        heteropraxy
    lived, "on the ground", 5, 15, 17, 45, 73,
        99, 121–2, 170
    monotheistic, 4, 6, 13, 57
    non-(mono)theistic, 2, 6
    philosophy of, *see* philosophy, of
        religion; analytic philosophy of
        religion
    as proper object of philosophy of
        religion, 5, 22n6, 73
    role of imagination in, *see* imagination,
        imaginings, religious

religious belief, believer(s), xiv, 170, 207;
        see also belief; certainty,
        subjective; faith; rationality
    irrationality of, 12, 23n12, 48, 79, 102n18
    as necessary for religious faith, *see* faith,
        doxastic models of
    as norm/ideal/paradigm attitude in
        religious life, 66, 72, 76, 129, 130,
        143n5–6, 148–9, 155, 157–8, 200

rationality of, 5, 11, 14, 23n12, 25, 47–48,
72, 79, 116, 182
and religious make-believe(rs), 129–30,
148, 153, 156–63
vs. religious non-belief/disbelief, 122n1,
149, 156–9
obsession with in APR, 3–4, 14–16, 39,
99, 120, 215, 219
and sincerity, 131
as socially-constructed fiction, 15,
23n12, 148–51
theistic, 4, 14–17, 47–8, 182, 207, 215
(*see also* theism)
as victims, 130
religious experience, viii, ix, 15, 17, 49, 78,
94, 101n10, 103n24, 124n12, 162,
213
religious practice(s)/praxis (participation),
xii, 15, 44, 50, 71, 73, 82, 84–7,
91, 156–7, 160–1
embodied, *see* embodiment
liturgical, ritual, 4, 51–2, 84, 92, 98,
127–8, 150, 160
primacy of, xi, 3, 46, 66, 72, 75, 83–5, 93,
97–9, 108, 116–17, 150–1
and religious belief, 149–50
and understanding, 3, 46, 56, 73, 85, 98
religious studies, 5, 22n6, 149, 197
reorientation, *see* orientation
representation
and imagination, 108–11, 120, 124n11
and models, 26, 30, 47, 53
resilience (of faith), *see* faith
resistance
epistemic, 36, 58–9, 62n20, 64
epistemology of, 58–59, 64
imaginative, 64, 115, 119, 121, 126n25,
169
mysticism of, 219
to evil, 51, 208
resonance, 34–9, 42n13, 127, 197; *see also*
disruption, dissonance; epistemic
frictions; reflective equilibrium
aesthetic/affective, 34–5, 39, 41n12, 55,
58, 65, 67n6, 85
in APR/AT, 45, 57, 58, 64–5, 96, 197,
215–17
cognitive/intellectual, 35–6, 58, 169
and harmony, 42n14

interdisciplinary, 59n2, 94, 197
and social dynamics of understanding,
35–7
revelation, 49, 60n6, 103n24, 220
reverence, irreverence, 130, 131, 141, 148,
155, 158, 162, 168
revolution, xi, 3, 167
Ricœur, Paul, 60n5
Riezler, Kurt, 138–9, 141–2, 163
rights, 55, 61n17, 65, 167
ritual, *see* religious practice/praxis
(participation)
RMB, *see* make-believe, religious
role-playing, 133, 140, 142n1, 163n1
Rosales, Harmonia, 125n16
rules
constitutive, 143n12
in make-believe, 134, 135, 145n20,
168
in play, games, sports, ix, 40n6, 132, 136,
141, 143n12, 170
rejection of by quasi-players, 140, 170,
171n2

sacred, sacredness, 130, 152, 162
salvation, 130, 159, 200
Sartre, Jean-Paul, 110, 124n9
Schilbrack, Kevin, 4, 5, 23n9, 59n2
Schleiermacher, Friedrich, viii
science(s)
models/theories in, *see* models,
scientific
philosophy of, 5, 27
and realism, 12, 27, 30
and religion, 2, 12, 25, 48–9, 65
social, 5, 14, 60n2, 197, 200
and understanding, 25–39
Scott, Michael, 78, 80–1, 83, 101n14,
101n8, 102n19, 104n37, 105n46,
158
secular, secularist, 2, 14, 22n2, 48, 53, 60n2,
65, 67n7, 210
self
deconstruction of, 208–11
and identity, *see* identity
transformation of, xii, 118, 127,
208–14
self-deception, *see* deception
Seligman, Adam B., 100n1, 144n16, 164n3

sensitivity, insensitivity
   aesthetic/affective, 34
   contextual, *see* context-dependence
   epistemic, 19, 20, 157, 196, 201
   meta-, 19, 195
   moral, 61n18, 196, 199, 201
      and religion, xii, 51, 57
      to suffering, 196, 198–9, 201, 215, 218
seriousness, 1–2, 122, 129, 137–42; *see also*
      earnestness; sincerity
Seuse, Heinrich, *see* Suso, Henry
Sikhism, 55
silence, 115, 184, 217
silencing, testimonial, *see* epistemic
      injustice
simplicity (as epistemic value), 17, 21,
      41n12
sin, 6, 180
sincerity, insincerity; *see also* authenticity;
      earnestness; seriousness
   as doxastic ideal, 130–1, 143n8
   and faith, 91–2, 96, 97, 104n37, 111, 151,
      156, 158
   and (religious) make-believe/play,
      129–31, 137, 147, 151, 156
situatedness, 19, 45, 47, 73, 94, 117
skeptical theism, *see* theodicy
smothering, testimonial, *see* epistemic
      injustice
social construction, 13, 15, 168
social epistemology, *see* epistemology,
      social
solidarity, xii, 51, 208, 214, 219
Sölle, Dorothee, ix, 196, 217, 219
Sollereder, Bethany, 189, 203n9
sophia, *see* wisdom
Soskice, Janet, 53
spoilsport, 3, 145n24, 167–71, 177
sport(s), ix, xiv, 1, 5, 40n6, 59n2, 88,
      102n23, 129, 131, 136, 138, 141,
      143n11, 154, 156, 159, 162
Stagel, Elsbeth, 209
Strevens, Michael, 40n4
struggle, religious/spiritual, viii, ix,
      182–200, 207, 211, 215, 219,
      221n11
Stump, Eleonore, 45, 60n6, 205n26
subjunctive (mood), 134, 135, 142, 152,
      155, 164n3

suffering, *see also* evil; theodicy; trauma
   faith-shaking trauma (FST) and,
      179–201, 202n6, 207, 215–19
   horrendous, 18
   innocent, 207
   insensitivity to, 196, 198–9, 201, 215,
      218
   "lay" Christian perspectives on, 185
   and the "purely intellectual" approach,
      187–91
   and theodicies, 180–1, 203n9
Suits, Bernard, 132, 136, 140, 143n12,
      144n15–16, 145n24, 147,
      170
Suso, Henry (Heinrich Seuse), 1, 126n22,
      207, 208–14, 220n1, 221n3–4
Swinburne, Richard, 101n12, 179
Swinton, John, 205n24
symbol, symbolism, 31, 37, 51–2
syncretism, syncretistic, 55, 167

Taliaferro, Charles, 4
testimony, testimonial, 18, 192–4, 199–200,
      204n20, 215–18; *see also*
      epistemic injustice, testimonial
tethering (of models to reality), 31–3, 37,
      47–53, 57, 112; *see also*
      correspondence; truth
theism, theistic
   belief, *see* religious belief
   classical, 4, 6, 7, 7n1, 11, 12, 17, 115,
      181
   perfect-being, ix, 4, 6–7, 7n1, 13–14,
      17–18, 20–1, 57, 63, 181, 196,
      216
   personalist, 7n1, 22n4
   and realism, *see* realism
theodicy; *see also* evil; suffering; trauma
   and anti-theodicy, *see* anti-theodicy
   categories of, 180–1
   moral and epistemic dangers of, ix, 3,
      177–201
   pastoral vs. philosophical, 189, 197,
      205n24
   and pregnancy loss, 183–7
   "purely intellectual" (PI) approach to, 3,
      171, 175–201
   skeptical theist approaches to, 49, 181,
      186

theology
    analytic, 6, 7n3 63–4, 66n2, 67n4, 151
    apophatic, 12, 22n3, 49, 66
    cataphatic, 66
    Christian, 6, 61n18, 64, 115, 119
    comparative, 6, 64, 94, 197
    declarative, 63
    feminist, ix, 6, 16, 64, 115, 200
    liberation, ix, 6, 16, 64, 85, 118–19,
        200
    mystical, 12, 208–14
    narrative, 109
    natural, 48
    non-Christian, 6, 7n3
    perfect-being, *see* perfect-being theism
    philosophical, 2, 6, 11, 12, 15, 190
    postmodern, xiv, 12, 13, 14, 66
    queer, 6, 16, 64, 200
theories, *see* models
Teresa of Avila, 101n10
Tillich, Paul, 12, 145n21
Timpe, Kevin, 4
transformation
    of APR, xi, 3, 26, 208, 214–20
    of models/frameworks, 53, 55, 58, 168
    personal/spiritual, xi, 36, 52, 117,
        118–20, 127–8, 155, 161, 208–14
    transformative criticism, in objectivity,
        37
    transformative experience, 78, 127, 220
transcendence, 12, 49, 51, 118, 142, 149,
    186
trauma; *see also* evil; suffering
    definition, 179, 202n7
    faith-shaking (FST), 86, 179–80, 182,
        187, 190–1, 193, 195, 200, 207
    psycho-physical, viii, 18, 119, 183–4
    religious/spiritual, 18, 103n25, 200,
        204n22
trifler, 140, 141, 145n23, 162–3, 170
Trinity, Trinitarian (in Christianity), xvii,
    111, 115, 119; *see also* God
trust, 18, 77, 84, 87, 90, 96, 97, 101n12–13,
    105n43, 114, 150, 186
truth
    -aptness/-conduciveness, 13, 22n8, 33,
        44, 47, 53, 168
    as correspondence, *see* correspondence
        (to reality) (*see also* factivity)

as epistemic value, 3, 26, 31, 33, 50
and knowledge, 26–28
as mind- or perspective-independent,
    11, 23n10, 27
and models, 26, 30, 33, 40n4, 49–50, 57,
    102n19
Truth, Sojourner (Isabella Baumfree), ix,
    117–20, 126n21, 167
turning (metaphors of), xi, 210–11,
    215–19, 221n5

uncertainty, *see* doubt
understanding
    discursivity/dynamic nature of, 37–9
    and exemplification, 31–2, 50–2
    as non-factive, 29, 30, 40n4, 41n9
    hermeneutical, 3, 43–6, 47–8, 61n9, 85,
        98, 99, 128, 162
    and intelligibility, 29, 116
    and objectivity, 37–8
    objectual, 28, 41n9
    and reflective equilibrium, 28, 36, 39,
        40n3, 58, 65 (*see also* reflective
        equilibrium)
    religious, 3, 43–59, 66, 85, 98–9, 116,
        167, 219
    scientific, 26–39
    and truth, 26–7, 29, 39, 122
    vs. knowledge, *see* knowledge
union (with God), *see* mysticism, *via unitiva*
unity (as epistemic value), 17
universality (as epistemic value), 17, 21,
    192, 194, 197

Vaihinger, Hans, 168
values (ideals, norms, standards), *see also*
    normativity, normative
    aesthetic, xii, 34, 41n12, 50, 55 (*see also*
        beauty; elegance)
    alethic, 3, 23n10, 60n3, 122, 201 (*see
        also* truth)
    American, 130–1, 143n8
    epistemic, 3, 17–18, 20–1, 24n16–18,
        25, 31–3, 39, 41n11, 43, 45,
        47–50, 122, 215, (*see also*
        epistemic value (of a domain);
        objectivity)
    internalization of, 95, 97, 113, 143n8,
        213

intrinsic vs. instrumental, *see* reasons,
    reasoning
  moral, 15, 34, 20, 45, 48, 55, 131, 160,
    178
  practical, political, social, 20, 33, 45, 47,
    55–7
Van Dyke, Christina, 123n6, 221n6
van Fraassen, Bas, 38
van Inwagen, Peter, 188–90, 196
Van Leeuwen, Neil, 125n20, 149, 154–5,
    156, 163n1
vice(s), *see* virtue(s)/vice(s)
virtue(s)/vice(s); *see also* close-mindedness;
    epistemic arrogance; epistemic
    cold-heartedness; epistemic
    traps; openness; humility;
    sensitivity
  epistemic/intellectual, xiii, 18–19, 38, 50,
    149, 153, 168–9, 171n1 189,
    194–6, 201
  moral, xiii, 31, 73, 160, 177, 180, 189,
    191, 195–6, 199, 201
  mystical, 208–10, 213, 216, 221n3
  religious/theological, 31, 50, 79, 155,
    158, 161, 208
vita activa / vita contemplativa, 99, 214; *see
    also* Eckhart of Hochheim;
    mysticism
volition(al), volitionality; *see also* will (the),
    willing
  and acceptance, 30
  and commitment, 15, 86, 88–90, 94–5,
    99, 104n33

and faith, 76–7, 86–91, 94–6, 99,
    103n29
and make-believe, 134–5
orientation/alignment, in religion, 15,
    46, 99, 103n24
vulnerability, 101n13, 200, 201, 204n20,
    218

Wagner, Rachel, 147
Walton, Kendall, 109, 126n25
well-being, 186, 199, 200, 130, 178,
Wettstein, Howard K., 27, 52, 102n20,
    161
Weyl, Hermann, 34
Wiesel, Elie, 181
will (the), willing, 15, 76–7, 85, 89–90, 94,
    96, 99, 103n24, 104n33, 116, 184,
    208, 213; *see also* volition(al),
    volitionality
Williams, Bernard, 24n16, 103n26
Wittgenstein, Ludwig, 127, 142, 169, 212,
    213
Wolterstorff, Nicholas, 23n11
Wong, David B., 24n18, 42n14
wonder (awe), 1, 12, 34–5, 41n12–13, 50,
    51, 141, 114, 141, 151–2, 161, 163
Wood, William, 4, 66n2
worship, 12, 51, 71, 86, 93, 98, 114, 128,
    150, 154, 182, 187

yirat shamayim, see wonder (awe), in
    Judaism
Young, Iris Marion, xiii, 24n16